AMERICAN POPULAR HISTORY AND CULTURE

edited by
JEROME NADELHAFT
UNIVERSITY OF MAINE

A GARLAND SERIES

Garland Studies in American Popular History and Culture
Jerome Nadelhaft, series editor

READING COMICS

LANGUAGE, CULTURE, AND THE CONCEPT OF THE SUPERHERO IN COMIC BOOKS

———————

MILA BONGCO

GARLAND PUBLISHING, INC.
A MEMBER OF THE TAYLOR & FRANCIS GROUP
NEW YORK & LONDON/2000

148748

Published in 2000 by
Garland Publishing Inc.
A Member of the Taylor & Francis Group
29 West 35th Street
New York, NY 10001

10 9 8 7 6 5 4 3 2 1

Library of Congress Cataloging-in-Publication Data

Bongco, Mila.
     Reading Comics : language, culture, and the concept of the
superhero in comic books / Mila Bongco.
          p. cm.
     Includes index.
     ISBN 0-8153-3344-7 (alk. paper)
      1. Comic books, strips, etc—History and criticism. 2. Heroes.
     I. Title.
     PN6714.B66 1999
     741.5'09—dc21
                                                                    99-046175

Printed on acid-free, 250-year-life paper
Manufactured in the United States of America

Contents

List of Figures

Acknowledgments

Many people assisted me in various ways in the course of putting this book together. The most important is Jan Philipzig, for his patience and unswerving belief in this book. He also wrote most of the material I translated for Chapters Seven and Eight. I also thank Milan Dimic who supervised my dissertation and encouraged me to have it published.

Other individuals who helped me directly include Mike Chow who lent me his comicbooks and gave feedback on some of the chapters, Gunnar Blodgett who also provided some comments, and Brent Simon and Lorne Tkachuk for technical help with scanners, CD burners, and the Macintosh. I want to acknowledge Pre Print Inc. for letting me use their equipment in scanning the images.

I gratefully acknowledge the permission given by the artists and publishers for the images in this book, without which reading this book will definitely be less interesting.

Most importantly, I wish to thank those who motivated and encouraged me during many moments of doubt: my family and friends from Manila, Bacolod, Munich, Dresden, Edmonton, Beaumont, New York, and California.

I regret the absence of illustrations from Marvel, and more illustrations from DC. I never got any response from Marvel, and DC would only allow one. It is unfortunate that bureaucratic policies prevailed over the value the illustrations would have had for readers.

Introduction

At the close of the twentieth century, the American comics industry seems to be facing a crisis. Sales had drastically declined since a renaissance in comics around 1986, and a burst of growth from 1990 to 1993. At the height of the boom in 1993, the total retail value of the comics market was estimated at over $1 billion. Three years later, this was just slightly less than half. In 1998, industry professionals say that sales are still declining, albeit in a much slower rate. The steady decrease in sales has affected comics shops which sprouted all over the United States and Canada around 1981. Audits from the two largest distributors in the comics market, Diamond and Capital City, show that in 1993, there were 9,400 retailers. In August 1995, the stores numbered between 6,100 and 6,500, and by July 1996, their records indicate about 4,500 stores. Since 1995, the biggest changes in the market have been the change in the demographics of its readership, a noticeably shrinking consumer base, and the shift in the distribution structure and sales strategy of comicbooks. All these have greatly affected the comics industry and have caused some apprehension in many publishers, retailers, distributors, and artists. Comicbooks have sprung back after dire predictions in the 1950s and 1970s. However, many say that the crisis in 1993-1996 is the biggest crisis so far in the comics market.

Interestingly, although sales are down, comics as an art form is flourishing. In the history of comics in North America, never have there been so many original contributions and innovative work being done in so short a time. There is no denying the sheer variety of material available in comics form today. The types of work being done vary from genre fiction to autobiography, to meticulously research historical fiction, journalism, dream work, essays, erotica, fantasy epics, and so on. The number of comics publishers has also increased, making it possible for cartoonists to escape the tyranny of big publishing houses in terms of style, recognition, and compensation. A choice in publishers has allowed authors and illustrators wider room for experimentation in expressing themselves, and this is apparent in the choice of comicbooks available today.

The current trend stresses the importance to distinguish between the medium's development aesthetically and its development as an industry. However, the relationship between commerce and art is complex and difficult to untangle. Any art form exists only in the environment that creates it and allows it to grow; and the art form sometimes changes as its surroundings shift. Analysing comicbooks within cultural studies highlights the interrelation between the medium and the society which fosters it. By their very accessibility and ubiquity, comics have necessarily contributed to the fashioning of the imagination of the society which contains them. Conversely, as a medium intended for mass consumption, the comics must cater to popular wishes and demands, including commercial and business needs.

This book outlines some developments in comicbooks since its inception until the 1990s. No claim for comprehensiveness is made, rather, the focus is on the following five important changes in the comics industry, how they affected the development of the medium in the last fifty years, and how they led up to the current conditions. The important changes were in the following:

a) Image and perception of comics
b) Format and overall appearance of comicbooks
c) Artists and publishers involved in the industry
d) Readership
e) Distribution and marketing of the products

The first chapter provides a sketch of the history of comics in America to provide a context for the earlier perceptions of comics that have been detrimental to the medium and the industry. This approach provides a more comprehensive critical framework for understanding the complexity of both the production and the reception of comics within contemporary cultures. It serves two purposes: to diverge from the traditional negative critique of comics and to circumvent the confining limits of traditional literary studies in investigating a cultural product such as comicbooks. The next chapter provides an outline of the responses to comicbooks in relation to the assumptions and ideological perspectives which inform the concept of popular culture. The focus is on showing how the perception of the "popular" as impermanent and inferior has had consequences for the reception of comicbooks, particularly in the critics' assessment of them.

Chapter Three elucidates on the language and grammar of comics, highlighting the study of comics as a narrative mode: it is a tangle of "competing languages," comprising both graphic and verbal signs. Reading comics involves the pictures and their meanings in addition to the accompanying words. The key to understanding comic art does not lie in the words or pictures alone but in the interaction between them. The expressive potential and uniqueness of the medium lie in the skilful employment of not one but two sign systems. Interestingly, the relations between the divergent "languages" of comics reflect the simultaneously competitive and complementary relationship which exists between comics and other genres, other popular forms of expression, other forms of literature. Chapter Four starts to focus on superhero comics. It utilises the concepts of genre studies to analyse superheroes by providing a short history of the context and activities in the rise of the superhero genre. In analysing the definition of a superhero, heroes such as Superman, Captain America, Spider-Man, and the Batman will be studied in the context of the form of masculinity offered in these texts. The portrayal of women in superhero texts will also be investigated, as well as their role in relation to the superheroes. It will be argued that superhero comicbooks delight in displaying chaos and criminality which belies the usual perception of these texts as merely espousing the ideologies of a dominant culture. Chapter Five follows this line of thinking and concentrates on analysing the generic changes in the portrayal and conceptualising of superheroes in the comicbooks of the 1980s. Factors that changed the superhero are also evaluated in context of the changes in the overall comics industry in North America. Textual examples for this chapter are culled from more recent graphic novels, particularly those labeled "Suggested for Mature Readers," which clearly exhibit different concerns from the prevalent escapist themes of more popular comicbooks. Examination of new characters and novel themes will be based on the works of Frank Miller,

Alan Moore, and Neil Gaiman, among others. The Batman, Black Orchid, the Sandman and the heroes in *Sin City* and *Watchmen*, will provide the main focus and examples for analysing the new breed of superheroes.

Chapter Six is a close look at *The Return of the Dark Knight* which is seminal in changing the direction of comicbooks, both aesthetically and commercially. There have not been many detailed interpretations of individual comicbooks to date, and there is a need for more critical studies on topics like the developments in the works of recent writers and illustrators, the handling of themes and topics within a particular period, or evolution in the narrative and graphic styles of a batch of artists. The last chapter provides developments in the comics scene after 1986, focusing more on the small-press and alternative publishers that sprouted in the mid-1980s. Works from various artists are mentioned, as well as specific elements that contributed to the innovations and different directions in comics.

Despite the downward trend in sales, comic art seems to be slowly shedding the cultural disdain normally attached to it and making its mark as an expressive new artistic form. Recently, comics have been attracting not only more serious critical attention but also more serious artists who are expanding the potentials of comics as a narrative medium while addressing more profound topics not usually associated with comicbooks. Respectable book clubs, such as the Book-of-the-Month Club and the Quality Paperback Book Club, now include selected comicbooks in their offerings. This recent confluence of good artists and good critical reviews in the area of comics may yet work to cast off decades of critical scorn and cultural marginalization that have long arrested the medium's development. As modern culture becomes less print oriented and more visual, the comicbook may become more and more attractive as a narrative form. Art Spiegelman, Pulitzer Prize winner for his comicbook *Maus*, once commented: "All media are as rich as the artists working inside them".[1] As comics comes of age in America, its potential may now be limited only by the creativeness of the artists willing to risk working in it.

NOTES

1. Interview with Art Spiegelman in *Time* (November 1, 1993): 65.

CHAPTER ONE

Comics and Cultural Studies
Sites for Struggle

> Once upon a time there were the mass media and they
> were wicked, of course, and there was a guilty party. Then
> there were the virtuous voices that accused the criminals. And
> Art (ah, what luck!) offered alternatives for those who were
> not prisoners of the mass media. Well, it's all over. We have to
> start again from the beginning, asking one another what's
> going on.

> Umberto Eco
> *Travels in Hyperreality* 1986

OVERVIEW OF CRITICAL ATTENTION TO COMICS

Browsing in bookstores, one sees an abundance of highly sophisticated studies of cinema, television, and popular fiction like detective novels, science fiction, and romances. There is, however, a
noticeable shortage in comparable studies about comics.
Superficiality has characterised much of the critical literature on
comics longer than on most other popular forms. I believe this
superficiality is closely connected to the nature of comics readership, generally perceived to be a group even more marginalized
than the consumers of film, television, or popular fiction: these are
children, young adults and, in non-industrialised nations, the poor
and not-so-literate. The association of comics primarily with children, adolescents, and the sub-literate is apparent in the profusion
of books, articles, reviews and outright attacks on comics that

characterised its body of critical studies for the longest time. These
attacks may be characterised as the "effects and influence tradition" of mass media critique that concentrates on the possible
harmful effects of substandard and unchecked entertainment on
malleable minds.[1] Traditional criticism about comics reflects the
pattern of ambivalence and censorious attitude toward mass media
in general. Among the most famous and virulent attacks against
comics is Fredric Wertham's *Seduction of the Innocent*, published
in 1954. Wertham criticised American comicbooks indiscriminate-
ly as inherently sensational, trivial and illiterate, depicting too
much sex, violence and anarchy. He asserted that the practice of
reading comics led to juvenile delinquency.[2] The only other two
lengthy discussions about comicbooks published before 1960,
those of Gershon Legman and Geoffrey Wagner, echoed Wertham's
disapproving appraisal of comics:

> "Legman, Wertham and Wagner compete in their merciless
> castigation of the comics, heaping blazing coals upon them
> for their excesses of violence and gore, their often unwhole-
> some treatment of sex, and their frequently low level of writ-
> ing and drawing."[3]

Legman, an authority on dirty jokes, the dirty limerick and
erotic folklore, focused on the action and violence in comics to
suggest a generic link between violence and adventure comics,
instead of placing these comics against the general background and
history of graphic brutality in mass media. Indeed, the eruption of
comics in the 1940s and 1950s was no spontaneous growth and is
better seen against the general backdrop of increasing production
and popularity of pictographs after the war. What was unique in
comics was their mass production and the easy public access to
them, not their content. Unfortunately, the rise of comicbook production coincided with a time of extraordinary attention to juvenile delinquency. There was an uncommon concern over criminal
behaviour infecting America's youngsters during the post-war
era—movies, dime novels, radio programmes, magazines, television shows and comics were all suspect. Of these, comicbooks
were the most affected as Wertham's provocative book, together
with his active crusade against comicbooks, incited public indig-
nation and set off a campaign which took the form of local pressure from parents' groups, religious groups, and school organisa-

tions. All this resulted in the public forum of the Senate Hearings under Senator Kefauver into possible links between the comics and juvenile delinquency.[4] The Senate Hearings on comics were a part of a bigger investigation into crime and adolescence that lasted a decade. Twitchell (1989) provides an explanation of why comics took the brunt of the repercussions of these delinquency examinations:

> The large media were protected from criticism in two ways. They were parts of American industry, important conduits for the flow not so much of information but of advertising. The sponsors of radio crime shows—cigarettes, toiletries, automobiles—were loath to give up their audiences. The movie industry could always claim its audience was self-selective, and in fact, the industry surveys of the audience of 1950 showed that only the people with sufficient disposable income and time to go to the movies were those between twenty-two and forty. Television was no menace—yet. Kids could not watch what was not there. Saturday morning TV did not carve out an audience until the late 1950s . . . The other protection for mass media was that audiences were as unwilling to give up their entertainment as advertisers were to give up their audiences. The democratising effect of electronic media meant that programming was done for the largest possible audience, and that audience, by its very nature, was too big to budge.

> Almost by elimination, the comics were left standing alone; they were never able to align themselves with any interested parties, having no untainted supporters who could vouch for them . . . But the real reason comic books proved such a huge target was that the hands turning the pages were so young, so male, and so easy to discipline—at least initially. Here was where the juvenile delinquency virus must be entering the body politic, and here is where it must be eradicated.[5]

Although the campaign against comics and the ensuing Senate Hearings did not lead into actual laws banning comics, the pressure forced many publishers out of business. More significantly, it set off a large comics scare and caused the self-censoring attempts of the comics industry. Although comics developed differently in Europe, North America, Asia and Latin America, the comics scare in the US in the 1950s—more specifically the crusades against

American crime and horror comics—rippled through to many other countries. In Britain, for example, the campaign succeeded in getting an Act of Parliament passed which made the publication or distribution of "horror comics" illegal. In many other countries, these American comics threw up shockwaves of anger and demands for censorship. Ireland, Canada, Australia, New Zealand, Italy, Denmark, Norway, Germany, and The Netherlands each had their national version of an anti-crime and horror campaign.[6]

The industry's self-censorship proved fatal to the medium's growth and development. In complying with the Code's insistence on "good" always vanquishing "evil," for example, comics tended toward the representation of oversimplified conflicts that led to thematic and generic stagnation. In part, the strict restrictions of the Comics Code did not allow comics the creative freedom enjoyed by the other media, and the comicbooks that flooded the market were trapped in the trifling problems and conflicts in a universe of costumed superheroes or "funny" talking animals. However, the Code cannot be blamed entirely for the minimal developments made in comics as a narrative form. In *Comic Books as History*, Joseph Witek analyses the effects of the Code on the development of comic books as a medium for a more sophisticated audience and reminds us that:

> To bash the Comics Code is easy enough: ...(B)ut it is important to remember that the Comics Code was not imposed on the industry by the government. In fact, its provisions make hash of the First Amendment and could stand no legal test. The Code's rules are not laws; they are self-imposed industry guidelines, and as such they simply codified the existing editorial leanings of most American comics. E.C.'s powerfully written war comics failed because of lagging news-stand sales, not because of the meddling of the Comics Code, and while the Code killed off most of the sophisticated American comic books, for many other comics the Code simply meant business as usual. The Code officially ruled out overtly mature treatments of adult themes in American comic books, but few such books existed anyway, and to blame only the Comics Code Authority for the lack of serious literature in comics form is to badly underestimate the puerility of the comic book publishers and of the mainstream comic audience.[7]

Partly as a reaction to the Code and the acquiescent attitude of mainstream comics producers and consumers, comic books that increasingly went beyond the thematic and narrative possibilities approved by the Code developed within the counterculture of the 1960s. These Underground comix, as they became known, cultivated an outlaw image and deliberately aimed to offend the sensi-

Figure 1. Just the title, *Dirty plotte*, calls attention to the lack of inhibition in this series. A page from *Dirty Plotte #1* showing influences of underground comix. Art and script: Julie Doucet @ 1990 The creator.

bilities of bourgeois America (*see Figure 1*). They defiantly opposed the sanitised views and values of middle class society proffered by their traditional counterparts. Instead, they offered biting parodies and satires of media and social customs as alternatives. Bound neither by the Code nor by any need to appeal to a wide audience, the Underground cartoonists had the incredible luxury of almost unrestricted artistic freedom. The "comix" became the principal outlet for the works of artists who were innovative and who rebelled against the restraints of the Code, thereby stretching the limits of what "comics" could be. Amidst the shameless obscenity and bad taste that abounded, several striking talents did emerge from this movement and much highly original work was accomplished. Though as a widespread cultural and artistic force, it lasted barely a decade, the Underground comix movement is a crucial phase in the development of comicbooks as a narrative form and a means of artistic expression. This was the first significant group of comic books in the United States aimed at an entirely adult audience. Many artists who are now major figures of comicbooks and who realised the potential of comics as a narrative form for serious themes and issues came from this movement. Industry insiders and critics agree that the roots of the new, fact-based comicbooks that have recently emerged in the United States can be traced to the Underground comix, "not only in the works of such established artists such as Robert Crumb, S. Clay Wilson, and Kim Deitch, who still create comicbooks, but also in a growing number of comicbook creators who take from the Undergrounds new visions of possibility for comicbook narratives but without that antagonism toward a general audience which so often led to the self-ghettoization of the Underground comix (*see Figure 2*)."[8]

For a long time after the late 1960s, much positive innovation in the comics was curbed by the conditions that dictated comics production and consumption: either they were mainly puerile adolescent entertainment or marginalized defiant magazines of the counterculture. Didactic comic books with definitely wholesome social aspirations also existed: these included biblical re-tellings, inspirational biographies, educational manuals, and historical legends. The most well-known would be the educational series by the Gilberton Company including the *Classics Comics* and *Classics Illustrated* which were redactions of literary works and popular

Figure 2. *Hate* is an example of a comicbook that treats sex candidly but nevertheless can appeal to a wide audience. *Hate #23*. Art and script: Peter Bagge @ 1996 The creator.

stories. However, these were generally more expensive and not as popular as the regular comics although many played on combining the informational and sensational with presentational patterns analogous to the comic-book industry's stock-in trades. The comics that held the public's attention, especially in the 1970s, were those that related to the two extremes: simplistic superhero fantasies or flagrant violence, anarchy and salaciousness. For critics concerned about comics at this time, it was uncomplicated to forego analyses of the artistic merits of comics and continue focusing on its "effects and influences" since the choice between approval and disapproval was almost prompted by the developments in the medium itself. Even in the absence of a specific critical rationale, critics judged the Underground comix as "bad," offensive and perverse in a condemnation that, despite its superficiality, was heeded by many.[9] By the mid-1970s, much of the force of the comix had disappeared just as the energy of the counterculture as a whole had dissipated. However, the practice of focusing on the capacity of comics to exert different kinds of influence over its readers persisted.

What is regrettable about the traditional critique of comics is that its fixed and enduring focus on morality has been maintained to the detriment of studies of other areas. More importantly, the various negative claims that have been made about the influence of comics were supported by insufficient data, and/or characterised by debatable methodology, in a way unimaginable for scholarship in other more established fields.[10] It would not occur to a serious critic to judge a novel on the evidence of a few paragraphs, nor a play on the basis of one or two scenes. Yet this practice is widely accepted in the criticism of comics. Such nonchalance and disapproval have also characterised works done on mass media and popular culture, most probably due to the stigma of "trivialization" that had been conferred on them from the start.[11] Since many studies on comics were included as part of works on mass media and popular culture, it is not surprising that comics were embroiled in the early struggles of these two disciplines to break out from the tangle of contentious claims about merit, validity, scope, terms, subject matter and so on. Scholarship in all these areas could not advance without a major shift in perspective from the frustratingly narrow and repetitive concerns about the apocalyptic views of seductive mass media and inferior popular culture.

By the 1970s, the popularity of comicbooks extended as their characters were transformed into action figures, masks, posters, ashtrays, mugs, boardgames, university mascots, and so on, to initiate a collection craze. The continuous rise in the number of comics being produced, sold, and read by the 1970s was accompanied by a substantial increase in the attention to American comics, both as strips and books, in journals, magazines and even books. In general, however, these publications are surveys and histories, mostly nostalgic and/or celebratory rather than analytical. One exception is Les Daniels' survey *Comix: A History of Comic Books in America*, which provides a sensible outline of major developments in comicbooks.[12] Another, and perhaps the most significant, analysis of American comics at this time is Dorfman and Mattelart's *How to Read Donald Duck: Imperialist Ideology in the Disney Comics*, a study of the Disney comics and an indictment of Disney as a prime carrier of "cultural imperialism."[13] This study is well-researched and well-argued, and is often cited as a paradigm of Marxist cultural analysis. In *Comics: Anatomy of a Mass Medium*, Reitberger and Fuchs culled examples from both comic strips and books and examined the social significance of comics, investigating broadly how comics propagate images and ideas that play up to prejudices.[14] Maurice Horn published thematic studies—*Comics of the American West* which is a heavily illustrated survey of the major Western comic strips and books and their basic symbolic themes; *Women in Comics* which provides an initial study on the representation and roles of women in comic strips and books; and *Sex in the Comics* which includes many illustrations, most of which come from the comics of the Underground culture of the 1960s.[15] Despite such studies as these, however, it remained clear that comics could not evade the notoriety established by some critics. The general tone of comics analysis underscored its role in the moral and cultural decline of modern society, and works on comics remained weighed down by the apprehensions of educators, parents, child psychiatrists, and moralists.

Meanwhile, in the 1980s and especially in the latter half of the decade, theorists of popular culture and media discourse started confronting the need to re-examine traditional thinking and expose the inadequacies of old conceptual moulds. This involved an active reassessment of the basis for the derision of popular culture in order to reveal the relativity or arbitrariness of the standards on which earlier conclusions on media influence were grounded. More current studies re-evaluate the terms, categories, presuppositions and methodologies with which mass media have customarily been thought of and call attention to the cultural hierarchies that attend the social construction of subjectivity and of standards.[16] Unlike previous approaches which mostly aimed to prove that media has the power to influence, or illustrate the effects of that influence, the more recent ones investigate the explicit and implicit logic and processes operating in these claims of media influence: What are the reasons behind the analyses? From which perspective are they being conducted? Who is doing the studies and for whom are they meant? What ideologies are being espoused or criticised in the analyses? New critics demand that current media discourse not simply stop at asking if media influence takes place and what the effects are; it must clarify HOW the processes are supposed to take place, explain how ideas, images, attitudes, forms and contents of a specific medium can exist within the texts and reproduce themselves in the readers.

This broader and more penetrating approach to communication and media studies, while having been very constructively applied in studying cinema, television, and the genres of melodrama, romance and detective fiction, is not yet as prevalent in studies of comics. An exception and an excellent example of the new breed of comics critic is Martin Barker who, through his discussion of comics, systematically re-examines claims about media influence and re-assesses many poor theories or empirical misrepresentations concerning the power of mass media in general, and comics in particular. In *Comics: Ideology, Power and the Critics*, Barker shows how, in the brief history of comics as a mass medium, critics have made all kinds of ideological claims about what comics supposedly exemplify.[17] He uses comics as a case-study to reveal the ways critics have investigated the mass media for possible "influences," while calling attention to the fact that there are literally thousands of works on how comics affect children without the authors acknowledging that they are coming from a particular ideological perspective. He also demonstrates how many standard concepts used in critiquing the media, such as "identification" and "stereotypes" for example, are not so much analytical tools as arguments from definable social positions.

In addition to cultural studies and media discourse, the rise of semiotic studies and an accompanying interest in the relations of verbal and visual languages also spawned some proficient analyses of comic books. There began an awareness of comics not only as a created product and social activity but as an artistic product which must be looked at in its own aesthetic terms. Will Eisner's *Comics and Sequential Art* is an important critical contribution by one of the central figures of the comicbook industry.[18] Eisner views comics as a distinct artistic expression with a literary-visual form. Using his own illustrations, he discusses his ideas on the potency of the medium for graphic storytelling and proceeds to discuss comics as a form of reading. Another fresh analysis of comics is Thomas Inge's *Comics as Culture* which shows the growth and development of comics as an important document of the twentieth century, and a distinct part of America's national heritage. In addition to demonstrating how comics have enriched and reflected the trends in American popular culture, Inge traces the influence of many American cartoonists in the world art scene and the relation of comics with other art and cultural forms.[19] Joseph Witek's *Comics as History* examines comicbooks for adults as narratives and provides a close reading of three examples utilising the methods of contemporary semiotics' reading of images and other nonverbal structures as texts.[20] Included in his study is one of the comicbooks responsible in large part for a revived interest in comics in the United States in the mid-1980s.

Published in 1986, Art Spiegelman's *Maus: A Survivor's Tale* is a comicbook recounting his parent's experiences related to their internment in the concentration camps in Auschwitz parallel to showing his strained, current relationship with his father. This comicbook caused a stir when it was nominated by the National Book Critics Circle for the biography category in 1987, and later won the Pulitzer Prize in 1992.[21] In the media attention to *Maus*, it was clear that North American readers were surprised by the topic, style, form, and length (2 volumes) of Spiegelman's comicbook. Spiegelman's innovative and intelligent exploration with comicbook form and content is not isolated. There have been other successful attempts in comics which break away from common comicbook formulas to maximise the rich formal and thematic heritage of the medium; much of these took place in Europe, primarily in France, Belgium, Italy and Germany, where a tradition of well-written and skilfully illustrated comic books designed specifically for adults have existed since the late 1960s. In the United States, where comicbooks are mostly devised for teen-age diversion, there have been notable changes in the comics scene in the last two decades as evidenced by the creations of, among others, Will Eisner, Harvey Pekar, Frank Miller, Alan Moore, Jules Feiffer, the Hernandez brothers, Art Spiegelman, Scott McCloud, Chester Brown, Seth, Donna Barr, Roberta Gregory, Kurt Busiek, Peter Bagge, Mike Allred, Jeff Smith, David Mazucchelli, Howard Cruse, Daniel Clowes, and more recently, Adrian Tomine (*refer to Chapter Seven, the section on "In the Shadow of the Speculation Boom" in this book for more information on these artists and their works*).

Artists, readers, and critics are developing an increasing confidence towards the capacity of comic books as a legitimate artistic form for expressing a wide range of ideas and emotions. As Witek observes:

> "the comic book, a widely accessible and commercially available medium, is now being chosen as a form by serious writers whose themes have traditionally been expressed in the forms of verbal narratives, or in films and other visual narratives . . . such that a general reading public now exists in the United States for narratives written in a medium historically considered solely the domain of subliterate adolescent fantasies and of the crassest commercial exploitation of rote generic formulas. Comic art is thus a literary medium in transition from mass popularity and cultural disdain to a new respectability as a means of expression and communication, and this new respect is evident first in the attitudes of the creators themselves."[22]

The popular success of comics as a mass medium has long obscured their pre-existence as an expressive form. Paying attention to the horde but ignoring individual examples, critics have seized upon comics as a sociological subject for clinical study, denying however from the onset that aesthetic qualities could be attributed to this medium. That comics can function as an artistic expression is proved by the presence of recently published comics which dynamically deal with larger aesthetic and psychological issues earlier unthinkable in the medium. As well, there has been a shift in critical attitude towards them to recognise that comics are a legitimate contribution to the visual and narrative arts of the world. One of the most comprehensive book dealing with comics as an artistic medium is Scott McCloud's *Understanding Comics: The Invisible Art*. This is a remarkable 215-page critical appraisal of the art in a comicbook form, using the medium of comics itself as a very innovative and effective way to study the art.[23] Robert C. Harvey's *The Art of Comic Book: An Aesthetic History* clarifies the form and language of the medium and illustrates the powerful potential of comics as narrative art.[24] Other examples of scholarship on comicbooks is *Adult Comics: An Introduction* by Roger Sabin which comprehensively chronicles the rise and development of these comicbooks in Great Britain and the United States.[25] For insight into superhero comicbooks and the environment where that created them, recent books published in North America that are worth mentioning are Gerard Jones and Will Jacobs' *The Comic Book Heroes* and Trina Robbins' *The Great Women Superheroes*.[26]

The emergence of comicbooks as a respectable literary form in the 1980s might seem unlooked for given the long decades of cultural scorn and active social repression but the potential has always existed for comics to present the same kinds of narratives as other verbal and pictorial media. Serious literature in comic book form may be a relatively concept in American culture, but in Europe, comics have long made broad inroads into highbrow culture, especially in France and Belgium and Germany where comics for adults have been published steadily. In Germany, it is not unusual to read reviews about comics in reputable newspapers, as well as magazines such as *Der Spiegel*. In France, comics have been reviewed in the literary pages of *Le Monde* alongside articles on semiotics and biographies of prominent cultural figures. Without having to go underground, French comics took on a highly critical sociological and political character in the 1960s and 1970s. University degrees on this topic may be had in France, Germany, Belgium and Italy. In fact, at the Sorbonne, comics as a distinct discipline was institutionally introduced by the Institut d'Art et d'Archéologie as early as 1972 and a special subject "l'Histoire et l'Esthetique de la bande dessinée" (Aesthetic History of Comics) has been taught by one of the leading figures in comics analysis, Francis Lacassin. Together with Jules Renard, Lacassin helped found the "Club des Bandes dessinées" in 1962 in Paris, which later became the "Centre d'Etude des Littératures d'Expression

Graphique," a Center which has consistently been crucial to the development and growth of comics scholarship. He also published *Pour un neuvième Art*, to date the most comprehensive description and analysis of the formal and structural aspects of comics.[27] Most of the early critical attention to comics has been provided by French, German and Italian scholars, who have even produced many of the most comprehensive studies of American comic strips and books.[28] Another difference in the attitude towards comics between Europe and the US is apparent in the perception of comics artists. The talents of Winsor McCay of *Little Nemo in Slumberland* and Harry Herriman of *Krazy Kat*, both American artists, were more fully appreciated in Europe before the US. At present, several comics artists in Europe are publicly acclaimed not only for their comicbooks, but for their achievements in other cultural forms as well. The French-Yugoslav star Enki Bilal and the Chilean Alejandro Jodorowski, for example, have recently made films, and Gérard Lauzier's plays have opened successfully in Paris. Other crossover artists include British novelist Doris Lessing, who is presently scripting a comic book, and Javier Mariscal, who is one of Spain's most famous designers, creating furniture as well as the 1992 Olympic mascot, Cobi.[29] Art Spiegelman notes the discrepancy: "In France, a cartoonist is one step below a movie director. In America, (a cartoonist) has only slightly more status than a plumber."[30]

Cultural attitudes towards the comics are changing in the US. Comicbooks with intentional literary and artistic aspirations may still be relatively rare but certainly prevalent enough to initiate new interests, including re-considerations of the traditional, more commercial comicbooks. One can finally see the development of a body of works attempting to assess comics on their own terms, measuring their worth against their own developed standards and aesthetic principles rather than by the yardsticks of other related art.[31] This is the most difficult area to write about due to present inadequacies in the critical vocabulary as definitions of the structural and stylistic principles behind successful comic art have yet to be formulated. Thus, there is still the tendency to rely on terms borrowed from other areas of creative expression. Apart from the necessity of formulating evaluative terms, there is as well the need to clarify terms without turning them into constraints.

The problems confronting the re-assessment of comics reflect the dilemmas which attend the study of other forms of popular culture: the attempts to smoothe the friction between refined aesthetics and mass popularity and the struggle to legitimise its status through critical academic approval—in short, preoccupations with acceptance and hierarchies which have long plagued the field. Much of the improved understanding and appreciation of popular forms may be attributed to the shifts in ideological inclinations used in analysing modern culture and society. Sanctioning and categorising are actions that have ideological implications, and paradigms and criteria that were earlier presumed sacrosanct are now being shown to be artificial, relative and subjective. Much of the exposure and re-evaluation of implied ideology in the analysis of popular culture is being undertaken within the framework of cultural studies and it is in this field that the current breakthrough of comics into mainstream scholarship must be contextualised.

NOTES

1 There have been intermittent attempts to sanitize the thematic and graphic contents of comics which have been directed for the most part against comicbooks, not comic strips (for a thorough investigation—and reinterpretation—of the major complaints against comicbooks, see Martin Barker, *Comics: Power, Ideology and the Critics* (Manchester: Manchester UP, 1989). The publication requirements of the latter—they are considerably shorter, usually appear in daily or Sunday newspapers, and are subject to editorial regulations of these periodicals which target a wider range of audience than comic books—have rescued the strips from the cultural hostility the comic books have suffered. On the other hand, these requirements have set more limitations for the comic strips and in general, the strips cannot match the graphic spectacle of the books.

2 Wertham, Fredric, *The Seduction of the Innocent* (New York: Rhinehart and Wilson, 1954). Seen from outside the context of postwar America of the 1950s, it is amazing how such an unsound and unscientific piece of research could have been so powerful. There are now many critics who probe the import of this book on comics. Among them, James B. Twitchell extensively quotes Wertham and illustrates the flaws and inconsistencies in his reasoning, as well as exposes some purposeful misreadings by Wertham. See "Disorderly Conduct Illustrated: The Rise and Fall and Rise of the Comics," Chapter Four of *Preposterous Violence: Fables of Aggression in Modern Culture* (New York: Oxford UP, 1989): 129–80. Wertham's book is also discussed at

length in Chapter Five of Martin Baker, *A Haunt of Fears: the Strange History of the British Horror Comics Campaign* (London: Pluto Press, 1984) especially in relation to the insiduous use of the concept of "identification" in the criticism of comics; as well as the problems this concept embodies.

3 Lupoff, Dick and Don Thompson, eds. *All in Color for a Dime* (New Rochelle, N.Y.: Arlington House, 1970): 17. The other two published discussions were sociological studies of comics by Gershon Legman, *Love and Death: A Study in Censorship* (New York: Breaking Point, 1949) and Geoffrey Wagner, "Popular Iconography in the USA," in *Parade of Pleasure* (New York: Library Publishers, 1955).

4 For information on the American campaign, see in particular James Gilbert, *A Cycle of Outrage* (New York: Oxford UP, 1987). A great deal of information and argument about this campaign is also to be found in any of the general histories of American comics. To be fair to Wertham, he never advocated a blanket censorship. In fact, he published his protestations about the arbitrariness of the Code and how America would be better off if it did not exist. However, by this time no one was listening. "Contrary to common belief Wertham's political orientation was in fact liberal. He is often painted as a puritan, even a fascist, but in his earlier life, he had campaigned against the abortion laws and for freedom of speech. He was a supporter of Civil Rights and opened the first psychiatric clinic in Harlem (charging less than the going rate because the locals were poor). Thus, in one sense, his opposition to blanket censorship was in keeping with his overall political philosophy" in Roger Sabin, *Adult Comics: An Introduction*, (London: Routledge, 1993): 280.

5 Twitchell, *op cit.*, 135.

6 In his Notes and References to Chapter I of *Comics: Ideology, Power and the Critics*, op cit., 303), Martin Barker provides information on articles relating to Australia, New Zealand, Canada and Germany.

7 Joseph Witek, *Comic Books as History: The Narrative Art of Jack Jackson, Art Spiegelman, and Harvey Pekar* (Mississippi: University of Mississippi Press, 1989): 50.

8 Joseph Witek, "The Underground Roots of Fact-Based Comics," in idem (1989): 48–57, p. 54. For more information on the Underground Comix, refer to Mark Estren, *A History of Underground Comix* (San Francisco: Straight Arrow, 1974); the second chapter of Thomas Inge, *Comics as Culture* (Mississippi: University of Mississippi Press, 1990); and the last chapter of Les Daniels, *Comix: A History of Comic Books in America* (New York: Bonanza Books, 1971). So far, Estren's book is the most comprehensive record of the comix; documentation of this movement is difficult because (a) the underground comix were too idiosyncratic in approach and too multifarious in subject matter to be eas-

ily summarised, (b) it must cover a wide expanse of the counterculture scene which spanned California to New York, and (c) there is a general reluctance among the artists to cooperate with researchers and critics.

9 Refer to the Mark Estren, *op cit.*, where he cites and counters numerous examples of objections to the undergound comix. For other reactions to the censorship of underground comix, see also, D. Donahue and Susan Goodrick, eds., *The Apex Treasury of Underground Comix* (New York: Quick Fox, 1974); and S. L. Huck, "Sex Comix: A Report for Adults Only," *American Opinion* 17 (1970): 15–20.

10 See, for example, Valerie Walkerdine, "Some day my Prince will come: young girls and the preparation for adolescent sexuality," in Angela McRobbie and Mica Nava, eds., *Gender and Generation* (London: Macmillan, 1984): 162–84; Clare Dellino, "Comics that set a bad example," *Sunday Times* (February 15, 1971): 19; Ruth Strang, "Why Children Read Comics," *Elementary School Journal* (1943): 336–342. For more examples and sustained analysis of poor approaches and methodology in comics criticism, refer to the two books by Martin Barker in the Bibliography section of this thesis.

11 Joli Jensen, *Redeeming Modernity: Contradictions in Media Criticism* (London: Sage Publications, 1990) especially Chapters Two and Three.

12 Les Daniels, Comix: *A History of Comic Books in America* (New York: Bonanza Books, 1971).

13 Ariel Dorfman and Armand Mattelart *How to Read Donald Duck: Imperialist Ideology in the Disney Comic* (New York: International General, 1976). Barker (1989) praises Dorfman and Mattelart as a "model of propriety when it comes to giving references" since a general frustration in studying comics is the incompleteness of references, especially inattention to details in dates and edition numbers of the original materials.

14 R. Reitberger and W. Fuchs, *Comics: Anatomy of a Mass Medium* (London: Studio Vista, 1972). Translated from the German Comics: *Anatomie eines Massenmediums* published by Rowohlt Taschenbücher.

15 Horn, Maurice, *Comics of the American West* (New York: Winchester Press, 1977); *Women in Comics* (New York: Chelsea House Publishers, 1980). This book provides good visual examples but disappoints in critical depth. A third one is *Sex in the Comics* (New York: Chelsea House, 1985).

16 For examples of the new approaches to media discourse, refer to the works of John Fiske, James Carey, Tony Bennett, Stuart Hall, Ervin Goffman, M. Gurevitch, J. Curran and J. Woollacott, among others, in the Selected Bibliography section of this study.

17 Martin Barker, *Comics: The Critics, Ideology, and Power* (Manchester: Manchester University Press, 1989).

18 Will Eisner, *Comics and Sequential Art* (Tamarac, Fla.: Poorhouse Press, 1985).

19 Thomas Inge, *Comics as Culture* (Mississipi: University Press of Mississippi, 1990). Inge is an important authority in the medium and played a vital role in the academic community's awakening to the art form.

20 Witek, *op cit.*

21 Art Spiegelman, *Maus: A Survivor's Tale* (New York: Pantheon, 1986).

22 Witek, *op cit*, 37.

23 Scott McCloud, *Understanding Comics: The Invisible Art* (Princeton, Wisconsin: Kitchen Sink Press, 1993).

24 Robert Harvey, *The Art of the Comic Book: An Aesthetic History* (Jackson: University Press of Mississippi, 1996).

25 Roger Sabin, *Adult Comics: An Introduction* (London and New York: Routledge, 1993).

26 Gerard Jones and Will Jacobs, *The Comic Book Heroes* (Rocklin, CA: Prima Publishing, 1997) and Trina Robins, *The Great Women Superheroes* (Northampton, MA: Kitchen Sink Press, 1996). There is also an excellent book in German about the medium in Andreas Knigge's *Comics: Vom Massenblatt ins multimedia Abenteur* (Hamburg: Rowohlt, 1996).

27 Francis Lacassin, *Pour un neuvième art* (Paris: Slatkine Editions, 1982).

28 European sources, mostly unavailable in English, have been included in the Bibliography section.

29 Margot Hornblower, "Beyond Mickey Mouse: Comics Grow Up and Go Global," *Time* (1 November 1993): 63–64.

30 *Ibid*, 64.

31 Refer to the works of Arthur Berger (1991); A. Dorfman (1983); S. McCloud (1993); D. Chavez (1988); N. Harris (9185); B. DeMott (1984); Pearson and Uricchio (1993); R. Sabin (1993), Harvey (1996), among others, in the Bibliography section of this study.

CHAPTER TWO

Responses to Comicbooks and the Concept of the "Popular"

This chapter focuses on how varying perceptions and discourses about popular culture are implicated in the discourses used in describing and evaluating comicbooks. My concern is not to come up with a definitive meaning of the "popular" but to focus on the languages in which comicbooks have been discussed, and the ways in which these discourses have affected the history and politics of the production and consumption of comicbooks.

Discussions of any cultural form inevitably involve questions of aesthetics, history, and politics. Clarifying the categorisation of comicbooks as a "popular" form, and analysing the traditional critical ambivalence in responding to sequential art as a valid cultural product, bring up aspects of the notion of "popular culture" that are best perceived as problematic rather than definitive. In the range of responses to comics and its by-product—in the press, by critics, by fans, or by cultural theorists—there is a level of energy which attests to a cultural and social debate that is connected to many other aspects of modern life such as technology, media, communication, and visual arts. That the majority of the criticism of comicbooks, except for the recent ones, have largely failed to produce new concepts for exploring cultural forms, social relations and hierarchies, or even acknowledged that they might be required, is a measure of the newness and the difficulty of the problems addressed in this study. This chapter, then, shall attempt to relate the development of critical discourses about comicbooks to the wider context of popular culture while questioning the usual impressions of the concepts, relations, hierarchies and standards in the social and cultural spheres of modern life.

The discussion will focus mostly on the responses to sequential art by American and British critics, theorists, and publics. Given the more substantial amount of research on sequential art in continental Europe, this may seem surprising. But the proposition that the development of political, literary and theoretical languages used to analyse popular culture has to be given the specificity of a national context cannot be emphasised enough. Sequential art, particularly comic strips, has been popularly acknowledged as an American form. And, although European comicbooks have previously outdistanced American ones in the range of themes, narratives, and forms of visual impact, the form and content of sequential art in the United States, Canada, and England quickly caught up in the mid-1980s.

Changes to the reactions to comicbooks in the United States reflect the radically changing tendencies in thinking about culture and the "popular." In the specific history and development of comic strips to graphic novels, for example, one sees the development of recognisable and distinctive responses to the medium, characterised by patronage, paternalism, and obsessive return to the "literary" or concepts in cinema criticism. This latter gesture is particularly ironic as a medium itself once labelled "popular"—the cinema—is now being used as a legitimising medium for sequential art.

In trying to evaluate comicbooks as a new cultural form, explicit and implicit cultural hierarchies must be examined. This examination will necessarily touch upon arguments or charges about cultural decline in a wider context. It would be difficult to understand the compelling influence of Frederic Wertham and the consequences of his attack on comicbooks in isolation from the American political context of the 1940s and 1950s that spawned it. We need, therefore, to examine the country's social and cultural ideals in order to decipher the rise and "need" for underground comix to rebel against the definition of the all-American boy, the family as an institution, prevailing middle-class bourgeois values, and so on. In the same vein, in evaluating the decline in sales of superhero comicbooks in the mid-1990s, we have to examine the impulses in the comics industry and its readers which led to its decline.

The most popular comicbooks read mostly by male adolescents present a specific and interesting commentary concerning the relations between culture, history, national identity, and social success. The unquestioning patriotism of superheroes unashamedly fighting for Uncle Sam while remaining assured of recurring and unfailing victory against the enemies of country and society provides an example of a social text worthy of examination. The representation of enemies and villains in these comicbooks is highly dependent on the social and cultural relations of the United States at any one time, as well as the prevailing ideas of unity and conformity. The study of comics necessarily invites investigation in this more sociological realm.

In looking at the development of comicbooks and the responses to them, one becomes aware of the problems the concept of the "popular" poses for debates within the dominant culture and the categories relevant to define it, e.g., history, national identity, institutional stability, monetary resources and productive power, among others. In previous studies, representations and ideas in comicbooks which suggest cultural hierarchies and differences have been usually cloaked in general cultural terms, as if these differences were simply a matter of audience, taste, or preference. Only recently have critical responses to comicbooks referred explicitly to the assumptions about class, age, race and gender which underlie the differences and reveal the biases in the environment in which they are received and reviewed. In tracing the changes behind responses to comics, one may perceive the complex and focal points of cultural studies in re-constructing the concept of the "popular" by accounting for cultural differences and practices NOT in reference to intrinsic or external values (how good, how beautiful) but by inferences to the overall map of social relations and practices (in whose interests, by whose estimation).

The sudden prestige granted to adult comics or graphic novels attests to the need for caution in evaluating new cultural forms strictly within the confines of either intrinsic or external values. Graphic novels increased both in quality and quantity since the

mid-1980s and are now part of a cultural landscape that would
have been unimaginable two decades ago. Their present cultural
status and favourable reception cannot be traced solely to the
refinements in their formal and structural features. The following
list, for example, provides a partial enumeration of some of the
changes in the production, distribution and marketing of comicbooks which have influenced the perception and reception of these
books: the amount of disposable income now available to former
adolescent comic fans; the increasing number of people who "grew
up" with comics now in positions of power in the publishing business; the spread of new scholars and critics who grew up in a
multi-media environment of learning and cultural refinement; the
growing appreciation of other graphic arts like films, videos and
television; the formation of an *auteur* system that gives the artists
more creative freedom; the sale of comicbooks in specialty stores,
bookstores, and over the internet rather than news-stands; developments in technology; the multi-media approach to promoting
comicbooks characters and stories; and finally, the increased contemporary awareness and availability of comicbooks from Europe
and Japan. All these and other factors have greatly influenced the
recent trend in comicbook sales in America, the changes in the
medium's form and contents, as well as its critical reception and
type of audience. Sequential art is gradually shedding the stigma of
triviality to establish itself as a genre capable of rivalling other narratives and signifying practices in the process of producing and
representing reality.

THE POPULAR AS INFERIOR

The reasons why comics have been described as a form of popular
culture show the ambiguities involved in conceptualising the "popular"; the reasons also recall the on-going dialogue about hierarchies and definitions in culture. First of all, sequential art is seen as
a popular form because it is different from the forms favoured by
the dominant or official culture. Critics constantly refer to its difference from literature, often comparing the experiences of reading
literature and "reading comics." Usually perceived as a visual
form, sequential art is deemed both inadequate and/or too explicit for a culture that confers pre-eminence on the written word.
Reading literature is seen as offering free play to the imagination,

while comicbooks are overtly explicit and thus produce passivity. Too many factors and other people intervene between the "creator" or author and the audience. Reading, according to this theory, should allow for direct access to an author's thoughts and language, whereas creative expression in comics, or other popular forms, is constantly hampered by the industrial and technical constraints of the medium. Furthermore, popular forms like comics are more sales or profit-oriented and thus are capable of compromising excellence or artistic merits for wider consumer appeal. Therefore, the creators themselves often concede creativity because they are constrained by factors external to the medium such as deadlines, editorial decisions, space allotment, sales statistics, and so on. This practice contrasts highly with the presumed purity of artistic expressions and the unrestricted range and freedom found in novels, poetry, and other forms of art deemed serious by the principal culture.

Comics, then, is a popular form by default because it does not meet the criteria for serious cultural significance when compared to works of literature which consist of the "finest human experience" and are capable of evoking a "genuine personal response."[1] Popular culture, collectively and commercially produced, is stereotyped, formulaic, anonymous, and deficient in "human experience" according to this view. Consequently, sequential art is described as an impoverished form of culture, hence "popular." Here, one sees the equation of "popular" with "base" or "inferior" which has characterised many discussions of popular culture. Such notions have also led to a rather extended rejection or trivialization of comics and caused a dearth of serious critical attention to it.

THE POPULAR AND IMPERMANENCE

Sequential art is also described as "popular" because of its ephemeral nature. Dominant forms of culture are institutionalised in libraries and galleries or in ways that will ensure their preservation and their centrality to the cultural debate. The institutions of comics, on the other hand, are notorious for their impermanence as objectified by their product's form, often referred to as "throwaway entertainment." Until recently, there also seemed a strange reluctance to engage with any notion of the history or continuity of this medium. Only now are there noticeably more attempts to document the popular or critical memories of comics and the comics industry. Unfortunately, a vast amount of primary material has already been irretrievably lost. Due to the scarcity of organised and existing accounts about the industry and the conditions and decisions therein, most research into the early days of comics must be constructed from the memory or perspective of "industry insiders." This ephemeral quality assures sequential art exclusion from those cultural discourses founded on the notion of continuity and tradition, and whose merits are gauged by their enduring qualities. Comics are thus largely denied the serious critical and theoretical attention given to other forms of communication and expression due to the long-standing fallacy of equating the most prevalent form of the medium—the physical comicbook—as BEING the medium itself. The wrong, but persistent, perception of the actual comicbook as the medium itself has prompted many changes in the present production, distribution and sales of comicbooks. There is currently a noticeable shift of emphasis on "books" rather than "comics," as evidenced, for example, in the re-naming of comicbooks to "graphic novels" as recent crops of comicbooks published in North America increasingly aspire to a "book-look," similar to the format of comicbooks in Europe and Japan. In the same vein, comicbooks are now sold in bookstores and specialty stores, which has enhanced their cultural status among the general public, and has likewise modified its group of readers. Much like any product subject to a semiotic reading, the socially determined place of appearance influences the decision of the comics reader, including its critics. Where comics are placed and seen, who reads and talks about comics, what comes before and after them and what surrounds the perception of the medium are all aspects which attest to the fact that the place of the medium is related to its meaning and that the location and environment of comics have semantic value.

While comicbooks themselves may be ephemeral, the medium and form are not. In fact, many acclaimed directors and scriptwriters of film, television and video admit their indebtedness to comics for refining aspects of their art. Many mythologies, characters, anecdotes and forms of humour which originated in comics are deeply ingrained not only in American consciousness but have found their way into a world-wide system of reference. The language, characters and narratives in comics do not exist devoid of ideologies, doctrines, and biases. Given the ubiquity of the medium and its influence on a large portion of the population, it is difficult to imagine that sequential art did not, in an enduring way, participate in or contribute to the cultural debates or struggles of the medium's surrounding social environment.

GENERAL ACCESSIBILITY SPELLS MEDIOCRITY

Comics are often described as a "popular" cultural form simply because they are well-liked and have most probably touched the lives of everyone at one point or another. This observation can be made in relation to comics as a whole, in relation to particular types of comics—superhero comics, humorous comics, science fiction, horror, and romance are among these at the top of the list— or in relation to by-products and spin offs from comics in whatever other form of merchandise. The power and popularity of comics and the characters generated from them as a whole, however, have generally been problematic for critics, simply because the other, more negative meanings of the "popular" are always present in the margins. Comics, for example, is seen as "popular" in its general accessibility (contrary to catering to a "cultured" or "cultivated" few), its pandering to mediocrity, and in its broad appeal to a general, acquiescent public which is characterised as unsophisticated and hence easy to cater to.

The debate between general accessibility and cultural authenticity is usually based on the concept of cultural authenticity in the sphere of the literary: comicbooks are measured against the narratives and characterisation found in the novel or are measured against a set of cultural values derived from literature. Given this criteria of evaluation, comics are naturally almost always found wanting. This attempt to designate the particular, historically specific modes of representation which have characterised the novel as a guarantor of the worth of all cultural forms cannot be impartial. Once more, this emphasis on the criteria of other literary modes is a testament to the importance of the "literary" as an articulation of agreed cultural values. Confronted by this tendency it would seem that there is no way to respond to the democratisation, or accessibility, represented by comicbooks and other popular forms of expression except in terms of decline, and loss of authenticity.

The frequent movement between the realm of literary criticism and the analysis of popular culture has tended to hamper the development of a specific language for the analysis of popular narratives in general, and sequential art in particular.

REPRESENTATIONS IN COMICBOOKS

One other way in which comics are implicated in discourses of the "popular" encompasses two seemingly contrary notions. They are seen both as (a) constitutive of and (b) rebelling against the ideas of the people and the nation. At any one time, readers are cognisant of a hegemonic or dominant mentality and, accordingly, comics are perceived as either rebelling against or catering to this mentality. Critics frequently echo this sort of construction, either attempting to align comics with those that assert legitimisation of the common or dominant cultural values, or criticising comics for falling behind the "standard American." Either way, the definition of prevailing ideas of "people" and "nation" are implicated. To what extent do comicbooks celebrate dominant viewpoints? Especially after the institution of the Comics Code, comicbooks are seen as offering constructions of social relations which make a certain unified notion of "the American people," the very same paradigms that are ironically de-constructed in more recent graphic novels.

Arguments about how comicbooks deliberately and playfully engage the interests of their readers will be discussed in more detail in the following chapters though it must be mentioned here that establishing a legitimisation/criticism dichotomy ignores the complexity of the issue. Argumentation itself, for example, may be more a matter of degree than of absolutes. And even the most fundamental social criticism appearing in mainstream media may, in certain instances, serve to legitimate social values and structures, albeit in the disguise of criticism. As Gitlin shows, oppositional movements can be "framed," their voice and arguments distorted and labeled as deviant and wrong, in such a way as to depoliticize them.[2]

Some critics reject the dismissal of all television as debased and corrupt, and try to establish a hierarchy within the forms of television, either in terms of different channels (shopping channel vs. all-news channel) or in terms of different genres (soap operas vs.

current affairs). The same is true now with sequential art.[3] Hierarchies are established between graphic novels and superhero series and humorous ones, bound volumes and loose-leafed or single issues, traditional superheroes and mature, ironic new ones, established artists and unknowns. Even the publishing houses are ranked according to putative value.

Unlike television, however, whose almost intrusive accessibility makes its representations of reality available to most members of all social classes, the differences in comicbooks are already visible at the point of consumption. Reading comicbooks entails more activity than watching television; it often requires the choice and purchase, and sometimes collection, of issues with variable publication dates and frequency. These activities are performed repeatedly, usually weekly or monthly, as opposed to the convenience of daily turning on a television in one of several rooms. There are also more representations of all kinds of social reality available in television simply because of the immense quantity of types of programmes available: newscasts, advertisements, game shows, documentaries and so on. Such programmes are aired almost twenty four hours allowing one to anticipate them for viewing or simply chance upon them while channel surfing. Representations in comicbooks are already circumscribed by the amount and type of periodicals purchased, and for the longest time the assortment of comicbook genres was not very broad. Even in the case of comic strips, the difference between the dominant and the marginally popular was never particularly visible at the point of consumption since strips began appearing in newspapers and, even presently, are still published within newspapers and magazines. Furthermore, the reading of comicbooks denies the possibility of the kind of interactive discussion and sharing which often attends group television viewing, or the reading aloud or re-telling of comic strips in communal settings—i.e., the sharing of newspapers within the home, workplace, and such public places as a doctor's office, trains, or subway stations. The audience perception of differing media concerning their content and significance is influenced by the differing circumstances which frame television and comic strips and which allow for communal forms of qualification by readers.

Like any other medium, comicbooks may be read on different levels, but in gauging critical responses in general, they seem to be more prone to be read as legitimising or rebelling against rigid social categorisations because of the lingering association of the medium with adolescents or the avant-garde. More nuanced assessments of cultural practices and differences, however, may be detected in aspects which were formerly identified as similarities and continuities in comicbooks. The labelling or classification of comicbooks has been getting increasingly difficult, as has the identification of its readership.[4] Earlier critical attempts to distinguish genres within comics and the connections between types of comics and readers were conducted in general cultural terms which tended to account for such differences as if they were simply a matter of age and taste, instead of examining and explicitly referring to the issues of social class, gender, and opportunities which underlie these differences and preferences.

In undervaluing the grounding of differences at the level of social dimensions instead of simply cultural ones, there is a tendency to see the popularity of comicbooks as a symptom, or perhaps a source, of a certain cultural homogeneity. Readers are united by the fact of their reading comics. Critics, government committees, and the comicbook industry admit to this by their insistence in giving an "identity" or definitive description to the "groups" who read comicbooks. The demographics of this homogeneity have been used as the basis for sporadic attacks on comicbooks by educators, child psychologists, and concerned authorities, as well as by those involved in the manufacture of the medium in order to plan for and improve their merchandise and merchandising strategies. Both camps endow more social and political substance to this unity, assuming that readers of comicbooks form coherent, non-hierarchical groups who share cultural and political values. This exemplifies the fluid shifts in the significance of "the popular"—from a term of legal and political relations to a synonym for the "general public." This is an interesting tension utilised in the discussions of sequential art as a form of popular culture. While one set of arguments tends to reproduce existing social and cultural hierarchies (culture in terms of "elevated" and "base"), the other tends to repress them in the name of the "audience" or the "man in the street" (as in wide and well-liked or trendy). Thus, difference and distinction can be acknowledged at the level of the cultural where they can be represented as natural, but are consistently removed from discussions of the social dimensions of comics which also tend to overlook what roles comic-

books might have had in the construction of notions of "the popular."

CULTURAL COLLAPSE

Evaluating responses to sequential art raises exactly the sorts of
questions about the relation between cultural forms and social and
political structures central to the attempts to find new categories
and new ways in studying cultural forms. Even the use of one
form, comicbooks as a case study, shows the difficulty of thinking
social, technological and subjective determinants simultaneously
and is a measure of the difficulty of breaking away from inherited
debates about social and cultural relations. Within the past decade,
a wide range of cultural critics, as well as literary and social histo-
rians, representing radically different ideological perspectives, have
pointed to the crisis within cultural life. They consider culture to
be no longer a unitary, fixed category but a decentered, fragmen-
tary assemblage of conflicting voices and institutions. They draw
attention to the prevailing awareness that an "official," centralised
culture is increasingly difficult to identify in contemporary soci-
eties. Although explanations for this development differ quite
drastically from theorist to theorist, as do their responses to it, the
common denominator remains a recognition that a "culture"
shared by all is continuing to fragment.[5]

As categories of literature and kinds of public continue to
diversify and multiply, "culture" becomes a fundamentally conflict
ridden terrain.

> The significance of this emerging school of cultural analysis
> comes from its recognition that all cultural production must
> be seen as a set of power relations that produce particular
> forms of subjectivity, but that the nature, function, and uses
> of mass culture can no longer be conceived in a monolithic
> manner.[6]

As the concept of "culture" splinters into varying directions,
the terms and the framework we use to understand it become
ambivalent, even arbitrary. Jim Collins proffers the observation
that our culture has become highly "discourse-sensitive" in that:

> how we conceptualise our culture depends upon discourses
> which construct it in conflicting, often contradictory ways,

according to interests and values of those discourses as they
struggle to legitimise themselves as privileged forms of representation.[7]

An on-going proliferation of popular narratives, the unpre-
dictable diversification of their publics, and the increasingly serious attention given to these forms attest to this "struggle for legitimisation." Amidst the rise of varied textual production and social
diversification, analyses of cultural forms must rest on expanded
definitions of culture, media and communication and changed criteria for the designation of valid objects of study. Cultural analysis must act on the democratic principle assumed by Raymond
Williams in *Culture and Society* that the discourses of all members
of a society should be its concern, not just those of an educated
elite.[8]

As more and more kinds of texts and forms of discourses compete to define for themselves their cultural and social space, the
connection between language and the distribution of power and
the role of discourses in the distribution of ideologies, become
more apparent. Critical studies of television and cinema have
exhibited much initiative in exploring these lines of inquiry. The
uses of cultural forms to maintain social control, the relations
between dominant and subordinate cultural forms, the possibility
of cultural authenticity, the necessary relations between technological progress and cultural decline, the corrupting effects of generally accessible forms of culture, the hierarchies imbued in categorising forms, and the gender roles in cultural production and
consumption are all areas which have been explored in this general critical project. Responses to comicbooks have only very recently started locating the medium and its consequences within such
discussions. Nonetheless even former ways of talking about
comics, when re-examined along the lines of these new perspectives, can be made to participate in the continuation and adaptation of debates about issues central to the evaluation and re-defi-
nition of culture, media and communication.

Much interrogation of the validity of comicbooks as a cultural form concerns the mass media's "effects and influence" or
"hypodermic needle effect" type. This form of cultural inquiry
concentrates on the effects of comicbooks in influencing moral and
social values, including political ones, and the medium's role in the
distribution of deficient and rebellious values relative to estab-

lished authority. To some extent, such questions are unavoidable since comicbooks and strips may be perceived as a widely consumed source of political and dramatic representations (though still far below the range and frequency of television). It is notable, however, as Denis McQuail has pointed out, that we do not ask such questions of other major institutions of communication such as the Church, or the Law, whose legitimacy and responsibility seem to be taken for granted.[9]

But while such establishments are more prominent, and certainly more powerful in creating partial representations of reality, it seems more reasonable instead to look at a less culturally pervasive medium such as comicbooks in terms of the ways it contributes to our conception of social and cultural relations, or about the types of experience or knowledge which these books either enhance or marginalise. There are some questionable presumptions underlying the traditional "effects and influence" method. This model treats its subjects as decontextualised, asocial beings who either absorb mass media contents or (luckily) resist them. It also frames the problems in terms of assessing the measurable "effects" of comicbooks on an otherwise stable political and cultural structure, running the risk both of simplifying the communication process and displacing an entire matrix of social transformations onto a single institution.

We must not forget that whatever the effects of comicbooks are, it cannot be assumed that the environment is otherwise stable in that it only receives without re-acting. Rather, it is more the case that the environment is a continually changing thing and much more complex in character than that which allows itself to be passively influenced. The truth is that the audience affects books just as books affect the audience, because consumers affect the product just as products affect consumers. Comicbooks have flourished at a time of increased diversity in society's composition and identity. Increased mobility and an attendant intermixing of people led also to the greater mixing of social ideologies and aesthetic preferences. This is reflected in the increasing variety of forms and types of discourses people choose to believe can reflect their reality or the reality they wish to see. People often utilise multiple discourses; those who read comicbooks, for example, usually also watch television and film, and avail themselves of other forms of print narratives. In the face of many factors that are constantly interacting, it is really quite difficult to blame such particular cultural forms as comicbooks with causing the moral deterioration and cultural decline attributed to it by many critics.

Overlooking the general instability of society as a factor is apparent, for instance, in the magnitude of response to Frederic Wertham's attack on comicbooks despite the unsound reasoning of his book and the gaps between his premises and conclusions censuring comicbooks for a range of deficiencies from juvenile delinquency to romanticising criminal and sexual deviance, and belittling authority. His charges occurred during a time and in an atmosphere imbued with changes and uncertainties about the structure and stability of social institutions. Due to its format and unfortunately close link to adolescents and children, comicbooks were easy targets as scapegoats.[10] From a very early stage, a particular and persistent equation was made between comicbooks and adolescence and, by extension, the moral and spiritual health of the family, society and the nation. This follows the tendency of criticism about media effects to see the family as the focal, and vulnerable, point of social relations. In the case of comicbooks, the family is particularly threatened because its most vulnerable members, children, are ingesting dubious values and ideas about ethics and authority through comicbooks. By 1954, when Wertham's *Seduction of the Innocent* was published, comicbooks were already long susceptible to outside pressure groups because of their child-oriented market.

The ability of pressure groups to influence a medium depends greatly upon its perceived vulnerability to such pressure. Comics were sufficiently vulnerable to outside criticism and pressure because it was perceived as a medium for children and adolescents, and for a long time, it was not clear that they were protected by the First Amendment.[11] Educators and psychologists endlessly debated whether comicbooks corrupt children. In 1940, one of the first descriptions of comicbooks in a professional journal (*Journal of Educational Sociology*) claimed that comics'

> crude blacks and reds spoil the child's natural sense of colour, their hypodermic injection of sex and murder make the child impatient with better, though quieter stories. Unless we want a coming generation even more ferocious than the present one, parents and teachers through-out America must band together to break the "comic" magazine.[12]

Quite early in its inception as a medium, the potential for out-side criticism from parents, educators, community and religious groups, and especially the government had afflicted comicbooks and already tended to "mainstream" content and discourage themes that might be viewed as corrupting.

In addition to this continuous outside pressure to "main-stream" content, two other factors influenced the content and for-mat of comicbooks in its early years, and steered the medium towards reinforcing dominant social values and institutions: a) the organisation of the comics industry and its preferred methods for production; and b) the war effort which increased the importance of reinforcing dominant values and institutions to solidify the U.S. sentiment against the Axis menace. It is easy to understand why World War II comicbooks exemplified the medium's purest expres-sion of dominant social values.

More indirect were the effects of the basic organisation of the industry and the way the medium was produced. As in any medi-um, there was tension between those industry practitioners who saw their product as a commodity and those who saw it as an artistic endeavour. After the enormous success of Superman in 1939-1940, the comicbook industry expanded suddenly and mas-sively as more and more businesses sought to profit from this new phenomenon. Many early comicbook organisations, especially the smaller companies, were owned by people who had earned size-able amounts of money during Prohibition, not always legally, and who sought to invest this money in easily accessible and successful industries.[13] Thus, in the industry's first decade, the scales were overwhelmingly tipped toward the commodities view where the philosophy of many of the early publishers was

> *do it cheap*. Find cheap labour, pay cheap prices. Low over-
> head. Tie up as little money as possible. Take out as much
> money as possible. The results were predictable—in a few
> years the bad drove out the good.[14]

By the mid 1940s, production was already highly routinized and the strict divisions of tasks between artists, writers, and edi-tors were not conducive to artistic innovation or autonomy. For artists, especially, economic incentives encouraged simple, quickly produced content. Many artists were teenage boys from modest backgrounds who were willing to work for low wages. They were

typically paid by the page which encouraged them to work quickly.[15] The publisher usually owned the rights to the finished artwork, and artists and writers were rarely credited. All these factors
encouraged the early comicbook creators to work quickly and to
put little artistic effort into plots, characterisation, and illustrations. Coupled with the main audience of the medium, children,
this reinforced the formulaic aspects and mainstream themes of
comicbooks. Comicbooks shied away from themes dealing with
sophisticated social criticism and instead opted for plots and characterisations that children could easily grasp. Through the 1940s
and early 1950s, comicbooks stressed simple themes such as good
versus evil, with clearly established rules for understanding which
characters were good and which characters were not.

Despite all these factors which sought to steer comicbooks
toward reinforcing dominant views and ideals, negative sentiments
reigned in the critical responses to the medium. The appraisal of
comicbooks as a serious threat to society culminated in the form-
ing of the strictest and most influential organisation ever to have
control over comics—the Comics Code Authority formed in 1954
and headed by former New York magistrate Charles F. Murphy,
who became the comicbook equivalent of the notorious movie censor Will Hays.[16] Once again, the Comics Code Authority was
explicitly designed to "mainstream" the values and messages presented in comic books. One rule, for example, stated that "policemen, judges, government officials, and respected institutions shall
not be presented in such a way as to create disrespect for established authority."[17]

Within its first six months of existence, the Authority
reviewed 5,000 stories, 200 of which were rejected and 1,300
were revised. Many comic book publishers were pushed out of
business. EC (Educational Comics) at first subscribed to the
Code but abruptly abandoned it after a story about a black
astronaut was to be rejected unless the character was
recoloured as white (44, p. 314). Like some other publishers,
EC then switched to a larger-sized black and white format that
was not subject to the Code.

> The Code was a setback for the art of comics, which was
> forced into essentially infantile patterns when its potential for
> maturity had only begun to be explored.[18]

There was nothing inherent in the nature of comicbooks that dictated its development as a cultural form economically and institutionally linked to children and adolescents. After all, the earliest comicbooks were bound reprints of strips earlier published in newspapers and enjoyed by adults and children alike. However, bereft of the surrounding seriousness of black-and-white columns of print about politics, sports, and current stock market reports, the same strips seemed to give a different impression. The very first comicbooks were given away as premiums for the purchase of children's products. Even these, however, were bound strips of "Joe Palooka" and "Mutt and Jeff," not specifically intended as children's fare. Undoubtedly, it was the 1938 publication of the first superhero, Superman, that launched and guaranteed the success of comicbooks as a medium for the youth. This success was reinforced by Superman's pervasiveness in other media such as syndicated newspaper strips, the sale of other commodities with the Superman character or symbol and, somewhat later, Saturday morning cartoons in the television. Superman stories were published in two periodicals, *Action Comics* and its sister publication *Superman*. By 1941, the two Superman comicbooks sold 1.4 million copies every two weeks.[19]

> Children regarded the early comic books as "their books," the first medium they exclusively could call their own. Ninety-five percent of boys and 91 percent of girls between the ages of six and eleven bought comic books regularly by 1943. Annual sales revenue reached $15 million, approximately 75 percent of which came from children's purchases.[20]

The implications of this new cultural form invading the privacy of homes and school playgrounds were received, and have since then been attached, with suspicion and head shaking among adults. Comicbooks were very quickly perceived as a "problem." The growth of a cultural form that was affordable, easily accessible and so popular triggered anxiety: how was control to be exercised over the consumption of such cultural forms?

The obsession with control and regulations was reflected in the critical discussions of comicbooks. As early as the 1940s, when comic books were beginning to be extremely popular, one can already find the elements that were to dominate the discourses which address comicbooks: a noticeable displacement of social problems onto forms of "the popular"—a strategy not unique to the reception of comicbooks but generally utilised in evaluating new forms of mass media. New popular forms are hardly primarily analysed for their aesthetics or intrinsic formal characteristics but are always evaluated in terms of their impact on society, more specifically, the extent of their merit or threat in upholding values and institutions already in place and in terms of how they conform to or rebel against authority.

Interestingly, the apprehensions and caution which greet new forms tend to revolve around issues related to sex and violence. Perhaps due to the general suspicion in perceiving new forms or because of the general apprehensive atmosphere of cultural decline in the twentieth century, discussions about effects and influences of the mass media and popular culture were usually examined in relation to the vulnerability of order and authority in society and very often became disguised treatises and attacks about sex and violence. A common critique of comicbooks, for example, could be summarised this way: the "problem" is seen as social decay, i.e., too much sex and violence; the "cause" found in comicbooks, and the "solution" is the imposition of one common set of social and moral values, presented in the name of peace and progress. A review of the responses to comicbooks reveals that a large percentage of the critical commentary follows an established pattern of investigation and evaluation. Previous studies of mass media, which correlate the expansion of popular forms and the deterioration of societal norms concerning the family and other social institutions, are reviewed and their negative findings re-articulated.

VIOLENCE IN COMICBOOKS

Studies done on mass media, especially in relation to sex and violence, are often predetermined by assumptions that bear on the very categories, methods, procedures, and therefore, results of the research. A pervading sense of cultural decline and social disintegration, for example, overdetermines or sets the tone for such studies. Morag Shiach, in relation to his analysis of television, critiques one of the most influential books on mass media criticism, Eysenck and Nias's *Sex, Violence, and the Media*.[21] Morag Shiach may be quoted at length here because it shows the same assumptions about sex and violence which inform most essays about mass media and popular forms and their role in the deterioration of modern society:

> Eysenck and Nias do not examine the history of the concepts of "sex" and "violence" in order to understand the cultural and historical specificity of identifying particular images or acts as "sexual" or "violent." Within any society there is a complex set of legitimate and illegitimate acts of violence, and the meanings of any particular representation can only be assessed in terms of such social norms. Eysenck and Nias ignore the fact that the meanings people derive from particular representations are to some extent culturally specific . . . . (advocate instead) restrictions amounting to an eradication of all images of sexuality and violence, not considering how violence is represented in a particular text, its relation to a particular narrative, or the extent to which certain forms of violence such as war, are culturally sanctioned while others, such as vandalism, are condemned. Eysenck and Nias merely assume that sex and violence are bad, and their representations dangerous.[22]

The representation of violence in comicbooks has been an overwhelming concern for most critics.[23] They suggest damaging effects from the profuse, repetitive and *graphic* depictions of violence in comicbooks which purportedly incite children to more violent and unrestrained behaviour. Critics also question the danger in portraying the triumph of individualism and wish fulfilment in the guise of comicbook characters, especially in the immortality of superheroes and even some favourite villains. The same critique is levelled at those comicbooks wherein the exploits of cunning detectives suggest by their very existence that the forces of government and law are not sufficient to contain outlaws and sinister powers.

Violence in comicbooks is often disparaged as pointless and its context irrelevant and irreverent, capable of threatening the innocence of children, inciting aggression, and endangering the stability of families because of the repetitive representation of certain types of authority and of the rebellion against them. There is concern that children lose their place and forget their proper relation to society because of too much fantasy. Thus, there is the danger of the erosion of proper and fulfilling relations between parents and children, between authority figures and those under their charge. Apparently, interest in comicbook violence was more inspired by aspirations of "social control" than appreciation and comprehension of the new medium.

This form of interest is also evident in methods of inquiry which do not follow the "effects" tradition. Standing opposite to this form of approach, for example, is the "uses and gratification approach" which argues as follows: the "effects" model treats the audience as a passively encountering mass media, insulated from other forces in society that might influence their perception and reception of the media contents. The uses and gratification approach recognises that audiences are already members of their society and interact with mass media by actively choosing what they will read or watch since they want certain things from them. In effect, the concern now is not what the media do to the audience, but what the audience does with the media.

As a reaction against the "effects" tradition, this approach to comicbook research took audiences seriously and searched for reasons as to why people watch television or read comicbooks. In effect, the "uses and gratification" approach sought to discern what needs these activities satisfied.[24] A famous, and often cited, piece of early research into comics-readership by Wolfe and Fiske came out of this tradition.[25] Wolfe and Fiske showed that children read comics progressively: they go through several phases in reading different kinds of comics—classified as Funny Animal, Superman-type, and True comics—which correspond to distinct phases of their development. The researchers also strongly implied that normal children generally outgrow reading comics in the process of maturation, and that this process may vary from child to child. However, even as they claim that comics "fulfil children's developmental needs," these needs are noticeably classified as ones to be got over as soon as possible. Wolfe and Fiske distinguished between "normal" readers, readers with "problems," and "neurotic" and "psychotic" readers.

The rather strange form of reader classification employed seems to suggest what the authors wanted to prove; that normal children have reading patterns and preferences different from those with "problems." Not surprisingly, they described children who became and remained comics fans as out of control and neurotic, ones "whose problems had affected their entire behaviour patterns."[26] Wolfe and Fiske portrayed comics reading itself as a neurosis: "The fan does indeed become neurotic, i.e., the habit and characteristics of comic reading gradually engulf his life and affect his entire behaviour patterns." Wolfe and Fiske also talk about fantasy as one of the phases a child goes through but must overcome to reach a "correct attitude" which is described as a "realistic interest in the world." For them, fantasy is escapism, and escapism, being lawless, is potentially dangerous. Anything "fantastic" that is read provides a link with uncontrolled tendencies. They concluded that the sheer fact of reading comics puts children at risk.

> For the normal child, then, comics are a means of healthful ego-strengthening and a source of amusement. Other children do not seem to be so eager to fortify themselves for the experience of life. They do not seem to have emancipated themselves from their parents to any great degree... But their belief in their parents seems nevertheless to have been shaken... They therefore search for a more perfect father-figure, a being who is omnipotent but, at the same time, tangible and feasible. And such a father-figure they find in Superman. These children become fans... For normal children, then, the comics function as an adaptation mechanism... For the maladjusted child, the comics satisfy, just as efficiently, an equally intense emotional need, but here the need itself is not so readily outgrown. The religion of comics is not easily given up...[27]

Wolfe and Fiske's research reveals the presumptuous arguments which characterise uses and gratifications research: timeless needs which explain why people use the media, and naive classifications of media content and type. Here, we see yet another approach to comics which does not seek to analyse comics themselves, and in addition, a method which already embodies prejudgements about that which it wishes to establish. Much like the "effects" tradition it is reacting against, the framework of the "uses and gratifications" method is problematic in that its very framework tends to produce or confirm the results already assumed in the initial theory. One such unexamined presumption in a great deal of existing studies about texts and readers of comics is the linking of violence and adolescent boys.

Critics who sought to establish a relation between exposure to violent images in comicbooks and subsequent acts of violence have tended to focus on adolescent boys, generally claiming to demonstrate that "high exposure to comicbooks violence increases the degree to which boys engage in serious violence."[28] Why the link between adolescent boys and violence should be self-evident remains largely unexamined, however. The underlying assumptions followed are simply that: a) violence is innate, b) adolescent boys are prone to violence, and c) comicbooks reduce inhibitions in relation to violent behaviour, and therefore, exposure to comicbooks leads to acts of violence or rebellion.

Seldom, if at all analysed, are the reasons why girls do not resort to acts of violence when exposed to such images on the same scale. That girls do not read as many comicbooks as boys do, however, is not a sufficient reason for the lesser tendency to transform comicbooks violence into real life. Martin Barker, in *A Haunt of Fears* and *Comics: Ideology, Power and the Critics*, examines how girls were just as interested in horror comicbooks and crime and detective stories until the mid 1950s when these comicbook genres started catering increasingly and exclusively to boys. Furthermore, girls are just as exposed to other popular forms of entertainment such as television and cinema which are censured for violence. Why is the influence of violence then so gender-specific? If, among girls, the interest in popular forms which depict violence does not transform itself into violent behaviour in female adolescents, perhaps there is a need to examine more closely the relationship between the formation of social and sexual identity and acts of violence.

Violence should not be assumed as an unproblematic and measurable category, ignoring the possible ways in which representations of violence interact with discourses of class and masculinity. In addition, the extent to which violent behaviour might be explicable in terms of environment and class should also be considered. By overlooking these possibilities, comicbooks are simply seen as expressive of social decline but, in the process of analysis, are removed from the social relations that constantly inflect their meaning and use.

RE-ASSESSING CATEGORIES

The identification of comics as "popular culture" represents a critique of the categories for the description of the cultural forms and relations in the twentieth century. Thinking of comicbooks in terms of the "popular" indicates a refusal or an inability to engage with many of the medium's varied forms of representations, since it undermines the complexity of the ways in which comics may be understood and the range of meanings it can produce. Clarifying the functions of reader/text relations cannot be defined outside the history and context in which specific texts—some more than others—have conspicuously functioned intertextually to make a plurality of different readings possible. Caution must be exercised in positing a notion of the audience as a social aggregate subjected to the effects and influences of representations in cultural forms, as well as in concentrating on the individuality of spectators whose distinct subjectivity is constructed by the various systems of meaning in which they participate.

By presenting a more comprehensive understanding of the relationship between culture and subjectivity than had been previously theorised, many critics have recently effectively rescued an enormous segment of cultural production from the oblivion earlier assigned to it by mainstream critics. Of note are feminist analyses of mass media, along with those certain British culturalists who, instead of assuming that readers are passive and can be subjected and influenced *en masse*, argue for the active participation of an audience otherwise thought of as a lobotomised media consumer.

But in focusing on the subjectivity and power of readers and viewers, there is the tendency to emphasise or claim a heterogeneity of the audience while assigning a fundamental homogeneity in the production of mass or popular culture; this then also results in a lopsided notion of cultural production. In evaluating reader-text relations, Jim Collins advocates the critical awareness of "conflictive textual production and reception in tension-filled environments;" he emphasises tension-filled and multiple environments to explain the differences in the reading constructed by media consumers. He also recommends awareness that numerous contentious qualities shape the very formation of the texts, as well as their ariticulation.[29] The "mediation" of texts begins at their inception; their original structure and development are shaped by an environment that influences the functions that popular texts would serve for diversified audiences.

The profusion of popular narratives presents different, and even contradictory, positions for potential spectators which merit critical analyses, not merely critical statements or pronouncements. Barker (1989) shows the deplorable fact that numerous studies about media influence hardly acknowledge that they are investigations of ideological effects, nor are the authors themselves aware that they are espousing a particular theory or ideology. This thesis agrees that inevitably, any discussion of mass media influence must involve ideas about ideology since hardly any form of popular culture (or culture in general, for that matter) is free of ideological domination. Positing a space beyond the reach of ideology—a space of "authenticity" where the dominant culture will hold no sway—is possible only within the terms and theory of cultural analysis, and may have no existence outside it. Nevertheless, investigations of mass media and popular forms can still aspire to relative objectivity, that is, a critical analysis characterised by appeals to standards and values that can be understood and shared, and the use of methods that are at least revealed to everyone.

This chapter has focused on an attempt to clarify how the origins of certain sorts of judgements about popular culture as debased or irrelevant must be seen in their historically shifting relation to dominant cultural forms. Implied in this analysis is the belief that popular culture matters: it has clearly mattered to those who have sought to classify it or control it, and should now matter to those who seek to challenge existing social, sexual and cultural relations. Examining any form relegated to the popular cannot escape ideological implications, especially in analysing reader-text relations, since factors such as class, gender, race, and age, as well as the conditions for text production and articulation, affect their definition.

Corresponding to this view, the following chapters will focus on examining a particular type of comicbooks—the superhero comics as a genre—tracing the development of the genre, to consider such questions as who reads such books, why and in what way. Examining the superhero comics as a genre will stress the manner in which the involvement of reader and writer could shape the contours of texts. Genres are interesting in that they represent a set of conventions whose parameters are redrawn with each new book and each new reading. Once one thinks of a text as an example of a genre, it can no longer be approached only as an artefact to be analysed in some form of contextless critical purity. Looking at superhero comicbooks as a genre will bring together a range of levels in which these forms operate in our culture, from the pragmatics of production to issues of ideology and language. The functions and dynamics in superhero comicbooks will be used as an example to illustrate how a particular form of discourse, one among the many discourses, competes to define its place and audience in the highly discourse-sensitive society we now live in.

NOTES

1 Leo Lowenthal, *Literature, Popular Culture, and Society* (California: Pacific Books, 1971): 18.
2 Todd Gitlin, *The Whole World is Watching*. (Berkeley: University of California Press, 1980): 44ff.
3 That such divisions cannot actually be related exactly to other social and cultural hierarchies is a problem for both types of critics, who constantly risk the ignominious slide into utilising the concepts of the problematic "popular."
4 Roger Sabin, *Adult Comics: An Introduction* (London and New York: Routledge, 1993): 2ff.
5 Refer to the Bibliography section of this study to studies done by A. Easthope, Gurevitch, T. Bennett, J. Woollacott, J. Fiske, T. Gitlin, and C. MacCabe.
6 Peter Davison, "General Introduction," in Peter Davison, et al, eds. *Literary Taste, Culture and Mass Communication, Vol. I: Culture and Mass Culture* (Cambridge: Chadwyck-Healey, 1978): viii.
7 Jim Collins. *Uncommon Cultures. Popular Culture and Post-Modernism* (New York: Routledge, 1989): xi.
8 Raymond Williams, *Culture and Society* (New York: Columbia University Press, 1983). See especially Chapter Two.
9 Denis McQuail, "The Influence and Effects of Mass Media," in James Curran, Michael Gurevitch and Janet Woollacott, eds., *Mass Communication and Society* (London: Routledge, 1977): 70–94.
10 There was a rise in crime and horror comics during the early 1950s which no doubt perpetuated the situation of raids and incessant negative attention. But even while Wertham himself was censuring only the crime comicbooks, the censoring board that was formed as a result, the Comics Code Authority, had blanket authority over all comicbooks.
11 Matthew Paul McAllister, "Cultural Argument and Organizational Constraint in the Comic Book Industry," *Journal of Communication* 40.1 (Winter 1990): 55–70.
12 Josette Frank, "What's in Comics?" *Journal of Educational Sociology* (December 18, 1940): 54–59.
13 Ted White, "The Spawn of M. C. Gaines," in Dick Lupoff and Don

Thompson, eds. *All in Colour for a Dime* (New Rochelle, N. Y.: Arlington House, 1970): 25.

14 *Ibid.*, emphasis in original.

15 Coulton Waugh, *The Comics* (New York: Macmillan, 1947): 350.

16 During this time, censorship in the movies and television were also getting increasingly stricter. The simultaneity of tighter control among the various popular forms may well be more a sign of general alarm at the pace and scope of the changes happening in society, most of which were perceived as threatening to a recognisable order, and were then projected as corrupting capabilities intrinsic in the forms themselves.

17 Sabin, *op cit.*, 251.

18 McAllister, *op cit.*, 62.

19 Jules Feiffer, *The Great Comic Book Heroes*, Volume I (New York: Dial Press, 1965): 238.

20 McAllister, *op cit.*, 57.

21 H.J. Eysecnk and D.B. Nias, *Sex, Violence and the Media* (London: Blackwell, 1978).

22 Morag Shirach, "The Changing Definitions of the Popular," in Gary Day, ed. *Readings in Popular Literature: Trivial Pursuits?* (London: Macmillan, 1990): 77

23 See, for example, articles on comics in the journal called *Childhood Education*, especially during the 1940s and 1950s. See also the *Report of the Royal Commission on Violence in the Communications Industry*, Vol. 4, (New York: Royal Commission on Violence, 1966).

24 The "uses and gratification" approach was also a reaction against the aftermath of research on propaganda during World War II. Useful introductions to this research approach are Jay Blumler and Elihu Katz, *The Uses of Mass Communications: Current perspectives on gratification research* (Beverley Hills: Sage, 1974), and Karl Rosengren, Lawrence Wenner and Philip Palmgreen, *Media Gratifications Research: Current perspectives* (Beverley Hills: Sage, 1985).

25 Katherine M. Wolfe and Marjorie Fiske, "The Children Talk About the Comics," *Communication Research: 1948–49* (New York: Harper and Bros 1949): 3–50.

26 Wolfe and Fiske, *ibid.*, 29.

27 *Ibid*, 34–35.

28 Wertham, *op cit.*, 54.

29 Collins, *op cit.*, 19.

CHAPTER THREE

On the Language of Comics and the Reading Process

> How can we recognize or deal with the new? Any equipment
> we bring to the task will have been designed to engage with
> the old: it will look for and identify extensions and develop-
> ments of what we already know. To some degree, the unprece-
> dented will always be unthinkable.
> But the question of what "texts" are or may be has also
> become more and more complex, has forced us to revise our
> sense of the sort of material to which the process of "reading"
> may apply.
>
> Terence Hawks
> "General Introduction to
> New Accent Books"

INTRODUCTION

The study of comics has a goal similar to the study of art and literature in general: to promote an understanding of the medium
that sharpens perception and awareness, leading ultimately to a
keener enjoyment of the form. Unfortunately, the lack of seriousness in the general attitude towards the medium as an art form has
been an enduring factor that has impeded the development of
comics. This situation may be summed up using the words of
Maurice Horn: "(Comics is) an original form whose intrinsic val-

ues must be objectively assessed. A thorough knowledge of the field must be obtained, with the same assiduity as is required of any other discipline; the *a priori* judgement that this is an inferior form only deserving of inferior scholarship is an especially galling piece of tortuous reasoning."[1] The concept of comics as a distinct art form must be an accepted premise in the analysis of comics as an art. In the absence of this principle, and without being accorded the status of an independent art form, comics will suffer as a poor relation of other literary or visual forms.

A close look at comicbooks reveals an ingenious form, with a highly developed grammar and vocabulary based on a unique combination of verbal and visual elements. This medium uses words and pictures in a way more completely integrated than illustrated or picture books. Reading a comicbook is as a complex semiotic process—it involves understanding how the interactions between words and images have been manipulated in order to achieve a story or joke. The appreciation of comicbooks is not possible without the recognition that its language and grammar consist of not one but two elements: words and images.

TEXT-IMAGE CONFLICT

The simultaneous presence of two mediums—words and images—neither started with comics nor is unique to them, yet their existence remains a contentious issue in studying comics. There are factors that seem to favour the valorisation of images over texts. In early studies about the origin and development of the medium, for example, a graphic history was usually provided and an "iconic archaeology," rather than a textual one, was instinctively assigned to comics.[2]

It is not difficult to focus primarily on the images in comics since graphic art is more striking than printed letters. Any comicbook is first perceived visually; readers are usually first struck by illustrations when choosing one comicbook over another. Studies have shown that people are initially attracted to illustrations more than to words.[3] Indeed, in some comics, words are even unnecessary—strips like *Henry* by Carl Anderson show that comics are possible without words. In other instances, words become secondary to images; some panels or whole pages of comicbooks are intentionally rendered without any text (*see*

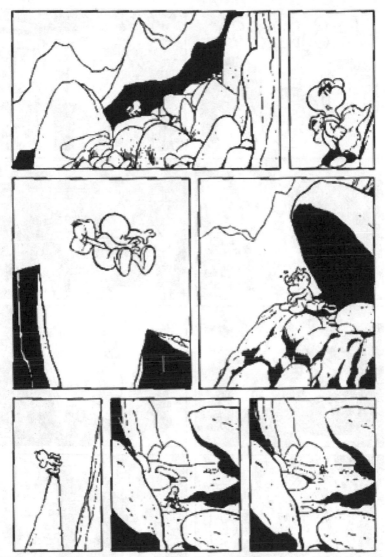

Figure 3. *Bone Vol. One: Out from Boneville*. Art and Script: Jeff Smith
© 1996 The creator.

Figures 3 and 4). It is not surprising that comics are often discussed on the basis of their graphic aspects alone. For example,
individual panels of Milton Caniff's comic strips have been dis-

Figure 4. "La Sorpresa" tells a story without text. Back page of *Luba #1*
Art and script: Gilbert Hernandez © 1998 Fantagraphics Books.

played in museums. This presumes that Caniff's art may be appreciated out of the context of the comics medium, since the illustrations were isolated from the context of the narrative they were initially intended for. The subsequent reviews of Milton Caniff's exhibition attest to the possibility of exclusively paying attention to comics illustration divorced from the textual cues and the context of the comic strip or comicbook stories. The appropriation of comics in Pop art by, among others, Roy Lichtenstein and Andy Warhol, has also caused comics to be re-submitted to pictorial, artistic criteria and to be perceived as viable museum pieces. While studies of comics abound which focus on the graphics, there are hardly any studies which focus only on the texts without referring to the illustrations at all. Indeed, it seems that images are more essential to comics than texts. On the other hand, since comics usually contain stories, some studies have focused on the medium as a narrative art. Comics are compared to fiction and, using methods of literary analysis, factors such as character, theme, and plot are evaluated.

In analysing comics, however, it is necessary to develop a new kind of understanding that goes beyond comparing and assessing verbal and visual structures separately. We must not lose sight of the fact that both pictures and texts are the fundamental basis of almost all comics, and to seek to understand one without the other is to misinterpret the substance of this hybrid genre. Reading comics involves the pictures and their meanings in relation to the language, and the key to understanding comics does not lie in the words or pictures themselves but in the interaction and relation-ships between them.

The crucial point is how effectively the linguistic and pictorial signs interact—how perfectly, how absorbingly and dynamically a story is related in pictures and texts. The interaction is all-impor-tant. The relation between text and image is a defining character-istic of comics, and the efficacy of the medium rests on the inter-dependence of the two mediums. As such, comics cannot help but demand of its readers the ability to decipher and "read" a new lan-guage of combined written and illustrated codes. In reading comics and appreciating its formal composition, words and illustrations form the language and grammar of comics. It is essential to under-stand why the relation of the two mediums is important and how it operates specifically in comics.

Until very recently, this was a difficult area to write about due to inadequacies in the critical vocabulary for the medium. In earlier studies of comics, there was a tendency to rely on terms borrowed from other areas and critical evaluation used the yardsticks of other related art. In order to assess comics on their own terms, definitions of the structural and stylistic principles behind successful comics art must be formulated. In addition to constructing evaluative terms, there is also the need to clarify terms without turning them into constraints.

DEFINITIONS

A clear definition of comics is indispensable in establishing a system for analysing the conventions specific to this genre. To articulate an aesthetic theory of comics, we need a vocabulary tailored *for* comics and derived *from* the most distinctive aspects of this art form. Until there is agreement on what this art form is, difficulty in specifying and evaluating its distinctive aspects will continue to plague discussions. If we consider the bewildering assortment of artistic and graphic styles, stories, characters, and purposes present in comics, a clear generic definition seems all the more compelling. We need a means of sifting through the wide variety of comicbooks to ascertain those features that may be deemed common and integral to the art form. The search for a definition of comics can help dispel many misconceptions and limitations of the medium. A proper definition will expand the popular connotation of "comics" as humorous or simple, illustrated reading materials. The search for this definition will also reveal the difficulties involved in the textual analyses of comics and the need for body of criticism to establish norms and standards.

Will Eisner, a prominent cartoonist intent in cultivating comics as an art form, suggested a new term for comics: "sequential art."[4] Sequential art has the advantage of avoiding the generic connotations of the word "comic" while sidestepping associations with the burlesque, the ridiculous and humorous which have burdened initial impressions of the medium. This problem does not exist in the "Bilderstreifen" of Germany, "bande dessinée" of France and "fumetti" of Italy, which have no immediate connections to the "comic" and, in fact, call attention to intrinsic qualities of the comics as a narrative medium. The desire to clearly define what comics are and to detach them from notions of the comical and humorous is one of the critical concerns in re-assessing comics. Stan Lee, renowned for the creation of Spider-Man and his other achievements at Marvel Comics, makes the following statement:

> "Consider the word "comicbook." I've been fighting a losing battle with the rest of the world over that word for years. Most everybody spells it "comic book" as if it's two separate words. As is, "comic" is an adjective which modifies the word "book," thus making it mean a comical book. Such an interpretation would certainly give a casual reader the wrong impression. . . Now, let's consider the single word "comicbook." Ah, what a world of difference! Suddenly, it is no longer an appellation indicative of humorous reading matter, but rather a generic term denoting a specific type of publication."[5]

In an interview for *Time Magazine*, Art Spiegelman had this to say: "But I spell it *c-o-m-i-x*, so you are not confused by the fact that comics have to be funny, as in comic. You think it is a co-mix of words and pictures."[6] Perhaps the most revealing definition is Martin Barker's assertion about the perception of comics: "a comic is what has been produced under the definition of a 'comic'. One cannot answer the question "What is a comic?" by formal qualities alone; a comic is what has been produced under that *controlling definition*."[7] Barker's statements underline the incessant efforts to censor and control what may or may not be produced under the name "comics" which have become powerful determinants of the products. In these instances, the definition of comics became a constraining force, requiring publishers and artists to abide by it and, in turn, sustain the limiting public concept of what comics are and can be.

In addition to associating comics with humour and "trivia", the usual definitions of comics in English also limit the stylistic of the medium by constant connection with cartooning and caricature. One dictionary meaning of comicbooks, for example, is "a magazine consisting of narrative cartoon drawings."[8] This definition perpetuates the drawback of limiting the style that may be employed in comic art. Comic strips, meanwhile, are defined as "a narrative series of cartoons, usually arranged horizontally in a newspaper, magazine or book" or "a form of cartooning in which a cast of characters enacts a story in a sequence of closely related drawings designed to educate and/or entertain readers."[9] Cartooning should not be included in defining comics. As Scott

McCloud appropriately asserts, "nothing in its definition should limit style or determine subject matter or range of topics to be covered," otherwise, the common unfortunate practice of mistaking the *style and format* of the most popular comicbooks for the essence of the medium itself shall continue (*see Figure 5*).[10]

There is another aspect of comics that is usually taken for granted, and its role as an indispensable feature of the medium is

Figure 5.   A proper definition of comics does not limit the medium. *Understanding Comics.* Art and script: Scott McCloud © 1993 The creator.

undermined: comicbooks always consist of "story situations."
Comicbooks contain accounts of people and ideas with a logical,
sequential progression in which "reading" plays an important role
(*see Figure 6*). This aspect is highlighted in the new terms that are

Figure 6. Essential in conceptualising comics is the idea of its being a
sequential art—not simply a visual stimulant but something that must be
"read". *Understanding Comics*. Art and script: Scott McCloud © 1993
The creator.

increasingly employed in recent discussions of comics, concurrent with the seemingly new status of the medium: *graphic novel or sequential art* are alternatively used for comicbooks to avoid the English terminology problems cited above.[11] Sequential art is further expanded by Scott McCloud to provide a definition for comics as "juxtaposed pictorial and other images in deliberate sequence." This definition is noticeably neutral. It does not limit the medium to a particular style of illustration or schools of art, a range of storytelling themes, technique and procedures in printing and publishing, and materials or tools to be used.[12]

The concept of comics has traditionally been too narrow and limiting for the medium. A proper definition, if found, would give lie to stereotypes and show that the potential of comics is limitless and exciting. Following McCloud's definition, some works of, among others, Maurice Sendak, Raymond Briggs, Edward Gorey and Shel Silverstein, branded and marketed as illustrated "books" could actually be classified as comics if it were not for the old notion of comicbooks as cheap, softcover magazines of serialised cartoons.[13] The following sections undertake to discern the conventions in comics largely based on narrative. The discussions contend that the primary function of the features of comics, particularly that of the peculiar text-image interaction, is to solicit narrative comprehension.

COMICS AND NARRATION

Narration, broadly defined, is the intent of comicbooks; their purpose is to tell a story. Because they aim at a large public, comicbooks have come to compete with older forms of popular narratives such as dime novels, pulp fiction, and magazine serials. While sharing many themes, images, and even characters with these other popular forms of expression, comics deviate in their narrational activity by using an intricate interaction of words and pictures. The relation of these two elements depends on the thrust of the narrative they operate it. Although image and text may affect the style, overall design and aesthetic effect of a sequence in comics, their interaction principally serves to aid readers to construct the story that the artist intended. It is in the activity of selecting, arranging and rendering story material—especially in the choice of what to illustrate and what to narrate—in order to achieve a narrative coherence perceptible to a receiver that the interaction of the two mediums is most vital to the artist and reader. Many cognitive activities are performed in making sense out of a narrative: a reader makes inferences that are open-ended, probabilistic and subject to corrections. Meanwhile, the reader often hypothesises about the story's ending—weighing the probabilities of future narrative events and testing his or her expectations as more information is given and more events unfold. The interaction between graphic and linguistic elements in comics aids the reader in executing operations relevant to constructing a story out of a sequence's particular depiction. Ignoring one medium leads to a misinterpretation of the story or worse, makes a sequence wholly incomprehensible. It is when images and texts are perceived together that they are more effective in realising the narrative in comics (*see Figure 7*). The

Figure 7. It would be difficult not to be curious as to what the characters are saying in these panels. *Soulwind #3*. Art and script: C. Scott Morse © 1997 The creator.

opposition, confirmation, and other interaction between the pictures and words reveal unstated premises for making inferences, and make possible the humour, surprise, or other such appropriate endings of the story fascinating to the reader. Since all narratives, in order to sustain a reader's attention, are composed alternately to reward, modify, frustrate or defeat a reader's search for story coherence, the play between text and image becomes even more potent. It is this very play which provides the irony, complications, double meanings, humour, suspense, melodrama, pun, parody, secret motivations, and other similar intentions in the story (*see Figure 8*).

By manipulating the interaction between the two codes which make up its language, comics have at their disposal the syntax of other literary and artistic forms: iteration, distortion, amplification, stylization, and more. There is, however, an idiosyncrasy in

Figure 8. The size of the small guy belies the sincerity of his response. *Bleeding Heart #5*. Art and script: Peter Kuper © 1993 The creator.

comics narrative due to publication or production requirements which differ from other forms subjected to narrative analysis, like books or even films. The flow of the story in comics may be marred by artificial or strategic narrative breakdowns caused by publishing requirements that reduce or cut up materials to intelligible daily, weekly or monthly instalments (quite similar to earlier novels previously published in serialised forms). Many cartoonists manage to turn this requirement into an advantage; they try to enhance the suspense or humour naturally accruing from each instalment by working deliberately toward a concluding panel to serve as a springboard of suspense to carry the story to the next issue (*see Figure 9*). The conventions of the art form are refined enough today that most contemporary books and strips can seldom be faulted for narrative breakdowns, while older strips sometimes offer examples of obviously flawed breakdowns. Even

Figure 9. We know there will be some fighting in the next issue because of the ending of this one. *Daisho*. Art and script: Patrick Debruin © 1993 The creator.

among the recent ones, in fact, there are still inept or awkward breakdowns which weaken the structure and projection of the story. Although narrative breakdowns reduce all action to discrete static moments, comicbooks can, nonetheless, be evaluated by the extent to which a smooth sequential progression and narrative coherence are achieved. This progression must be served by both the visual impact and the nuances of the story, and its assessment must embrace both the pictures and the texts used. The next sections will discuss the elements that are utilised in the creation and process of "reading" comics. These are: 1) panels, which include the concepts of gutter and closure; 2) the use of balloons and the art of lettering in comicbooks, and 3) the use of panels and text balloons in signalling the rhythm of the narrative, which also addresses timing and duration in comics.

NARRATION IN FRAMES: THE USES OF PANELS OR VIGNETTES

The image-text conflict may be circumscribed by taking the panel or frame as a unit of signification. In comics, images are drawn and accompanying texts provided are usually framed together. Since both image and text are contained within one panel, taking this as a single unit attenuates the dispute regarding the advantage of one medium over the other. Instead, image and text may be given equal interpretative weight as they need not be analysed separately. The panel provides an enclosure, a unified field wherein images and text may be analysed in relation to one. The panel, in fact, *graphically* and *diegetically* unifies image and text in the comics: it forms a graphic unit which represents one moment, one instant of an action in the narrative. Then, one frame interacts with other frames to create a sequence which constitutes the syntagmatic discourse of the story. The panel is the smallest unit of "comics grammar" in which the complex interaction of text and picture operates. It is a process of organising sensory impressions into intelligible patterns wherein the panels' lines, sizes, and shapes offer cues or criteria for perceiving meaning as intended by the artist.

The use of panels has been credited as responsible for the narrative unity in comics.[14] It is a graphic technique specific to the comics which effectively synthesises two distinct mediums to optimise expression. In addition to its unifying function, the panels also signal the relevant time and space dimensions in comics narrative whereby a series of "framed" views interact to cue and channel the reader's construction of a meaningful story.[15] Frames enable the writers to surmount problems in presenting complex narratives within the static, two-dimensional space of the comics world. The progression of time and action are simulated by varying the contents and size of each frame in order to move the story forward.

The utilisation and perception of space is of paramount importance in comics. Instead of relying on textual clues, narration in comics depends considerably on the effective positioning of the viewer with respect to a production in/of space. Discourse becomes a series of views, having their source in the viewer's position (strategically controlled or manipulated by the illustrator). One of the artist's primary concerns is always: How is the space of the story to be presented and where is the spectator in relation to it? The ingenuity of a comics' artist lies in the manipulation of the contents and sequencing of panels in order to most effectively express their narratives. The primary function of perspective should be to purposely manipulate the reader's orientation in accord with the author's narrative plan.

Another use of perspective is to manipulate and produce various emotional states in the reader. The reader's response may be influenced by his or her positioning as a spectator, so that a scene depicted from above may evoke a sense of detachment—depicted from below, a feel of inferiority or fear (see *Figures 10 and 11*). Concurrent to the angle of presentation, the size and shape of the panel may also be used to elicit different levels of involvement or response from the readers, i.e., a narrow panel could trigger a sense of confinement, whereas a wide one inspire freedom or escape.

A panel must have a coherence and balance on its own, but it is always only a part of a bigger design which follows and exhibits patterns of narration, a rhythm of the unfolding events, and a recognisable space and time dimension. Panels form units which mark the rhythm and tempo of the narrative's unfolding, control the points of view and angles of presentation, signal to the reader which perspective is being given or made sympathetic, as well as signal the story's space and time dimensions (*see Figure 12*). Joined

Figure 10. This man looks threatening because of the angle in relation to the reader, as well as the fact that he extends past the gutters. *Daisho*. Art and script: Patrick Debruin © 1993 The creator.

Figure 11. The same man looks non-threatening at all because the frame is smaller, and we see him from a bird's eyeview. *Daisho*. Art and script: Patrick Debruin © 1993 The creator.

side by side, panels form a system of signs that becomes coherent by orienting the reading of the narrative. The manipulation of the various aspects of the panels provides almost unlimited means of manoeuvering the plot and gives rise to numerous narrational possibilities (*see Figure 13*).

Comicbook composition and layout may be evaluated by looking at individual panels, a sequence of panels, at one full page, or a double-page layout. An essential guiding feature to gauge the effectiveness of the composition and layout in comics is narra-

Figure 12. The overlapping of the frames and the shift from one small frame to another signals the speed with which all of the actions happen. *The Tale of One Bad Rat*. Art and script: Bryan Talbot © 1995 The creator.

Figure 13. The layout of the smaller frames mimics the action of our hero.
The Maxx #1. Art and script: Sam Kieth © 1993 The creator.

tional clarity—in how the choice and organisation of panels function to advance the story. Controlling the focus of the reader is
important; one way to effectively do this is to select a "camera"
distance so that each panel contains only the minimum essentials
of a scene while maximising story-telling. This corresponds to
what Robert Harvey calls the "graphic centre of narrative focus:"

> Most composition in the graphic arts have what I call a "cen-
> tre of focus"—a place to which the arrangement of the ele-
> ments of the composition forces our attention (not necessari-
> ly the geometric centre of the composition). In the most effec-
> tive comic panel composition, our attention should be
> focused on whatever element in that panel that contributes
> most to the telling of the story. That place in a panel I call
> "the graphic centre of narrative focus"—*graphic centre*
> emphasising the visual nature of the medium, and *narrative*
> *focus* embracing the storytelling function of comic art.[16]

In comics, panel composition does not necessarily follow the
"geometric centre of composition" of most graphic art because of
constraints such as: 1) having to arrange speech balloons and their
corresponding characters in reading order, 2) the inclusion of cap-
tions, 3) the need to change camera angle to vary perspective in a
sequence, and 4) an artist's preference or ability to draw close-up
or wide angle scenes. To overcome such constraints, a skilled cartoonist can also use his or her understanding and appreciation of
the readers' "visual literacy." With each decision of what to
include or exclude, an artist presumes knowledge of some visual
competence which is mostly based on experience and memory. The
artist must supply sufficient cues in each panel so as to activate the
remembrance necessary for comprehension, without providing too
much so as to take the pleasure out of recognition and participa-
tive reading (see *Figure 14*).

One of the principal skills of comicbook narration lies in
selecting, from among a potentially infinite number of choices, the
most effective points and moments to match the thematic movement of the story. Each moment depicted in comics is the outcome
of a narrative choice which will then set the tone of the narrative,
present a privileged angle, or determine the truth and ideological
claims in the story being related. Analysis and comparison of texts
must take into account a complex set of prior narrative choices
that establish the field and boundaries of each particular telling of

In a given series of panels wherein the frame encompasses only the head, a 'visual dialogue' occurs between the reader and the artist which requires certain assumptions growing out of a common level of experience:

The slim head (A)   The fat head (B)
implies a slim body.   implies a fat body.

Subsequent views of the characters will of course substantiate these assumptions. Illustration C, however, serves to demonstrate that there can be a misreading of the artist's intentions unless a more skilled drawing is executed in the panel itself or a prior panel has established what it is the reader is viewing.

Figure 14. A visual dialogue between the reader and the artist requires certain assumptions growing out of a common level of experience. An illustration from *Comics and Sequential Art* by Will Eisner © Poorhouse Press.

events. As an example, Joseph Witek provides an analysis of two comic books depicting one historical event: The Battle at Fort Sumter. The two versions vary widely in point of view, in tone, and in the ideological implications each draws from the events it is narrating. Witek points out how the title and the initial panels of each comicbook already direct the interpretation of an event: *First Shot* rendered by Harvey Kurtzman, Joe Severin and Will Elder starts with an exploding cannon ball which fills more than half of the first page. The succeeding four panels show the trajectory of the shot and its subsequent explosion. Meanwhile, the other version, *April 1861: Fort Sumter*, by Jack Kirby, opens with a more conventional rendering of battle showing soldiers and officers, drawn with a demeanour of rationality, sensibly discussing their next moves and possible surrender. In contrast to the impression of destruction that opens *First Shot*, the latter version lends an air of rationality to the battle. Witek warns against hasty judgement of the precision of one over the other, however. Instead, a better focus is to investigate the varying ways in which these narratives deploy the conventions of sequential art to make truth claims about an event already weighted with cultural significance, previously established readings, and individual associations.[17]

A more common, though largely unnoticed privileging of an ideological tone or truth claim is performed by presenting the narrative through the perspective of the lead character. In most popular American comicbooks, this is usually the ubiquitous crime-fighting superhero/ine. Specific narrative devices grant superheroes narrative centrality and often cede to them narrative authority through point-of-view frames, first person narration, and other textual and graphic cues which foster reader identification with them and their exploits. In the process, reader acceptance of the superhero's hegemonic role and function is encouraged, notwithstanding the fact that some superheroes resort to "illegal" means of solving crimes or upholding justice, and that the presence of superheroes attests to flaws and lacunas in society's legal and policing system.[18]

GUTTER AND CLOSURE

One important and distinct feature of comic art narration and panel composition is the concept of the "gutter." As panels form borders to enclose material for narration, so do the same borders work to exclude the surrounding space. Much of the story in comics takes place in these intervals between the frames, in the gaps which separate the panels, called the gutter. From past experience and sense-making that one naturally employs while reading, readers fill in gaps in information and cues supplied to them. In sequential art, although nothing is provided either textually or graphically, experience tells us as readers that something must be there and so we make the leap ourselves from one panel to the other. We provide the intervening actions and do this no matter how long or large the interval is between one panel and the next. The type of leap to be made dictates the flow and pace of the narrative. The rhythm or the narrative in turn depends upon the difficulty of the transitions the readers are asked, or rather, forced to make, as the amount of bridging material that must be supplied in moving from panel to panel to comprehend the story is set.

Scott McCloud has categorised these "leaps" into six different levels in a transition scale for narrative movement and comprehension in comics: 1) moment-to-moment, 2) action-to-action, 3) subject-to-subject, 4) scene-to-scene, 5) aspect-to-aspect, and 6) non-sequitur (see *Figure 15*). He also graphed the frequency of the transition techniques used by well-known comics artists internationally and showed that the breakdown proportion of transition types used is consistent among different genres of the medium, and very similar even among artists with very different styles, designs, and subject matter (see *Figure 16*). McCloud proposes that the proportion is an

Figure 15. McCloud identifies six kinds of transition most commonly used in comics narrative, each one differing in the amount and range of leap in bridging the sense from one panel to another. *Understanding Comics*. Art and script: Scott McCloud © 1993 The creator.

Figure 16. There are similarities in the proportion of the transition strategies used in American and European comicbooks. *Understanding Comics.* Art and script: Scott McCloud © 1993 The creator.

important, albeit invisible, structural crutch used widely in comics in order to provide readers with minimum signals to mentally construct a continuous, unified reality from a medium which depends on reading and understanding "empty spaces" (see *Figure 17*).[19]

As part of further experimentations with panel and page formats, many artists started "violating" the gutter space as early as the mid-1960s. Text and graphic art would sometimes extend into the gutter although the squares designating the panels are kept intact. Sometimes, the borders of the panels are eliminated altogether and images spill into the gutter without, however, totally obliterating the spaces which signal the transition between panels. In addition, various shapes other than the traditional squares or rectangles are used to mark the panels, therefore incorporating the

Figure 17. The reader makes the leap from one panel to another; here, one assumes that the sound in the second panel is somehow connected to the death threat in the first. *Understanding Comics*. Art and script: Scott McCloud © 1993 The creator.

gutter more graphically into the narrative and total page lay-out. The functions of this procedure are variable, but accentuating key moments in the narrative or rendering panoramic images are two of the most common (see *Figure 18*).

Figure 18. The clothesline used to separate the first and second row of panels also serves as an escape device for the fugitive. In the centre row, Eisner also manages to depict succeeding moments without any change or break in the brick wall. An illustration from *Comics and Sequential Art* by Will Eisner © Poorhouse Press.

TEXT READS AS IMAGE: LETTERING AND BALLOONS

Similar to the use of panels, the use of balloons is a defining characteristic of the comics. Nowhere is the inter-relation of image and text in comics more apparent than in the imaginative use and continuous transformation of words and text into graphic status through the use of balloons. Balloons started as a rectangle delineating speech in a frame, usually employed to differentiate direct speech from narration. Narrative texts not placed in balloons are usually utilised to supplement images, as in providing additional information about critical persons or objects, expounding on the intervening events in the interval between panels, or reveal the internal thoughts of characters (see *Figure 19*). In some serial publications, there are even special panels for narrative texts at the beginning and/or end of instalments—summarising previous actions or foreshadowing future ones—to ensure continuity. However, the majority of comicbooks, past and present, combine the use of narrative texts and balloons in presenting the story.

When introduced, the use of balloons made the third person and invisible narrator superfluous. The characters can speak more directly and a more conventional, less stilted style of dialogue could be used. Thought balloons also made introspection more direct and personal. In reducing or sometimes even totally omitting narrative text, the use of balloons is also effective in propelling the plot forward in terms of actual reading time. Through time, balloons have developed into a graphic component intrinsic to sequential art. Its development, which allowed for the integration of texts into images in one imaginative fashion after another, has marked the differences between other "illustrated texts" and the comics.

Eisner has called balloons a "desperation device" which "attempts to capture and make visible an ethereal element: sound."[20] Corresponding to the increased sophistication in the medium and its artists, the balloon developed from a simple enclosure to take on additional meaning to become an important narrational device. It soon gained independence from a merely functional role to become aesthetically imbedded and part of the whole vignette as more and more artists experimented with and manipulated its appearance and content.

Now, balloons themselves constitute an essential element as part of a new pictographic code. The various forms and contours

Figure 19. Instead of a speech or thought balloon, Seth uses a separate narrative text to reveal the thoughts of his character. *Palookaville #4*. Art and script: Seth © 1993 The creator.

of the balloons enhance both texts and image in expressing emotions, movement, sound effects, abstract concepts, tone of dialogue and secret motivations or intentions (see *Figures 20* and *21*).

Figure 20. The thought balloons here show a series of images instead of text but just as clearly convey what our hero is thinking. *Madman Comics, Yearbook '95*. Art and script: Mike Allred © 1995 The creator.

Noticeable too, is how artists have rendered the lettering, both within and outside a balloon, such that the letters function as an extension of the imagery. The choice and design of the typeface convert the normally mechanical aspect of type or font into a component of supportive involvement in the imagery which can provide the mood, a narrative bridge, and the implication of sound. Text, rendered in concert with the art, shows how the "reading" of it can evoke and influence specific emotions and modify the perception of the image (see *Figure 22*).

The ability of verbal signs to be transformed into graphic signs through the use of balloons is international, and works even in cultures with different figural tradition like Japan, China and Thailand. Indeed, it is possible that, to an extent, the Japanese and Chinese are predisposed to more visual forms of communication because of their calligraphy which evolved from ideograms and fused drawing and writing. Comics—*manga* or *komikkusu* in Japanese—make up 30 percent of Japan's total production in books and magazines, and over one billion Japanese comic magazines and books are sold annually.[21] Japanese comics are not mere western importations but belong to a century-old tradition of pictorial narration which can be traced back to the picture scrolls of the 19th century. Japanese comics contain highly developed symbolic systems and conventions that are mutually understood by

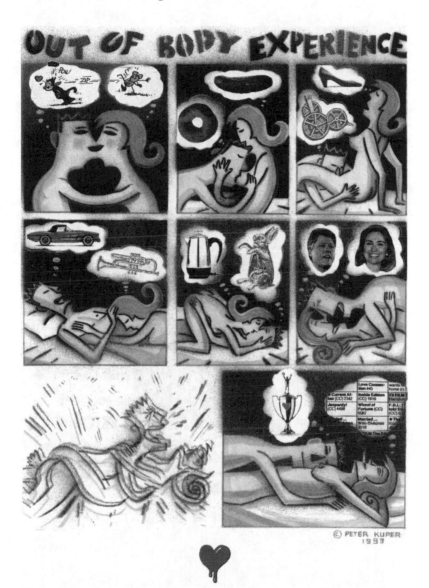

Figure 21. Images inside the balloons instead of texts tell a story just as effectively in this example. Back page of *Bleeding Heart # 5*. Art and script: Peter Kuper © 1993 The creator.

Figure 22. The word "Shoom" fills this page and mimics the reverberation of the sound beneath the sea as the creatures get nearer and the sound gets louder and louder. *Soulwind #4*. Art and script: C. Scott Morse © 1997 The creator

artist and reader and accepted as typical story elements, but which prove to be bewildering to foreigners.[22]

Japanese comics are highly susceptible to graphic manipulation because of the Japanese language. Depending whether one lives in the western or eastern hemisphere, Japanese comics are or are not read "backwards," that is, all panels and pages move sequentially from right to left. Usually, the writing in each dialogue balloon is vertical and is read from top-to-bottom and right-to-left. But in fact, the language can be written in any direction except from bottom of the page to top. This flexibility can work as an aid in creative lay-outs, setting of tone, signalling other things both iconically and verbally. The dialogues and onomatopoeic words, for example, can be directed to enhance and control the visual flow of the page.

> What gives the page even more flexibility is the fact that the Japanese language employs not one, but four entirely separate writing systems: ideograms imported from China, two different syllabic scripts, *hiragana* which is cursive and *katakana* which is more angular, and the Roman alphabet... Japanese people normally write a blend of all four systems, but by being selective an artist can create different moods.[23]

RHYTHM OF THE NARRATIVE: TIMING AND DURATION

No matter how illustrative the texts are rendered, there remains a paradox in the use of words to accompany images in telling a story. While texts help the narrative to move forward—by providing more information, directing the reader's attention, bridging gaps in time and movement—the presence of the text itself *delays* the reading of the story. The duration it takes to read the text already increases the time a reader may spend with one frame rather than if that frame were wordless (see *Figures 23* and *24*). But more significantly, texts demand that readers process more information, the meaning of the words alone, and then in relation with the pictures, which itself initiates further re-thinking of already formed inferences, the making of new hypotheses and so on. Since all narratives unwind in time, this process of retardation is unavoidable in any narrative structure.

Figure 23. The wrestling match seems to go faster due to the absence of text. *Whoa, Nellie! #1.* Art and script: Xaime Hernandez © 1996 The creator.

Figure 24. This fight scene seems to take longer because of the presence of texts which retard the readers eye movement from panel to panel. *Daisho*. Art and script: Patrick Debruin © 1993 The creator.

Retardation is more complicated in comics narration because the perception of texts and images is different. Images are perceived instantly and may be experienced at once. Reading requires time since prose must be read in a linear, time-based sequence. In cinema and television, where the motion of images is now seen simultaneously with the sound of the accompanying texts, the two narrational elements, through the use of sight and sound, may attain a synchronicity of comprehension not available to the medium of comics.[24] In comics, images are static and thus may be perceived immediately while the texts must be *read* through time; furthermore, both actions require the use of the same organ for perception. In addition, images in comics are part of a sequence of other images and must then be comprehended in relation to a series of images. Thus, time elapses from the instant of seeing the events and information illustrated, through the process of relating this information to the whole story and framing hypotheses to confirm or disconfirm moments upon reading the text. This intervening time may be deliberately manipulated by the artist to suit his or her own graphic style and narrational purposes. The delaying of the reader movement from panel to panel due to the necessary unfolding of the text in time, for example, can be used in marking and controlling the timing and duration of the story in unfolding and may be a means of holding reader interest.

Most of the time, texts are used to complement the accompanying images. Texts provide subtle shades of meaning too complex to be contained in images; they clarify strange, imaginary and other unfamiliar situations and scenes; they re-direct the reader's attention, and signal the continuation of the action and the duration of time. On the other hand, graphic images may be presented which are disconfirmed by the verbal information, or vice versa. While everything included in a comic strip is related to a specific story, some codes are intended to evolve and function in diverse, even opposing parameters in the process of creating engrossing or interesting narratives. Even within one frame, there are multiple codes which do not advance in the same time, nor even in the same direction.

The order in which one perceives the various textual and pictorial elements of a single panel—not to mention a series of panels—depends on eye movement. Interestingly, eye movement in a panel is determined in the West by both the left-to-right, top-to-bottom conventions of reading and by the freer patterns associated with the contemplation of pictures. A good comics artist knows how to work the two seemingly unrelated eye operations to his advantage. The tendency for a series of panels to move the eye along in a prescribed pattern suggests the second facet of ordering in comics—duration. The concept of duration refers to the period of time depicted in the panel drawing, whether it is a single instant or a longer interval. Duration also refers to the time allotted the viewer to perceive each panel picture (including the length it takes for one to read the text). The time to be spent in reading each panel is carefully controlled, in that the text actually *determines* the amount of time spent viewing the scene. Depending on what the text says, readers eagerly proceed to the next panel, search the current one for confirmation, or refer backwards to whatever was missed in the previous panel. Each panel, however, no matter how many verbal and pictorial elements are included in it, eventually pushes the reader forward into the next panel, according to the flow and pace of the story's continuity. Each drawing in comics has its allotted reading time, without which narrative continuity would be severely hindered.

The power of the panels to establish duration holds true in a variety of situations. A panel may represent a single instant—a fist hitting an assailant—or it may depict a scene that would take several moments to obtain—a conversation among two or more characters. But in either case, the number of panels and the presence of text will influence the amount of time in the reader's act of perception. A long-panel may actually be divided into multiple frames, usually cut according to the various segments of conversation. The panel with a series of pictures becomes in fact a tableau, a frozen scene that comes to life in segments. Each segment comes alive the moment the reader pays attention to it and only so long as the reader's attention is on it; each group of conversants is in motion only during its speaking moments, and only as their lines are being read. Due to the graphic impact, however, the semblance of continuous conversation and the appearance of a single unbroken scene exist simultaneously, creating the effect of a single, united scenario out of a scene that actually unfolds in time (see *Figure 25*). Graphic cues utilised in the picture blend easily into our perception of the whole—so easily in fact that we are hardly aware of the mental gymnastics necessary to coordinate the time frames. The ease of the reader's perception is ordered by the text so that

Figure 25. Each segment comes alive only as the reader moves from one speech balloon to another yet there is the illusion of perceiving the whole panel as one unified scene. *Zot! Book One*. Art and script: Scott McCloud © 1990 The creator.

eye movement and the pace of the story are both controlled. In this case, the text both creates and controls the illusion of running time, the "duration" of the scene.

The instantaneous effect of image-perception, meanwhile, allows for the maintenance of the illusion of perceiving a whole. Both the reading of texts and the viewing of cinema involve control over the revelation of the next scene. In the case of comics, readers may take in the whole graphics first which may influence the interpretation of the texts, and may even stimulate them to read faster than their usual rate in anticipation of the next panel in the page. Thus the role of the text in ordering visual perception is not merely one of influencing eye movement but also of controlling the temporal aspect of perception.

In comics, time is a function of space, and panels may serve as divisions of time. The succession of panels in comics is the mechanism by which timing is achieved, and carefully controlled timing enhances the drama of every event (see *Figure 26*). The narrative flow (how the author conceives of the passing of time in a particular sequence) and time flow (how it is perceived by the reader) are seldom coincidental. Both must be weighed against actual reading

TIME

A simple action whose result is immediate . . . seconds.

TIMING

A simple action wherein the result (only) is extended to enhance emotion

Figure 26. An illustration from *Comics and Sequential Art* by Will Eisner © Poorhouse Press.

time. The presentation of images and words must always correspond to the intentions of relating a story, where some information may be privileged in order to create the desired narrative effect.

Although the control and manipulation of information is characteristic in any storytelling, there is an added dimension in comic art because it is primarily visual and the format of comics is such that the reader can actually read any one panel he or she fancies. The comics artist must rely on a tacit agreement in reading competencies built up in reading comics so that readers will follow the pattern set up for the best presentation of the story. The reading manners in western and eastern countries, for example, differ in direction such that even "instinctive" eye movement would also vary.

Another distinct consideration of the temporal aspect in comics is the seemingly limitless and open-ended concept of time in it. Time, for instance, may also be reversible. Often characters will go back decades or more in time and start the cycle all over again potentially thrusting the narrative in a different direction. Comics are also ahistorical in that there is almost complete absence of teleology. Events that took place in the past usually do not have the slightest influence on the events taking place in the present, at least not in a strictly causative sense. Radical changes may be introduced in one issue that completely contradict information provided in earlier ones. In addition, the most popular comicbooks often provide the feeling of an eternal present tense; characters do not age with their "celebrity life" while the background and settings which are ambiguous and fantastic may rarely be equated to any particular time period.

The sample narrative analysis provided for Frank Miller's *The Dark Knight Returns* in Chapter Six illustrates the role of panels, gutters, and duration in comicbook narrative. But before this textual analysis, Chapter Four discusses superhero comicbooks within genre criticism in order to further clarify more distinctive features of the medium.

NOTES

1 M. Horn, *Seventy-Five Years of the Comics* (Boston: Boston Book and Art, 1971): ix.
2 I. Pennachioni, *La nostalgie en images* (Paris: Libraires des Meridiens, 1982): 22.
3 Rolf T. Wigand, "Toward a More Visual Culture Through Comics," in Alphons Silberman and H.-D. Dyroff, *Comics and Visual Culture* (Munich: K. G. Saur, 1986): 28–61; H. Culbertson, "Words vs.Pictures: Perceived Impact and Connotative Meaning," *Journalism Quarterly* 51.2 (1974):226–237.
4 Will Eisner, *Comics and Sequential Art* (Tamarac: Florida: Poorhouse Press, 1985).
5 Stan Lee, "Introduction," in Les Daniels, ed. *Marvel: Five Fabulous Decades of the World's Greatest Comics* (London: Virgin, 1991): iii.
6 *Time* (November 1, 1993): 68.
7 Barker, *op cit*, 8. Italics mine.
8 Patrick Hanks, ed. *Collins. Dictionary of the English Language* (London: Harper and Collins, 1978).
9 *Ibid.*
10 Scott McCloud, *Understanding Comics: The Invisible Art* (Princeton, Winsconsin: Kitchen Sink Press, 1993): 17.
11 A note of caution must be made regarding the term "graphic novel." Graphic novels existed long before the term itself was coined and became popular around 1986–7. The term is now used mostly to refer to a particular type of adult-oriented comicbooks published in expensive album-format and sold not only in comics stores but regular bookstores as well. Comics scholar Roger Sabin, in *Adult Comics: An Introduction* (London and New York: Routledge, 1994): 236–50, states that "a graphic novel is a comic in book form, but not all comics in book form are graphic novels" and aspects to be considered in determining which comicbooks may be regarded as graphic novels include, among others, thematic unity and perception of a finite story (in cases of collections); length of narrative, number of pages, the pacing of the narrative, and so on.
12 McCloud, *op cit.*, 22.

13 In his discussion of graphic novels as a definable category of comics, Sabin (*op cit.*, 237) already includes Raymond Briggs in his list of prominent authors of the graphic novel, therefore placing him within the tradition of comics for adults.

14 Antonio Lara, *El apasionante mundo del tebeo* (Madrid: Ed. Cuadernos para el Dialogo, Sociedad Anonima, 1972): 35ff.

15 Ruben Gubern, *El lenguaje de los comics* (Barcelona: Ediciones Peninsula, 1972): 115.

16 Robert Harvey, "The Aesthetics of Comic Strips," *Journal of Popular Culture* (Spring 1986): 650.

17 Joseph Witek, *Comic Books as History: The Narrative Art of Jack Jackson, Art Spiegelman, and Harvey Pekar* (Mississippi: University of Mississippi Press, 1989): 22ff.

18 The hegemonic roles and functions of superheroes, and how these are implied or emphasized through various narrative devices in comic books, will be discussed in more detail in Chapters Four and Five of this study.

19 McCloud, *op cit.*, 70ff.

20 Eisner, *op cit.*, 26.

21 Frederik Schodt, *Manga! Manga!* (New York: Kodansha International, 1988): xx.

22 Schodt, *ibid.*, 55–60.

23 Schodt, *ibid.*

24 Shows that are sub-titled require a different process for understanding, compounded by the linguistic abilities and literacy levels of the viewers. Silent films, meanwhile, are also another matter because they contain separate panels of text which often interrupt the temporal flow of the images.

Chapter Four
Superhero Comicbooks

Commodities like mass-produced texts are selected, purchased, constructed, and used by real people with previously existing needs, desires, intentions, and interpretative strategies. By reinstating those active individuals and their creative, constructive activities at the heart of our interpretative enterprise, we avoid blinding ourselves to the fact that the essentially human practice of making meanings goes on even in a world dominated by things and by consumption. In thus recalling the interactive character of operations like reading, we restore time, process, and action to our account of human endeavour.

Jane Radway
Reading the Romance 1984

Since their inauspicious debut in the newsstands of New York in the 1930s, comicbooks in America have been published in billions of copies for audiences of countless millions. It would be fair to say that most who grew up since the introduction of comicbooks to popular culture have come under its pervasive spell at one time or another. Not until the arrival of television was there a sharp decline in comicbook sales. On the other hand, television enabled the instant transmission of comicbook-inspired material on Saturday mornings and prime time. Eventually, television would help propel the sales of comicbooks and also extend the production and manipulation of comicbook products into an increasingly multimedia base. Today, the comicbook continues to manifest

itself, although in different forms than its 1930 prototype. This
chapter will discuss how the changes and development in comicbooks, especially the construction and properties of superhero
comicbooks, can be correlated much more closely with the fantasy wishes and consumer caprice of readers than most other common forms of popular narrative like television, cinema or romance
fiction. Some reasons for the close relation between comics and its
readers are: the cheapness of comicbooks as a commodity; the general low opinion of the product which bonded those who favoured
it and also fostered a strong underground movement; its well-
developed community of fans; the way comicbooks were produced
and distributed; and, most importantly, the nature of the superhero
figure and his adventures and exploits which made it easy and possible to incorporate almost any "neat" idea proffered by those in
the industry as well as its readers.

At the height of its popularity in the early 1940s, the superhero comicbook was a unique visual phenomenon. In most cases,
it was in a standard 64-page magazine format and celebrated the
exploits of superheroic characters in action-packed, vividly
coloured covers that children found hard to resist. The superhero
dominated the pages of the early comicbook. These were mostly
muscular men[1] in brightly coloured tights shown performing
remarkable feats of strength and defeating strange villains one
after another. The heroes also had all the traits a child could dream
of: speed, strength, power, and knowledge. The recurrence of this
sight and theme in the minds of thousands of children and adolescents over a fifty-year period must have helped the American
(male) youths to a better understanding or recognition of their fantasy goals as they related to their personal ideals. Interestingly,
what primarily appealed to the visualised fantasies of childhood
provided the twentieth century with a pantheon and mythology
comparable to those of previous cultures. The superhero figure has
developed into a lasting and vigorous presence in American and
European popular culture such that the recognition of the Batman
or Superman, for example, by millions who have never read a
Batman comicbook or seen a Superman film is ensured.[2]

The lasting popularity of superheroes is rather unexpected if we
consider the characteristics most familiar to superhero comics:
a) the plot, characterisation, and theme are relatively simple; b) they
rely frequently on formulaic plots and traditional symbols; c) there

is an interpreting narrator to direct the stories; and d) simple, cartoon-like illustrations with bright, primary colours are used. While their generic similarities and obvious evocation of archetypes make them easy to remember, most superhero texts seem to be quite undetailed. The stories are so similar to each other, possess very few qualities distinct enough for durable impressions, and do not seem substantial enough to allow permanence over the years. Yet, despite their sameness, superhero comics have endured, have crossed over to other media, and have managed to maintain their almost worldwide presence in popular culture. Closer scrutiny of the genre reveals that the persistence and popularity of certain superheroes and particular texts belie the seeming interchangeability of these comicbooks. In fact, thousands of devout comicbook fans could enumerate differences in detail that would quell any doubts about the uniqueness of each text. Then again, careful analysis of the particulars of these "differences" shows that they are often appreciated in relation to their unexpectedness or deviance from a recognisable convention of a superhero text. This enjoyment derived from the manipulation of established conventions indirectly acknowledges the existence of a "model" or a "paradigm" for such texts. The shifts between repetition and uniqueness, between imitation and imagination in superhero comicbooks will be emphasised in this section which, by using genre criticism, will discuss superhero texts within the framework of cultural studies. The aim of the analysis is to study the central core of repeated patterns and restated meanings gleaned from a wide variety of superhero texts and evaluate the comicbook form within a cultural perspective. Some central points are: what are the defining traits of a superhero; what kinds of superheroes are popular during the important stages in the genre's development; what social realities are most reflected in this type of narrative; who are its producers and readers and how do they participate in shaping the genre; what social trends affect the genre most; in which direction does the genre seem to be headed?

In discussing superhero comicbooks within cultural studies, a number of paradoxes will be immediately apparent: a) the superhero comicbook is a popular art form traditionally known for its apparently hegemonic and sometimes overtly authoritarian texts; b) it is a publishing genre which began to gain a degree of cultural respectability by ducking the 'underground' label at least partially for greater distribution; c) it is an art form which has been handled (if at all) with disdain by the literary establishment, and yet has built up its own heuristic critical discourse through what is still rather misleadingly know as the "fan press;" d) it consists of a body of contemporary mythology from which television and Hollywood have plundered and distributed material; and finally, e) critical perception of the formal and narrative patterns and meanings of comicbooks is often based on an appeal to a common culture although the culture of comicbooks is not necessarily shared by students and scholars of literature. The culture of comicbooks seems to be in a power relationship with dominant literary norms, exposing notions of contradictory norms and power. Looking at how superhero comicbooks have survived and developed in the last fifty years will reveal some of the reasons and purposes for the paradoxes outlined above. Once we think of comics as an example of a genre, we can no longer approach it as only an artefact to be analysed in some contextless critical purity. We need to ask who reads such books, why and in which way, seeing them as "texts-in-use" that are accompanied by the pragmatics of production as well as issues of ideology and language.

THE USE OF GENRE STUDIES

It is important to clarify some points about the concept of the genre before plunging into the comicbooks themselves. The word genre conjures up different sets of associations. Often it is used in the context of popular literature, where it frequently implies "not literature" but rather some low-level formulaic production. But it may also be traced to formalist academic literary critics, for whom it meant established literary forms, with definite rules where a writer's art was shown in their faithful observation of or artful departure from these rules. Some types of literary criticism have come to decree that great writing is to be unique and *sui generis*— literally, each great work creating its own genre. But such conditions of uniqueness and transcendence of the generic would cause problems for evaluating comicbooks which are clearly formulaic and archetypal. The advent of cultural studies and the corresponding increase in attention to varying forms of popular narratives have caused the re-examination of genre and genre criticism. Once again, we are aware of the importance of genre, now not as a set of rules that ought to be followed, but as a framework that is always present to some degree. All texts are dependent on and grow out of other texts such that all texts are variations of previous models that contain rules, structures and patterns that make storytelling possible and the stories recognisable. Nonetheless, the importance of the rules may be that they are there to be broken.

Jonathan Culler (1981) defines genres as groups of norms and expectations that help readers assign functions to the various elements in a work.[3] The readers know what to expect and why: each genre has its codes and conventions. If we read crime novels, for example, we expect a mystery, an investigator, and a solution. If we read romance we expect a leading man, a leading lady, and true love. In superhero comicbooks, we expect a hero with superpowers, a villain, a confrontation, and a conclusion where the hero wins. However, norms and expectations are not inscribed within texts forever but are dependent on the readers' and writers' knowledge of the codes. Hence, one is not necessarily always sure which conventions to read by. For example, no one reading Frankenstein in 1818 could have thought they were reading science fiction, but with a history of science fiction we now can read it differently.[4] Genres represent a set of conventions whose parameters are redrawn with each new book and each new reading. The concept involves a contract between authors and readers. Generic conventions are especially important in superhero comicbooks as a way of understanding and constructing a triangular relationship between the producer, the text, and the reader. As John Fiske remarks:

> Genres are not to be seen as forms of textual codifications, but as systems of orientations, expectations, and conventions that circulate between industry, text and subject.[5]

Generic conventions are the structural elements that are shared between producers and readers and they are crucial to the pleasures a genre offers its audience. This can be clearly seen in superhero texts where repetitions in orientation, expectation, and conventions played an important role in keeping the genre alive. The market of superhero comicbooks was such that publishers could reckon with a fast turnover which made repetitions easy, even necessary. Many of the heroes that exist today have survived at least forty years of publication, and have undergone changes while retaining what may be termed the "key components" of their identity and the core ideas of their individual narratives. Many of the patterns and meanings which emerge from current texts, as well as the play which is derived from them, rely for their fullest impact on the readers' cumulative sense of significance of the similarities and differences among the individual elements within texts. There is a strong element of intertextuality among superhero texts which forms a progressive series of cumulative knowledge among their readers. This knowledge is developed through reading and following comicbooks, in acknowledging certain texts while disputing or dismissing others. There is a general agreement among Batman fans, for example, that the campy Batman television series with Adam West in the 1960s is not at all part of the bat-texts which comprise the key components in defining Batman's identity and psyche. Another example is the way fans ignored the Captain America texts which were published briefly in 1954. On March 1964, Captain America's revival showed him awaking from being frozen in suspended animation since 1946, totally excluding whatever text was written between 1946 and 1964.

Comics accumulate sign and meaning possibilities that do not depend on one book, but rather on a series of on-going short narratives. There is a complex intertextuality in comicbooks which opens a greater availability to different readings on both the synchronic and diachronic levels since the genre has existed for a long time. Simultaneously, its nature dictates a drive for perennial contemporaneity. In the context to be used here, a genre is defined less through its conventions and rules, and more as a shifting provisional set of characteristics that are modified as each new example is produced.

GENERIC CONVENTIONS OF SUPERHERO COMICS

A logical place to start in ferreting out the characteristics of the superhero narrative is in scrutinising its two most apparent features: the hero and his adventures. For this purpose, John Cawelti's description of the basic structure of a hero's adventure is very useful, pertinent to the point that it begs to be included here:

> The central fantasy of the adventure story is that of the hero ... individual or group... overcoming obstacles and dangers and accomplishing some important moral mission. Often, though not always, the hero's trials are the result of the machinations of a villain, and, in addition, the hero frequently receives as a kind of side benefit, the favours of one or

more attractive young ladies. However, the interplay with the villain and the erotic interests served by the attendant damsels are more in the nature of frosting on the cake. The true focus of interest in the adventure story is the character of the hero and the nature of the obstacles he has to overcome. This is the simplest and perhaps the oldest and widest appeal of all formula types. It can clearly be traced back to the myths and epics of earlier times that have been cultivated in some form or other by almost every human culture. At least on the surface, the appeal of this form is obvious. It presents a character with whom the audience identifies passing through the most frightening perils to achieve a triumph. Perhaps the most basic moral fantasy implicit in this type of story is that of victory over death, though there are also all kinds of subsidiary triumphs available depending upon the particular cultural materials employed: the triumph over injustice and threat of lawlessness in the western; the saving of the nation in the spy story; the overcoming of fear and defeat of the enemy in the combat story. While the specific characterisation of the hero depends on the cultural motifs and themes that are embodied in any specific adventure formulas, there are in general two primary ways in which the hero can be characterised: as a superhero with exceptional strength or ability or as "one of us"—a figure marked, at least at the beginning of the story by flawed abilities and attitudes presumably shared by the audience.[6]

Seen against this basic hero formula, the construction and appeal of the comicbook superhero become obvious and apparent: being pure fantasy, it can cover all kinds of fantasies and triumphs enumerated above that evoke the mythical and span the range of themes from moral conflicts to combat stories. Furthermore, superheroes embody the two types of hero mentioned since they are usually endowed with a dual identity being simultaneously a super-power while also being "one of us." Superhero narrative is simple and formulaic, held together by rapid action of one such character or a group of such characters. A mystery or dilemma is confronted with violence. Women are victims to be rescued. Heroes are tough and honourable. The law needs the hero's help. There are elaborate fight scenes whose winner is almost inevitable. Language is masculine. Plotting is precise and often predictable. Dialogue is short and punchy until the elaborate schemes of the villains need explaining. The conclusion is foreseeable. But despite the predictability of the stories, for some inexplicable reason, the "willing suspension of disbelief" in readers becomes inexhaustible. No matter how many times Superman, the Batman or Spider-Man achieve their triumphs, the next adventure captivates again, and reader suspense and involvement is always successfully manipulated. The play between predictability and innovation must account for some of the reading pleasure in the texts, and may lead one to the conclusion that the form is not as restrictive as is often thought.

Classic superhero narratives usually start with a disruption of the status quo and proceed to a discovery and eradication of the perpetrator of this disruption. Usually, the "establishment," namely, the police, and the judiciary, are the forces given credit for restoring order and stability, since the Superhero usually works with them. In classic superhero fiction, the disruption takes place in closed hierarchical communities—a "named" and identifiable, albeit imaginary, locale like Metropolis and Gotham City. The problem is solved by the superhero who is generally known as an establishment figure. The comicbook ends with the restoration of the old hierarchies. The superhero from this position could thus be seen as the last bastion of imperialism and outmoded class attitudes, sanitised violence, racism, sexism; he has too much respect for authority and an unhealthy tendency to see moral issues in absolute terms. However, attributing to superhero narratives such conservative forms tends to imply rather negative reasons for the prominence or persistence of the genre among its readers. It would suggest that its readers are those attracted most by repetitive genres with conservative implications.

But this view is erroneous. It is based on a too scanty knowledge of the history of superhero comicbooks, and a far too rigid interpretation of the superhero genre, at least an outdated one in view of the more recent re-makes of many of the genre's characters and narratives. More and more, one can assert that the boundaries of the superhero are relatively fluid. This genre does not necessarily have conservative implications since only an extraordinarily fertile and productive genre could have spread and caught the attention of readers world-wide for so long. It is true that classic superhero texts tended to end with certainties—chaos is vanquished and stability is restored. In the past, the classic superhero figure also tended to be an establishment figure which seemed to imply that the forces of law and order were always good and unproblematic. Nevertheless, it is possible to make a convincing argument that the outcome of the fights is often only secondary to the unfolding of the disruption and its effects, the ensuing confrontation with the villains, and the development and expansion of the superhero character in each issue. Even in a "classic plot" involving rather uncomplicated protagonists, there are at least two problematic elements: a) the depicted society is always in danger and its institutions for law enforcement are deficient, otherwise it would not need a superhero; and b) the restoration of peace and order is only temporary since recurring threats to a superhero's domain are intrinsic to the genre. In some cases, popular protagonists are even deliberately left to escape and their probable return is implied. In addition, many superheroes operate outside the law—the Submariner, the Hulk, Plastic Man, the Spirit, and countless others—helping powerless and worthy people to defend themselves against criminal and evil forces in areas where the official system of law and order has proven ineffective. The ending is moreover usually perfunctory, a necessary ending, but hardly equivalent to the complex fight scenes, the elaborate illustrations and interactions which preceded it, as well as to the flamboyant and memorable villains and rogues who litter superhero narratives. In reaching the end, all sorts of unexpected things can happen just as all sorts of unexpected things are introduced. After all, crime involves the disruption of normalities (superheroes themselves are already a disruption of normalities), and superhero narratives are often the consequences of this disorder. While the plots are naturally geared towards the restoration of law, they are also about the breaking of the law, about the transgression of normal rules. Viewed from this perspective, the narratives become more interesting and take on more dimensions especially in relation to power and control. It is possible to perceive the genre as actually dealing with the transgression of the law, portraying the play between breaking and restoring law, or at the very least, showing an ambivalence about law and order.[7] After all, if the police were efficient and sufficient in maintaining law and order, superheroes would be unneccessary. The presence of superheroes to augment the establishment's capacity to uphold the law lends a distance between the hero figure and aspects of establishment. Moreover, the superheroes of today have evolved a great deal from the unabashed patriots of the 1940s and 1950s. Since the early 1970s, they have been shown routing out scientists, politicians, priests, and other establishment figures who turn out to be in league with criminal elements. With the sophistication of the more recent graphic novels, the once reassuring form of traditional binary oppositions and simple disputes in the older texts have given way to a multitudinous and pluralistic range of images that fit our contemporary existence. Newer texts like *The Dark Knight Returns*, *Watchmen*, *Astro City*, and *Madman* tackle complex moral dilemmas and diverse political shifts where changes and contradictions cannot so easily be labelled and appraised. Often, the superheroes themselves question their role in upholding the law in a world where those in powerful and institutionalised positions have debatable intentions and morality. The world is very different from that of thirty years ago: the bases of power have shifted, and so have ways of understanding them. Old certainties have gone, though new and perhaps equally repressive authoritarianisms have emerged. These, in their turn, must be challenged. This present world of uncertain directions and kaleidoscopic and contradictory images is increasingly reflected both textually and visually in comicbooks.

There is one other essential feature of usual adventure or hero stories that is used quite differently in superhero tales: these are the trials designed to test if the hero should really be a hero, if he is a match for the tasks set before him, if, for example, he can cheat and triumph over death. But superheroes were conceived to be intrinsically indestructible. That a superhero never dies is a tacit agreement between artists and readers for otherwise, there would be no subsequent issues of that comicbook. The superhero's immortality, however, is directly proportion to its popularity which then dictates which comicbooks will be further published. Such narratives are not really geared towards an innovative ending other than the hero's triumph. The innovation and variability of each text is actually in presenting a variety of villains and in cooking up the "distortion" of the law. The originality and creativity of the artists lie in making up and developing transgressions that provide the plot in each issue. In a way, it is actually crime and the supervillains that keep the superhero in business. The proliferation of crooks and chaos is allowed as long as core ideas of the origins and identity of the hero are maintained. Committed comicbook readers have come to expect this, and letters to the editor often applaud or rebuke these "innovative repetitions," implying that the readers accept some rules governing story-construction and superhero definitions.[8]

SHORT HISTORY OF SUPERHERO COMICBOOKS

The first publication to call itself a comicbook in the US came out in 1917 from the Saalfield Publishing Company and consisted of collected reprints from newspaper comic strips. Its size and format looked very much like the Sunday comic section of the newspapers, except that it was mostly black and white. It would not be until 1933 that the comicbook in the format we know it today appeared, produced by the Eastern Color Printing Company as give-aways for companies like Proctor and Gamble, Wheatena, Milk-O-Malt and Kinney Shoes.[9] Although now in full-colour and magazine format, the comicbook was nevertheless still a compilation of popular Sunday comic strips, with neither original material nor an extended narrative featuring one character. By 1938, reprint comicbooks had become the norm. For the most part during these five years, early comic-book publishers were content to continue raiding the Sunday comic pages and had come up with neither a major original character nor concept.

But two teenagers would be responsible for changing the history and development of comicbooks in the US for all time. Despite refusals from major comic syndicates—the concept was a major departure from the idea of comicbook content—Jerry Siegel and Joe Shuster managed to have an original character called Superman published in *Action Comics 1*. This comicbook laid the groundwork for the transformation and growth of the largest and most successful comicbook genre that would assure the future of comicbooks. *Action Comics 1* (dated June 1938) hit the newsstands in early Spring 1938. There were two succeeding issues but no immediate success was noticed by its publishers until the fourth issue when Action Comics sold about half a million copies while other titles would be selling approximately two hundred thousand copies per issue. DC's owner, Donenfeld, unsure of why the comic-book was doing so well, ordered a newsstand survey and found that the children were not asking for *Action Comics* but for the comicbook "with Superman."[10]

Action really stood out from the other dozen or so comic-book
titles on the stands that month. Its cover pictured a muscular
man wearing a brightly coloured red-and-blue costume with a
cape, lifting a car over his head as criminals flee in terror.[11]

Donenfeld had ordered Superman out of the cover after the
first issue, worried that the character was too fantastic and ridiculous. But after the survey, he ordered him back on the covers and
watched each succeeding issue sell out.

So unexpected and rapid was the success of Superman that it
would be almost a year before he was joined by serious imitators.
Although some superheroes would later be given more elaborate
origins that may be traced back to Egyptian, Norse and Greek
mythological beings who helped in the affairs of mortals, the roots
of the early American comicbook superhero can be found in the
popular fiction magazines of the early 1930s. Characters like the
Shadow, Doc Savage, Dr. Mystic, and the Spider were all popular
pulp-magazine characters with secret identities, costumes and
super physical powers. Since many comicbook creators were also
writers of the pulp adventure stories, and many comicbook publishers originally published pulp hero magazines, the similarities
were not coincidences.[12]

The Golden Age of comicbooks is generally acknowledged to
have begun in 1938, but it was hard to tell this by looking at the
other comicbooks published that year. Most early comicbook publishers did not have a regular staff of artists and writers, and books
were packaged by comicbook studio shops which littered
Manhattan at this time. It took almost a year before the industry
caught up to Superman's popularity, but when it did, superheroes
multiplied by the hundreds and comicbook sales increased to millions of copies sold. Stan Lee of Marvel Comics remembers the
time when a variety of superheroes were being introduced almost
every week as publishers sought to launch a superhero that would
capture the readers' imagination like Superman, Batman or
Captain Marvel did. "It seemed that unemployed costumed heroes
were turning up almost daily at the Marvel office, and more loi-
tered in the streets of Manhattan..."[13] In 1939, there were fifty
comic titles, by 1941 there were 168 and over eighty percent of
these had superhero adventures in them.[14] Despite the seeming
inertia in the industry due to the war shortages in paper and labour
which limited the growth of the industry, comicbooks surged in

popularity during the war years. One publisher alone, Faucet Publications, sold nearly forty-seven million comicbooks in 1943, more than double its sales of the previous year. In 1944, its most popular superhero title, *Captain Marvel Adventures*, sold over 14 million issues during a twelve-month period, almost three million more than the previous year.[15] Increasing numbers of American servicemen became comicbook readers to the extent that comics were reported to have outsold popular magazines such as *Life* and *Reader's Digest* at a rate of ten to one on army bases (1949).[16] Propelled by the rising sales, more and more superheroes were published. World War II initiated a big push for patriotic heroes. It provided the superheroes with a new set of enemies and supplied a complete working rationale for the world view of a super-patriotic hero such as Captain America who epitomised American values during World War II (first appeared in *Captain America 1* (1941).[17] In the Summer of 1941, Nazi-bashing superheroes began in earnest—with propaganda and slogans included in the pages of the comicbooks.[18] The war also induced an element of realism into the comicbooks, and publishers adapted historical events or biographies of war heroes into comic-book stories. Fantasy, however, still ruled as seen in the spiralling powers granted to the superheroes, in the visual renditions of their strength and fighting capabilities, and the contraptions and gadgets used both by the superheroes and villains. To name a few, Captain Flash, Captain Atom, Doctor Solar and Dynamo provide a clue to the artists' and readers' fascination with scientific and futuristic curiosities. *Wonder Woman* (published by DC) broke the sex barrier in Summer of 1942, Marvel quickly followed with *Miss Fury* (Winter 1942) and Fawcett also added *Mary Marvel* (December 1945), a superheroine counterpart of Captain Marvel.[19] The summer of 1943 brought the first parody of the superhero comics in the form of *Plastic Man* created by humour artist Jack Cole for *Police Comics*. As Plastic Man stretched and slithered after criminals and transformed himself to all kinds of imaginable objects, he was played strictly for laughs, and his adventures were refreshingly different from the deadly serious crimefighters of the day.

After the war, superhero comics soon lost two things: its servicemen readers and Nazi/Japanese villains. It is generally agreed that the golden age of comics and superhero comics in particular lasted from 1938 to 1949 after which the bulk of superhero comics folded due to falling readership. Only the Batman, Superman, and Wonder Woman came through without a break in publication during the lean years of the early 1950s when interest had shifted to crime, western, and in particular, "horror and gore" comics. Ironically, the excess of gore and horror, which initiated the censorious attacks of Dr. Wertham and the Congressional hearings on comics and juvenile delinquency, also led indirectly to the renaissance of superhero comics.[20] Very few comics publishers weathered the implementation of the Comics Code which clamped down excessively on crime and horror comics. DC and Marvel were two of the few which survived, and for both, the revival of superheroes seemed safe within a Code which upheld authority figures and stipulated that law enforcement leaders should always be shown in a respectful and sympathetic manner. The year 1956 then sparked one of the most significant trends in comicbook history—the revival and updating of original comicbook superheroes for a new audience. A re-born and re-costumed Flash appeared in *Showcase* 4, October 1956 (the date usually regarded as the beginning of the so called Silver Age) and paved the way for the Green Lantern who returned in the *Showcase* 22, October 1959; a new heroine Supergirl also appeared, and then a whole superhero team in the shape of the Justice League of America who first appeared in *The Brave and the Bold* 28, March 1960. Norse Gods and legends were added as Thor first appeared in *Journey into Mystery* 83, August 1962. In March 1966, the comic was retitled *The Mighty Thor*. Horror wedded to the superhero format materialised in the form of *The Incredible Hulk* who burst on the scene in *The Incredible Hulk* 1, May 1962. Golden Age characters like Captain America and the Submariner were brought back out of retirement as well. The superhero revivals were carefully planned and published; the superheroes were featured in teams and groups as a chance to bring them all back at once, as well as to gauge from reader response which ones might be given their own issues or cover titles.

Marvel dominated the scene in the 1960s and early 1970s, but it was DC who benefited from the enormous appeal of the 1960s Batman television series. Almost immediately after its January 1966 premiere, USA went "bat-crazy." The show achieved tremendous ratings and was broadcast twice a week. This event had a great impact on comicbooks. Sales of all superhero comicbooks rose as a result of the show, and the Batman comicbooks in particular reached a very impressive circulation of close to nine hundred thousand copies, the largest circulation of any superhero comicbook since the 1950s.[21] Soon, the Batman was featured prominently in all DC comicbook covers, while both Marvel and DC rode on the wave of a new superhero popularity. By 1969, Batman and Superman titles made up nine of the ten best-selling comics in the United States.[22] Although the second heroic age of comicbooks, the "Silver Age" is acknowledged to have begun in 1956, it is difficult to determine exactly when it ended. Nevertheless, 1967 might be a good year to mark the beginning of the end of the second superhero boom. Almost every comicbook published in 1967 had lower sales than the previous Bat-year. The Batman fell in circulation by nearly one hundred thousand copies and many other titles experienced a ten to twenty percent drop in sales.

The next interesting landmark in superhero comics would be 1971 when *Spider-Man* (issues 96 to 98) defied the Comics Code Authority by featuring an anti-drug story, reflecting the new social consciousness of the young writers and artists working on the books. Because of Code prohibitions against any portrayal of drug use, this *Spider-Man* issue had to be distributed without the seal of approval from the Comics Code Authority. However, as a result of the industry's desire to present anti-drug messages, the Comics Code reviewed its 1954 standards and modified them so that such topics could be treated. At the same time, the Code relaxed the prohibition against the use of horror in comics, and the treatment of law violations. Before 1971, Spider-Man also introduced another innovation for the superhero genre—despite the fact that he was not originally intended to star in a series, he became the epitome of the radical innovations that characterised the Marvel Age (1961-70) when he started to analyse his motives for being a superhero:[23]

> "Can they be *right*? Am I really some sort of crack-pot, wasting my time seeking fame and glory? Am I more interested in the adventure of being *Spider-Man* than I am in helping people??? Why do I do it? Why don't I give up? And yet, I *can't*! I must have been given this great power for a *reason*! No matter how difficult it is, I *must* remain *Spider-Man*! I pray that some day the world will understand!"[24]

Marvel editor Stan Lee used Spider-Man to challenge the very concept of the superhero. Spider-Man was neurotic, compulsive and profoundly sceptical about the whole idea of becoming a costumed saviour. He was constantly struggling with himself while others continued their valiant fights against whichever villain was currently wreaking havoc in their spheres.

By the 1980s, the Comics Code had become a spent force. Both Marvel and DC had started to advertise insouciantly many of their comics as "Suggested for Mature Readers,"[25] offering comic-books dealing explicitly with violence and sexuality. Such confidence in the labelling bespoke the strength of their adult readership. In the mid-1980s, DC asserted itself as the leading comic-book publisher by launching a new line of comics (DC Vertigo) specifically for adults; by initiating a shrewd and imaginative revamping of classic titles, and by promoting bold and innovative work both in the superhero genre and in the linked genres of fantasy and horror with titles such as *Hellblazer*, *Watchmen*, *Sandman*, *Moonshadow*, *Shadows Fall*, among others. The current crowd of superheroes are much more mortal and more complex, especially in their psychological constitution.

Despite the introduction of new characters through many years, the Batman and Superman still remain the most popular superheroes.[26] They are popular with a variety of audiences who have grown up and embraced the superhero genre through a collage of different media manifestations during a fifty-year history. The Batman and Superman, together with many other superheroes, have come a long way from being related to the mystery men of the 1930s and 1940s pulp fiction, as well as from being patriotic do-gooders of the war years. Although almost all of the original superhero concepts were developed between 1938 and 1943, the superheroes have definitely grown up, and so have the genre and its readers. Looking at the characteristic features of superhero texts as gleaned from Superman and the Batman, we will be more able to appreciated the changes in superhero comic-books that have happened in the last ten years.

CHARACTERISTIC FEATURES OF SUPERHEROES

The concept of an invulnerable character with superhuman strength caught the fancy of a nation as Superman's arrival created a whole new genre out of a very coarse set of materials. Today, many aspects of the first Superman and its narrative approach have the appearance of a cliché. Indeed, much of what would become central to the superhero genre was already established in the thirteen pages of the first Superman issue. The first issue introduces readers to a distant, dying planet and explains that a "scientist" placed his infant son in a spaceship, launching it towards Earth. The "sleeping babe" is discovered and delivered to an orphanage (Clark Kent's parents were a later addition to the mythology). On reaching maturity, the young man discovers he has considerable powers, (though modest compared to the god-like capabilities that he would later acquire in his fifty-year career). He decides to dedicate his strength to the service of mankind, and becomes Superman—"Champion of the oppressed, this physical marvel who has sworn to devote his existence to helping those in need." All these facts were contained in just the first page. The next five pages relate how Superman prevents an innocent woman from going to the electric chair, how Clark gets an assignment from the (yet unnamed) editor of the *Daily Star* (later to be renamed *Daily Planet*) and assigned to cover the feats of Superman, and how Superman intervenes in a wife-beating scene.

Then, as Clark Kent, he meets his colleague Lois Lane who agrees to a date to "give him a break, for a change." It was a disastrous date, interrupted by a challenge to fight from a "hunk" called Matson who disdains Clark's pacifist attitudes, and later bundles Lois Lane into his car as she angrily leaves the club by herself. The car's getaway was blocked by the imposing figure of Superman who tips both Lois and the roughnecks out of the car, and then trashes the vehicle (this is the panel which provides the subject matter for the first *Action Comic*'s famous car-throwing cover). Clark's problem, in that his second identity steals the affections of Lois, starts here; the very next day, Lois treats him more coolly than ever. Meanwhile, Clark is assigned to stir up news for the *Star*'s front page and is told to go to the small South American republic of San Monte. But instead, as Superman, he takes the train to Washington to investigate corruption in the US Senate.

The actions and motifs in this first issue reveal the influence of usual hero-adventure narratives, as well as establish much of what will be staple to the superhero genre. Some of the features that would be repeated countless times in other superhero stories could be listed as follows: a) aberrant or mysterious origins, b) lost parents, c) man-god traits, d) a costumed, secret identity, e) difficulties with personal and emotional relationships, f) great concern for justice, and g) use of superpower in politics. Similar to Superman being forced to leave Krypton, the usual superhero adventure begins with someone from whom something important has been taken away—home and/or family, a loved one who dies, normal human constitution because of an accident, the sense of security is threatened, the feeling of complacency is lost because of the awareness of a "difference," and so on. In the usual hero-adventure story, the hero then undertakes a mission to recover what has been lost, to avenge a wrong, to discover some life-giving elixir or all of these together, usually fulfilling a cycle of departure and return.

For the true superhero, this cycle is rendered impossible by the nature of their "repetitive narratives," not to mention commercial demands, which dictate that they should battle again and again and thus bar any return to a former, calmer existence. The superhero cycle is simply comprised of discovering the cause of disorder and defeating the transgressor. However, even the ensuing peace and calm is often illusory, contradicted by an intrusion from the comicbook editor who advertises the next issue(s), directing the readers to upcoming battles and cancelling any pretence of a complete cycle.

Another basic motif of hero adventures utilised in this genre is the departure from one condition, usually psychological immaturity or physical dependency, in order to achieve individual and communal success. As in the folktale world, a superhero's coming into his inheritance or the acceptance of his "difference" and consequent role in society may be seen as a symbol of coming to a condition of moral autonomy. One favourite technique in obliging superheroes to confront autonomy is the loss of parents or a loved one—the Batman, a.k.a. Bruce Wayne, is haunted by the murder of his parents; Superman hails from a dying planet and is raised by human foster parents; Spider-Man's closest relative is his Aunt Mary who is also murdered; Wonder Woman starts as a lifeless sculpture created by her mother and she later renounces her immortality to remain in this man's world; the Submariner lost both his parents in a clash between humans and the inhabitants of Atlantis; Daredevil starts working out to avenge his father's death.

Although heroes in the folktale and comicbook worlds may be

said to be already earmarked for great deeds, many superheroes are different from folktale heroes in that their status is not gained by undergoing trials and tasks; most of them start out as a result of freak accidents (Spider-Man, Captain America, Dr. Manhattan, the Fantastic Four, the Hulk) or they are born somewhere else which gives them special powers on Earth (Superman, Wonder Woman, Mighty Thor, Iron Man, Submariner). Through no conscious desire of theirs, they find themselves thrown into an advantageous or extra-ordinary position. Some possible exceptions are Daredevil and the Batman who decide to transform themselves physically and mentally, driven by vengeance for their parents' murder. In dedicating over twenty years of his life to changing his physical and intellectual prowess, the Batman achieves what other superheroes already possess: some special powers that are either physical, magical, attributable to a weapon or device, or, most frequently, a combination of the above. We must not forget that supervillains may also have certain powers and the motivation to be supreme. What separates the two types of superbeings is the moral triumph that drives the hero in contrast to the egotism of the other. The implicit high moral of these avenger-type heroes provides a critique of the customary institutions of law and order in society, and expresses a desire for a fiercer and purer authority that would arise to punish evil, without the delays and corruption of constitutional law. In varying degrees of severity and explicitness, the presence and polarity of superheroes and the superhero genre involve a critique rather than a celebration of a given society's judicial system. If society does enjoy a distinct and central power source, then why the need for aberrant heroes? The code of the superheroes reveals a transcendent sense of justice that throws into question the accepted civil justice and the nature of "law" itself. As each superhero takes the "law" into his own hands, an alternative sense of justice is presented which implicitly or explicitly problematises the nature of "law." Acceptance of laws and social order should negate any need for independent crimefighters who are sometimes adversial to both state police and criminals.

That superheroes usually want to remain unknown to both crooks and cops attest to a preference not to favour (or trust) either side. A superhero has to assume another identity or an alter ego for reasons of privacy and protection. Having to assume dual identities, however, usually means entering into a series of com-promises, learning to be selectively deaf and blind to inconvenient realities. This may sometimes prove problematic for the super-hero's alter ego because, whether in his private or "public" life, readers have come to expect a high morality in the superhero char-acter.

One essential feature in superhero comicbooks that is used to differentiate the private man from the superhero is the use of cos-tumes. Costumes perform an interesting function in both defining and camouflaging a superhero, not only visually but in their bear-ing and outlook as well. Bruce Wayne's suave, playboy personali-ty effectively covers his nocturnal activities as the Batman; Clark Kent's shyness and fumbling speech hide Superman's invincibility; Diana Prince's eyeglasses and dowdy clothes cover Wonder Woman's curves and cunning; Dr. Blake's lame leg distracts from Thor's god-like perfection; and the list goes on. There is no mis-taking when each is functioning under their superhero or human capacity, and the most immediate sign to this is their costume. It would be no exaggeration to say that perhaps the most distin-guishing trait of the comicbook superheroes is their costume.

COSTUMES

From its inception, colour has been a chief selling point of comics.[27] By 1939, comicbooks were a full-colour medium and creators borrowed the colourful costumes of circus performers and acrobats to dress their heroes and make striking covers to attract buyers (which at that time were mostly children).[28] Because of the acrobatic stances of the heroes, it was convenient to draw them in tights which did not encumber the emphasis on the muscles and the anatomy, in general; capes added grandeur to the visual lines as the heroes dangled in mid-air or swooped upwards or poised for a fight.[29] The costume also served another important purpose. It allowed for easy identification of the characters especially consid-ering the graphic quality of early comics. In the poorly drawn and printed pages of pre-war comics, for example, costumes distin-guished a superhero from other characters or other superheroes. As more and more superheroes were introduced, costumes became a crucial sign of super-heroism that marked out heroes (and vil-lains) from by-standers and other characters who did not wear cos-tumes. In this sense, the costume functioned as a uniform which

bound together all super-beings and costumed characters in contrast to the non-costumed ordinary world. The appearance of a
costumed character in a story will generate a specific set of expectations—it signals, for example, that the figure is now operating in
his superhero identity and at any moment will be involved in violent conflict with villains. Costumes also increasingly indicated an
individual hero's character and powers. The colours, shapes, and
ornaments in the costumes, as well as other implements, show the
features essential to the hero's identity, powers, and capabilities—
Thor's hammer, Wonder Woman's lasso, bracelets and tiara,
Captain America's shield, Wolverine's steel claws, Silver Surfer's
board, and so on.[30]

Changes in costumes have also been used within the gambit of
character development as in *The Wasp* who brought a different
kind of rhetoric to her varied disguises. Her repeated costume
changes were purely for the sake of appearances, aimed to emphasise her femininity and served to blur the boundaries between the
superheroine and her alter ego, Janet Van Dyne, a socialite and
fashion designer. Due to the constant variation of her attires, The
Wasp lacked immediate visual identification and was established
more through contextual elements. Wonder Woman's characterisation also changed as her ornaments were discarded: her powers
and way of thinking had to be re-defined due to the loss of some
abilities dependent on her tiara and bracelets. Part of her origin-
stories had to be re-written because these ornaments were special
gifts from Aphrodite, the main goddess of the Amazon's Paradise
Land where Wonder Woman comes from. A member of *The
Avengers*, Henry Pym became variously known in costume as the
Ant-man, Giant Man and Yellow Jacket as he underwent costume
changes in an effort to refine his own powers and superpowered
identity. Ultimately, Pym's problem centred on justifying his place
in a super-team full of far more powerful and more charismatic
super-characters. Pym's failure to find any definitive version of his
costume placed him firmly in the ranks of secondary or back-up
characters. He was never featured in his own comic-book and was
only viable as part of a superhero group, The Avengers.

The discourse implicit in superhero costumes is far from being
an arbitrary set of conventions, so much so that the popular heroes
are recognisable even just in their silhouettes or in more abstract
renditions, and are identifiable through colour and/or shape com-

binations. To change the costume of solid superheroes like Captain America or the Batman would mean redefining a precise iconographic configuration. Captain America who burst forth on the comics scene in 1941 in a series of patriotic adventures against the Nazis, became Marvel's most popular superhero during the 1940s because he captured the essence of a World War II patriotic fighting hero.

> "Captain America was very much a reflection of his time. He was patriotic when the country was patriotic. He was willing to fight for his country when his country was getting ready to get into a horrible war. We saw him as a political statement fleshed out to be an active force (Joe Simon, co-creator of Captain America)."[31]

Inconceivable outside the circumstances which fashioned him, Captain America was suitably clad in the colours and shapes found in the US flag. The Batman's dark, bat-like costume is one utterance within the costume code that elegantly articulates the proper range of associations they were meant for: night, fear, the supernatural. It also suggests Batman's mode of operation: stealth, concealment, surprise.

Many texts about various superheroes have explored the contrast between the costume and the person behind it, the problems in dealing with split personalities, and the burden that the heroic identity places on them.[32] The man inside the costume is repeatedly called upon to earn his right to the powers which the costume confers on him. The costume somehow becomes a source of power, to wear the costume is to *become* the superhero or the super villain. In fact, the costume is very closely linked to the over-all make up of the hero so that a fraudulent use of the costume usually ends adversely for the usurper. In *Batman: Prey* (1992) a psychiatrist who is obsessed with Batman dons a bat-costume very similar to that of the hero in order to get to "know" Batman better.[33] He also deludes himself, no matter how slightly, that he gains some powers of the Batman when he wears the costume. In *The Reign of the Supermen*, despite all signs pointing to the contrary, Lois Lane doubts the claim of the Last Son of Krypton to be the real Superman (three other "Supermen" are making the same claim) because "Superman never hid his face behind glasses! And he didn't wear black like an executioner!"[34]

The role of costume as narrative device is a state of affairs which the writer and artist can work with or against, but which cannot be left wholly out of account. Costumes must be recognisable and make a formal statement about the hero's personality and character development. Even more recent texts, such as *The Dark Knight Returns* and *Watchmen* which make playful intertextual allusions to other superhero comics do not by and large break the rules of the costume system of signification.[35] Rather, they play a knowing set of variations with the audience's established pattern of responses, based on a shared knowledge of the rules of costume, and what might be said to constitute a violation of these rules.

> (in *Watchmen*) the deconstruction of costumed superhero values is pursued as part of the deconstruction of the costumes themselves. Dr. Manhattan, omnipotent super-being, spends his 25 year career shedding piece by piece the all-enveloping costume provided for him by the US government. At the end of the book, he chooses to go naked. And the semiotic function of superhero costume can be unpicked in more ways than one. Superhero costumes are either sexless, denying the humanity of the hero within, or garments of great erotic significance. Nite Owl reveals the fetishism implicit in the design of most superhero costumes, during his exceptionally well-realised first sexual encounter with Laurie Juszpeczyk, the Silk Spectre [36]

The sexual encounter between Nite Owl and Silk Spectre, which only took place when they both had their costumes on (*Watchmen* VII, 28), reveals a subtext present since the very first superhero story. Superman's prowess in defeating Butch Matson is only the earliest of many examples of the sudden virility and sex-appeal gained when a character changes into a "costume." As mentioned earlier, women always prefer the character with the costume on rather than the alter ego. It seems that donning the costume is more than just a sign of the inner change from ordinariness to a super man. A costume also endows some sexual power and attraction. In this regard, one of the most interesting parts in the use of comicbook costumes may be seen in its relation to female heroines.

The most well-known superheroine is Wonder Woman whose iconography of whips and chains became the jumping off point for the sub-genre of "Good Girl" art where superheroines were depicted scantily clad and in provocative and alluring poses. Although some girls also read them, comicbooks were generally written for boys. In comicbooks, characters are drawn according to a highly coloured and simplified scheme, and female characters were in general more loosely imagined than men and less invigorating to identify with. There were few major roles for women within the pages of such magazines. Most females are "girlfriends" of the hero and serve two functions: trying to learn the hero's identity and always getting into trouble so that the hero has someone to save. Or, they wear skimpy outfits, thus producing what is termed as "good girl art" in the comicbook community (see *Figure 27*)[37]

> Good Girl superheroines of the 1940s operated in the wider context of the Vargas pin-up girls, the Just Jane cartoons and sweethearts of the forces such as Betty Grable and Rita Hayworth. Good Girl art takes the signs of pornographic dis-course (whips, chains, spiked heels, beautiful but blank faces) and integrates them into the context of non-pornographic story structures. In this way, the sign of pornography (never explicitly delivered) comes to stand in for an entire porno-graphic sub-text, a series of blanks which readers remain free to fill in for themselves. And it is within the neo-pornograph-ic texts of Good Girl art that the distinctions between cos-tumed heroes and villains can first be seen to break down, a change that in turn influenced mainstream superhero comics.[38]

The "girlfriends" of the superheroes are always portrayed as well-behaved, alert and intelligent. Nevertheless, they are also marked by extreme vulnerability to harm and hopeless infatuation. This theme was already present in the first issue of *Superman*, and Lois's obsession with the superhero continues today. But although Lois has lived just as long as Superman, she has never achieved equal star status in comicbooks.[39] The pages of comicbooks abound with unflattering clichés about women's powerlessness and isolation which in turn provides a reason for the superhero to come to their aid. Lead female characters in more current comic-books are portrayed to be more aggressive and more dangerous—for example, Vampirella and Lady Death—but in general, the ide-ology remains the same.

This common theme crosses over to both heroines and female villains, blurring the boundaries between them. There are many

Figure 27. Good girl art continues today as lead female characters are still illustrated in scanty outfits and provocative poses. *Lady Death: The Reckoning*. Writer: Brian Pulido, art: Steven Hughes. © 1995 Chaos! Comics.

female antagonists who are shown to be victims of their circumstances as women, and later atone and change over to employing
their superpowers at the service of justice. Catwoman started as a
well-known Batman adversary, in the league of the Joker and
Penguin, even conniving with the Batman's enduring foes. She is
revealed to have been a streetwalker who turned to crime partly to
help those in the same plight and others oppressed by poverty.
Although she still works outside the law and is often wanted by the
police, she now leans more and more towards being a superheroine
than a villain. Spider-Woman, like many other superheroines,
started outside the law as Hydra, an agent for an unknown spy
organisation, under threat of death. As her powers increased, she
became a superheroine who was featured in her own comicbook.
Many of Wonder Woman's female enemies turn out to be under
hypnosis or under somebody else's power, usually that of a male
scientist. A featured villainess who appeared in a series of Wonder
Woman comicbooks, Baroness Von Gutenberg, was only acting for
the Nazis because they kidnapped her daughter. The Baroness had
to be helped out of this hostage situation and thereafter became
Wonder Woman's ally. Red Sonja enjoyed super-powers because
she hailed from the majestic kingdom of Hyrkania which she was
forced to flee after her parents were slain and she spurned the
advances of the pillagers' king and slew him.[40]

Especially in the early years of comicbooks, it seem that
women could not be portrayed as extremely evil as some male villains were. There are hardly any female antagonists who remain as
vile and unscrupulous throughout their comicbook career as some
well-known male villains. Although by the 1950s, many sultry and
hard-hearted female villains were created in reaction to the honourable and competent women of earlier comicbooks and strips,
there was neither conspicuous menace in their intentions nor gruesome violence in their adventures and fight scenes. During the
years from the 1950s to the early 1960s, there were many heroines
who adopted the aggressive, face-smashing attitudes of their male
predecessors—instead of a man bursting through the door and
executing an impressive jumpkick to his adversary, it was a
woman. But in spite of some sympathetic, independent heroines
and some socially satisfying plots, their acceptance of the individ-
ualistic and machismo codes of violence were highly problematic.
Most of these heroines were conceived by men, drawn mostly by

men, and targeted for male adolescents, resulting in "good girl art." The comicbook industry was so dominated by men for so long and so little attention was paid to the polysemy of comicbook texts that most of the differentiation of female characters remained in the visual level; the code, message and way of thinking were clearly male and simply transposed into the mouths and minds of heroines (*see Figure 28*).

The "reduction" of female protagonists may also be seen in the usual underestimation of their capabilities by both policemen and crooks. The intervention of female heroines seldom seems to evoke the deference from lawmen or terror from criminals (regardless how reluctantly) that herald the arrival of male superheroes in critical situations. Similarly, a female antagonist has yet to create a distinct and memorable response of fear or loathing among the superheroes the way the Joker has, or Lex Luthor, or even J. Jonah Jameson. By extension, women in general have been relegated to minor roles in superhero texts, and presented in ways that give priority to men and the idea of adventure; women have their assigned places in the men's lives and are made secondary to what passes between a man and other men. Women provide motivations for the men's great deeds, but superhero texts eschew the idea of intimate relations with women.

EXSCRIPTION OF WOMEN

Typical of many superhero stories, in so far as the narrative closure in each book goes, show the heroes reject or never really win the love of the woman they want. The Batman/Bruce Wayne finds himself attracted to perceptive women who understand the concept of "Batman" and find the vigilante interesting and honourable. These are, however, usually the same women who remain aloof to, or even slightly disdainful of, Bruce Wayne's playboy lifestyle. At the same time, Bruce Wayne harbours some hesitation in pursuing such attractions, to keep up with his projected cavalier treatment of women, and more importantly, for fear that his well-kept secret identity will be revealed. Often, love and intimacy demand a choice or conflict between their super-powers or possessing the woman they really love, as is the case also with Superman, the Hulk, the Mighty Thor, to name a few. To enjoy intimacy would entail disclosure of their super-identity which

Figure 28. *Naughty Bits #26*. Unlike the weak portrayal of female characters in superhero comicbooks, current comicbooks written by women present both female protagonists and antagonists in a more realistic manner. Art and script: Roberta Gregory © 1998 The creator. Her web page is www.robertagregory.com

would open the superheroes to some vulnerability, and somehow transfer power and control over to the women.

Regardless of how intelligent and positive these women are portrayed, they remain in the background and do not exist outside of their relation to the superhero. The most popular among them, Lois Lane, epitomises the secondary role of women in superhero texts who, in a typical piece of ideological double talk, are taught to admire and desire that which rejects them:

> (Lois Lane is) hopelessly in love with the Man of Steel, while at the same time haughtily spurning the sheepish advances of Superman's alter ego, Clark Kent. The Freudian implications of this weird menage-a-trois were never fully realised by the authors, but this story device projects a neurotic parable: while Superman was deemed too good for any woman, no woman would consider Clark good enough for her. Thus, in both of his impersonations, (as super-hero and super-schlemiel) , Superman-Clark Kent could find no sexual fulfilment (and neither could Lois).[41]

The subtle rejection of women is presented as a necessary element of the plot in most superhero texts. Women are perceived as threats to male independence and masculinity. Sentiment and emotions among superheroes is presented as a weakness that would detract from the masculine business of adventure and power. Women's concerns and their desire for intimacy are the repressed aspects of masculinity that must thus suffer reiterated narrative rejection. The hero's possession of such "weakness," however, and the constant need to conquer or deal with it, is naturalised as part of the masculine problem. The repetitive rejection of the woman is the narrative exscription of the feminine towards an ideology of masculinity that demands a rejection of the feminine in order to foster male bonding. By granting male relationships narrative centrality, and portraying adventure and the resolution of crime primarily as male business, the superheroes (and supervillains) sustain a defined relationship protected from the threat of female intimacy. Their bond is goal-oriented and not relationship-oriented; it depends more on action than on feeling. Relationships are there to serve a purpose, mostly to show the need to depend and care for others as externalised onto a goal and concrete actions, less as an internalised and basic need of the male. In issue after issue, the superheroes' concern for friends or family, their hometown, or planet Earth and its inhabitants propel them to confront almost anything, always at the risk of their lives. These external causes are deemed more worthy than true love and intimacy, enough to convince heroes to hold on to their identities and/or power which they risk losing if they succumb to women. However, the avoidance of intimacy places the superhero in a terrible isolation, and may present him as insensitive and less human—hence the need for higher action-oriented goals and legitimised, non-threatening male bonding which can be validly prioritised over the continuous agony of repeatedly unfulfilled relationships while not totally excluding the latter.

The exscription of women and the vague stance on intimacy in superhero texts is more understandable when viewed in relation to the superhero comicbooks' main audience—adolescent boys—with their burgeoning and ambiguous concept of dealing with the female and the feminine. It is not too difficult to understand why excessive signs of masculinity in an exaggerated and compensatory display would appeal to adolescent boys still denied the social means to exercise the power that society imparts as the prerequisite of their masculinity. Hero figures are popular among those whose bodies are not yet strong enough to grant them the power that they desire and which is conceived to be a sign of masculinity. For the same reason, advertisements for bodybuilding gadgets litter the comic pages, as well as ads for bicycles, toy cars and guns, and devices for home experiments. All of these are ways in which adolescent boys can vicariously access the strength of superheroes which is frequently presented as extended by cars, guns, machinery, and technical know-how. For some heroes, these extensions of physical strength are even essential to their identity, for example, Iron Man, Silver Surfer, and Night Wing; and for some, extensive knowledge of advanced technology is essential, for example, Batman, Dr. Manhattan, Ozymandias, and Adam Strange. In general, there is a close link between strength and control, privilege and virtue, power and humanity. All superheroes are in someway or another privileged by their super-status. Nonetheless, assiduous control of their emotions is a condition, as well as selective use of their might only for the benefit of mankind. Otherwise, there would be nothing to differentiate them from super-villains who may also be endowed with wealth, cunning and technology but are unscrupulously greedy and driven by their pursuit of power to madness.

In scrutinising the "identity" of a superhero, it is evident that masculinity is a principal concept in defining and distinguishing an enduring hero. Masculinity, however, is a social concept that goes beyond being muscular and excelling in brute strength. Being male and masculine manifests itself more in how effectively a superhero uses mind and/or muscle to resolve various power struggles, thereby displaying authority and self-sufficiency, and gaining public recognition. Superheroes share three traits: scruples, extra-ordinary strength, and financial self-sufficiency. They are also endowed with varied abilities that allow them to excel and assume authority as a masculine force: physical or mechanical power, planning and leadership, cunning and advanced or specialised knowledge, and so on—a variety of powers which provide readers with multiple entry points for their identification with a hero. The variety equally allows different ways of prioritising the concepts and abilities that constitute masculinity for adolescents, who, relative to the social concept of being "male," are as yet ambiguously situated in society.

IDENTITY AND MASCULINITY

Although all superheroes have developed throughout their comicbook careers, there are defining qualities tacitly agreed upon by both comics creators and consumers that constitute a superhero. Most of these have been established in the first issue of Superman, who remains the norm against which other superheroes are measured. The "true" identity of Superman may be scrutinised in a long series featuring his (formerly unthinkable) death, a narrative sustained in weekly issues which lasted almost a year.[42] It started with *The Death of Superman* which was first published in magazine form in February 1992, and extended to two other successive series—*Funeral for a Friend, The Reign of the Supermen*, ending with *Superman: Back for Good* issued in October 1993. As Superman became increasingly powerful throughout the years, his invincibility had taxed the encounters with the only element known earlier to be able to defeat him, Krypton: therefore, Doomsday had to be invented. Doomsday, portrayed as incredibly strong, possesses one of the most compelling, shrouded-in-mystery origins of any comics character yet and this kept the fan letters pouring into the DC editorial office. Introduced as pummelling his way out of a vault buried 100 feet underground in the middle of nowhere, Doomsday's genesis was intentionally kept rather vague and not necessarily evil. He was well-loved by fans, especially as he pushed the stories to become grittier and much more graphic, ultimately ending in the defeat and death of Superman.

Although surprised and saddened by the outcome, many of the fans indicated in their letters that Superman warranted such an end—by a worthy villain like Doomsday rather than through an inanimate substance, Krypton.[43] Some typical fan mail read:

> Dear Metropolis Mailbag:
>
> When America heard that Superman was going to die, fans crawled out of the woodwork to cry out in disbelief and outrage. They asked "why?" They asked "how?" The concept was beyond them.
>
> When I heard of Superman's impending death, however, I understood. Good people die: Martin Luther King Jr., John F. Kennedy, kings, queens, popes, my grandfathers, my grandmothers. All of them good people. All of them have now passed on.
>
> Why is Superman going to die? Because, although it is not a desirable ending, death is a natural process. It is inevitable for everyone. Some ask why Superman has to die now. I simply inquire when is it ever a good time to die?
>
> How will Superman die? It doesn't matter who kills him. It doesn't even matter that the Man of Steel could be killed. The true importance of that question is the manner in which Superman will die. I simply say that Superman will die the same way he lived: bravely, heroically, and with honour. That's just the way it is.
>
> Rest in peace, Kal-El.
>
>   Christopher Roestler Sparks,
>   NV

> . . . I am eagerly looking forward to the remainder of the "Doomsday" (and follow-up) storylines. I have absolute con-

fidence that the death of Superman, as well as the aftermath, will be sensitively, intelligently, and entertainingly handled. From what I've seen so far, I think that you're doing a great job. It's obvious you understand that it's important Superman not be killed by some silly gizmo like Lex Luthor or by some random natural catastrophe. You have pitted Superman, seemingly, against his opposite number . . . a battle against such a foe, even one that costs a hero his life, is an ennobling battle.

Jon E. Hecthman
Mt. Laurel, NJ[44]

Together with other fan mail in reaction to this series, these two share an underlying presumption: a superhero is entitled to a fair fight and not simply to be defeated by circumstances over which he has neither power nor control. With the annihilation of the sup- posedly invincible Man of Steel, death, success and triumph for superheroes were portrayed and perceived as neither easy nor always guaranteed. But in relishing Doomsday, no matter how reluctantly, the readers demanded at least that virtue should still pay off, that cause and effect be given their due, and the levelling of a legend not come from some divine intervention or magical force.

Even after Superman's burial, there was still general shock and disbelief about his death, and very shortly thereafter, the hero was sighted simultaneously in different parts of Metropolis. The people who testified seeing him varied in their descriptions and agreed only on one point: a "Superman" helped them out of a critical sit- uation and prevented a life-threatening crime or accident from happening. Indeed, there were about four or five costumed char- acters claiming to be the real Superman, and as each one is revealed to be an impostor, what constitutes the identity of a super- hero may be seen. The first one is "The Man of Steel" (introduced in *Superman* 22: late May 1993) who was easily discredited because he wore a very different costume from the real Superman. It was metallic and covered his entire body, including his face. "The Man of Steel" had to don this suit of armour because he was Black and had to hide his face. Accosted by Lois Lane, he also did not know anything about Superman's personal life, and his pre- tence could not last long, because there was not much with which to keep the readers guessing. Another one is "The Last Son of Krypton" (introduced in *Superman* # 687: June 1993) who is actually the nearest to the real one. His story was also the most plausible as, in some invisible elemental form, he was shown actually retrieving Superman's body from the casket. Among the others, he was also the only one with a clear knowledge of Clark Kent, and Clark's affection for Lois. However, he rejects this part of Superman and rejects Lois Lane as well. In doing so, suspicions are cast in readers' minds about his verity. Another impostor was called "The Metropolis Kid" (introduced in *Superman* 501: late June 1993) who is, however, too young, too immature, and juvenile to capture the readers' interest. He is portrayed as continuously craving publicity and too indecisive in his choices of girls/women. He is also easily discounted because he lacks the loyalty, temperance and courage that Superman exuded. The last Superman is "The Man of Tomorrow" (introduced in *Superman* 78: June 1993), half-machine, half-man whose DNA structure even matches those of the real Superman. However, being a cyborg, he is too mechanistic and too unformed in his humanity, relying too much on mechanical power which goes against the true Superman's nature. Moreover, he sets Doomsday free and destroys a whole city—questionable actions which betray his identity and intentions to everyone.

Reviewing the reasons or characterisations which invalidated the personalities described above from being Superman, we can say that superhero texts abide by the following precepts: a) a non-white person, even if male, is too marginal to be THE superhero for the mainstream comicbook consumers; b) a superhero usually maintains an object of love, which renders him more human and personal, and more attuned to his second identity (the Last Son of Krypton reveals his loss of humanity by his inability to love Lois Lane and by extension, by the rejection of his alter ego, Clark Kent); c) a superhero does not exhibit youth, immaturity, impulsiveness, and lack of mental and physical control; and d) a superhero is never too mechanical and never employs his powers for destruction and self-gain. All these precepts revert to the social concept of masculinity and control and power discussed above.

The concepts of identity and masculinity revealed in earlier superhero texts may be re-evaluated in more contemporary comicbooks which drastically changed the superhero, its adventures, its ideology and position in the narrative. There are many factors that contributed in revolutionizing this figure which came hand in hand with changes to the conventions and form of the medium itself. The next chapter will discuss the factors that changed the superhero comicbook seen against the backdrop of changes in the industry itself, especially in the production, distribution and reception of comicbooks.

NOTES

1 Although the muscular bodies of earlier superheroes were a novelty in comicbooks then, these were modestly drawn compared to the bulging muscles and overall exaggerated physique today.

2 Although Batman is known in both America and Europe, he is still more ingrained in the minds of North Americans. The producers of the Batman film did not realise this when they advertised one of the Batman films in Europe: the sneak preview showed only the Batman insignia. The promotion did not succeed as expected since the Batman emblem and colors were not as recognisable in Europe as in America.

3 Jonathan Culler, *The Pursuit of Signs: Semiotics, Literature, Deconstruction* (London: Routledge, Kegan and Paul, 1981): 123.

4 See Introduction by Maurice Hindle to Mary Shelley, *Frankenstein* (London: Penguin Books, 1985) which interestingly treats the novel as science fiction.

5 John Fiske, *Television Culture* (London and New York: Routledge, 1987): 111.

6 John Cawelti, "Notes Towards a Typology of Literary Form," *Journal of Popular Culture* 10.1 (1976): 34.

7 This is not very surprising since many people in the comicbook industry also felt their marginality in the printing and publishing industry. There were times when some even took pride in being "different" and sticking to working for comics which was not considered as a "real" job but simply a transition or entry point into more serious writing or illustrating jobs. A certain rebellious streak might also be due to the youth of many of the people who were working there (see interviews in Les Daniels, *Marvel: Five Fabulous Decades of the World's Greatest Comics* (London: Virgin, 1991); also, H. Kurtzman, *My Life as a Cartoonist* (New York: Simon and Schuster, 1988); and *The Comicbook Rebels* (1986).

8 In carrying out research on the comicbook audiences, Martin Barker shows some distinctions between committed, regular and casual comicbook readers and the correlating differences in their reactions to comicbooks. The more committed the readers, the "more likely they relate to

the comics as a *friend*." The implication of this is that they have a complicated social relationship to it. There is a kind of dialogue between comicbooks and readers in which the comic is seen as having a personality. See *Comics: Ideology, Power and the Critics* (Manchester and New York: 1989): 55-60.

9   Mike Benton, *The Comic Book in America* (Texas: Taylor Publishing, 1993): 14.

10 Ron Goulart, *Ron Goulart's Great History of Comic Books* (Chicago: Contemporary, 1986): 34.

11 Mike Benton, *op cit.*, 23.

12 Russell Nye, *The Unembarrassed Muse: The Popular Arts in America* (New York: The Dial Press, 1970): 56.

13 Les Daniels, ed. *Marvel Book of Superheroes* (New York: Marvel Comics, 1992): 112.

14 Judith Duke, *Children's Books and Magazines: A Market Study* (New York: Knowledge Industry Publications, 1979): 116.

15 Jeff Rovin, *The Encyclopedia of Superheroes* (New York: Facts on File, 1985): 38-9.

16 Bernard Rosenberg and David Manning, eds. *Mass Culture: The Popular Arts in America* (Illinois: The Free Press, 1957): 187. The Armed Forces, in fact, used the comic format in training material distributed to the troops. One comic artist who worked within this educational medium for a long time was Will Eisner, creator of the Spirit.

17 The first story is reproduced in Jules Feiffer, *The Great Comic Book Heroes* (New York: Dial Press, 1965).

18 Les Daniels, *A History of Comic Books in America* (New York: Crown Publishers, 1971): 56.

19 Later, other female heroes entered the arena like *Black Cat* (Harvey: June 1946), *Doll Man* (Quality Comics: December 1951), *Supergirl* (Action Comics: May 1959), *Spider-Woman* (Marvel: April 1978), *She-Hulk* (Marvel: February 1980). However, the superhero field was about ninety-percent male, which seemed to be about the same demographics as the readership of most superhero comics. (Benton, *op cit.*, 176).

20 The so-called Silver Age of superhero comics is agreed as having begun in 1956; there is no agreed terminal date but most would accept that it lasted until around 1967-70.

21 Patrick Parsons, "Batman and His Audience," in Roberta E. Pearson and William Uricchio (eds). *The Many Lives of Batman: Critical Approaches to a Superhero and His Media* (New York and London: Routledge: 1991): 66-89.

22 Benton, *op cit.*, 177.

23 Daniels, *op cit.*, 95.

24 Stan Lee, *The Amazing Spider-Man #4* (September 1963): n. p.

25 This labelling drew criticism from some artists, such as Frank Miller, who believed that classifications drew an artificial and unnecessary lines within comic readership.

26 In the Fall of 1998, a comics magazine and price guide, *Wizard*, undertook an on-line survey: Who is the greatest superhero of all time? Of the 500 e-mails they got, Batman was first with 25%; Superman and Spider-man tied at second place with 24% each.

27 In fact, the comics spawned the term "yellow journalism." *The Yellow Kid* (1896) by Richard Outcault is generally acknowledged to have been the first newspaper comic strip. It also marked a breakthrough in printing techniques because of its use of the colour yellow which made full-colour reproductions possible in newspapers for the first time. This strip became a major success, boosted the circulation figures of the *New York Journal*, and started a highly competitive campaign between two legendary magnates of the New York Press—Hearst and Pulitzer—for the ownership of the "Yellow Kid," as well as other comic strips which were regularly being featured in the comic supplement pages. The unscrupulous piracy of comic artists between New York's leading newspapers during this time, in particular for the Yellow Kid, is generally acknowledged as giving rise to the term "yellow journalism."

28 Alan Aldridge and George Perry, *The Penguin Book of Comics* (Baltimore: Penguin, 1971): 27. There were also some artists who played with the convention of portraying costumed superheroes, foremost of which is Jim Steranko who hails from the Underground comix movement.

29 Interview with Marvel editor, Stan Lee in Les Daniels, ed. *Marvel: Five Fabulous Decades of the World's Greatest Comics.* (London: Virgin, 1991): 112.

30 One of the more interesting of the 1940s comicbook characters was *The Spirit* by Will Eisner, created exclusively for a newspaper syndicate that wanted a superhero for its Sunday comic pages. *The Spirit* had a mask and dual identity but no superpowers. It is generally hailed in the comics scene (although not so popularly known among the general public) as one of the best written and illustrated comicbooks, known for its atmospheric stories, grotesque characters, gentle sense of humour, as well as satire and parody. *The Spirit* made its debut as a weekly Sunday comic book that was distributed for twelve years. It bridged the gap between comic strips and comic books by appearing in a coverless 16-page comic book that circulated with the Sunday funnies in newspapers.

31 Interview with Joe Simon in Les Daniels, *op cit.*, 72.

32 In Chapter Two of Richard Reynolds, *Superheroes: A Modern Mythology* (London: Batsford, 1992), Reynolds provides a prime

example of a superhero contemplating the burdens and demands of heroism on the hero's alter ego, in his close analysis of a page from *Iron Man 108*. In the last two panels, Tony Stark (Iron Man) thinks to himself: "Why should Joe and Jane America care who - or **what** - is inside this metal suit as long as **Iron Man** gets the job done?. . .As long as I risk my life to bring them **Peace of Mind**?. . .Peace that I, myself, have never **known!**"

33 Doug Moench, Paul Gulacy and Terry Austin. *Batman: Prey* (New York: DC Comics, 1992). Originally published in single magazine form as *Legends of the Dark Knight*, No. 11-15 (1990-91).

34 Roger Stern, Jackson Guice and Denis Rodier. *The Last Son of Krypton is Back (Born Again)*, *Superman 687* (New York: DC Comics, 1993).

35 Frank Miller. *The Dark Knight Returns* (New York: DC Comics, 1986). Originally published in magazine form as *The Dark Knight Returns, The Dark Knight Triumphant, Hunt the Dark Knight, The Dark Knight Falls*, all from DC Comics, 1986. Alan Moore and Dave Gibbons, *Watchmen* (New York: Warner Books, 1987). Originally published in twelve issues in magazine form by DC Comics, 1986-1987.

36 Reynolds, *op cit.*, 33. The first sexual encounter between Nite Owl and the Silk Spectre fails but this time it succeeds, enhanced by the costumes and the "other" identity that comes with their disguises (*Watchmen, op cit.*, 28.)

37 The trend of illustrating women in provocative outfits and postures has not changed, as may be seen in one of the comicbook heroines currently popular among adolescent boys, *Lady Death* (Chaos! Comics).

38 Juanita Coulson, "Of (Super)Human Bondage," in Don Thompson, ed. *The Comic Book Book* (New York: Arlington House, 1973): 230.

39 There is a weekly television show which began in late 1993 entitled "Lois and Clark" which now features Lois Lane and Clark Kent/Superman in equal billing.

40 Red Sonja's tale is reminiscent of the Brunhilde motif: she retains her powers only so long as she remains a virgin, and she can only yield to a man who can beat her in fair combat.

41 Maurice Horn, *Women in the Comics* (New York and London: Chelsea House Publishers, 1977): 91.

42 As comicbooks increasingly blurred the gap between the fantastic superheroes and the current realities of modern society, death among superheroes became an interesting theme beginning with the 1970s. Marvel initiated a trend by publishing—successfully—the death of Captain Marvel from cancer. Since then, the immortality of a superhero was not a certainty anymore.

43 Many fans were resigned to the pre-ordained death of Superman and were also certain that he would be revived. Even during the Doomsday

stampede, some were already writing in their suppositions and theories on how the editors would restore him. The coming of the series *Reign of the Supermen* shifted the readers' attention to guessing who the "real" Superman was among the four or five claiming to be him.

44 The first letter is from *Superman* No. 12, and the next is from No. 15. Both letters won a Baldy and a Platinum edition of *Superman # 75*, prizes for the best fan letter in an issue as decided by the Editors.

CHAPTER FIVE

Factors that Changed Superhero Comicbooks

I am, I am Superman
And I know what's happening
I am, I am Superman
And I can't do anything.

> R.E.M.
> "Superman"
> *Life's Rich Pageant*

    —not only do we no longer know if it is really (the familiar superheroes) we are watching, or a group of borderline psychotics, wearing the same costumes, playing a similar game, but driven by entirely different motivations that might push them over the edge at any moment.

> Jim Collins
> "Batman: The Movie,
> Narrative and the
> Hyperconscious"

THE FANS GROW UP

The superhero genre is tightly defined and defended by its committed readership—to the point of exasperation for many comics writers and artists who proclaimed it a worn-out formula as long ago as the early 1970s. Nevertheless, comicbook authors had to continue churning out the same tired narratives due to commercial demands of twelve- to seventeen-year old boys who have traditionally constituted the bulk of superhero fandom. Up until 1944, the number of girls reading comicbooks was almost the same as boys, especially between the ages of 6 to 11. From this year on, however, there has been a steady decline in comicbook readership among girls, particularly in the superhero comicbooks.[1] Although girls continued to patronise funny animals and romance comics, in total numbers, there were noticeably more boys steadily reading comicbooks, coinciding with the persistent popularity of superhero comicbooks relative to general comicbook sales.[2] That the readership of superhero comicbooks since the 1940s was primarily male and adolescent has had much to do with the shaping of superhero characters and narratives.[3]

The readership took a passionate interest in the content, details, and occasionally in the form of what they were reading. The readers steadily communicated these concerns with each other, as well as the comics writers, illustrators, and editors. Letters poured in daily to Marvel and DC from fans who continually monitored and made suggestions concerning comics, providing a very direct line of communication between the industry and its committed readers. If a superhero performed out of character, if a change in plot line was unsatisfactory, if there was a small mistake in art work, the fans did not hesitate to express their feelings. In the columns of the comics themselves, fans and artists and editors exchanged views, accepted compliments, justified story lines, and reacted to previous letters. This communication has remained active until the present as comicbook producers receive constant enthusiastic feedback from comicbook readers. Through the years, the letters columns increasingly reflected an articulate readership which also signalled the rise of the age level of committed readers. Dennis O'Neil, one of the most prominent figures in the comicbook industry and who had been an editor for both Marvel and DC, comments:

> "(We) try to make the letters representative, an accurate sampling of fan opinion. If 75 percent of our mail hated a story, we will reflect that in the letter column. Most of our readership is articulate. If you go out to schools, as I do, you will find that the kids who read comics are the bright kids, the ver-

bal kids. And then our marketing information shows that our average reader is twenty-four and male and very literate, so it is not surprising that we get a pretty high percentage of articulate, literary letters. That is one of the changes that has come about. I no longer feel very much need to write down to anybody when I am doing a comic book. I feel a very large persistent need to honour the tradition out of which I am working, but I don't have to worry about using big words anymore or even big concepts."[4]

Fan culture grew to parallel the commercial success of superhero comicbooks. What began as columns in the latter pages of the magazines, regular swapping or sharing of comicbooks, and some sporadic membership to clubs advertised within its pages, developed into a sense of fellowship later fostered through "fanzines" (fan magazines) and gatherings where stories, personalities, and ideas are discussed and debated. The fans cultivated a sense of community where shared and cumulative special knowledge about comicbooks is acknowledged and esteemed. At present, specialist comicbook stores, comic marts, and full-scale comics conventions are the outward signs of a certain cohesion among highly loyal and knowledgeable comic fans. In addition, there are price guides, comic forums and chat rooms, magazines and journals[5], and a highly organised market-place including internet auctions, for buying, selling, and collecting old comics.

In the 1960s, the fan movement was generally acknowledged as having shaped part of the resurgence of superhero comicbooks after the Comics Code of 1954 halted the production of horror and crime comics, and subsequently damaged the industry as a whole by stigmatising comicbooks. After this, the comics industry would never totally regain the same amount of consumer demand it enjoyed until 1954 because of television which lured readers away from comics. As sales dwindled, the comics industry started experiencing difficulties with its normal distribution system which made it pay more attention to fans. In the 1970s, news-stand distributors did not give comics much priority and thus hampered sales and expansion. Until then, the industry's sales strategies were not favourable to promotion and advertising which was becoming more necessary to attract new readers. The strong competition from television, the loss of convenient sales outlets, and the very limited approach to advertising reduced the industry to depend on hard-core fans and collectors. The comics industry was then forced to pay more attention to their fans, and initiated and encouraged more interaction with followers who were getting to be increasingly knowledgeable about their comicbooks and were somewhat older than the general comics readers.[6] By the late 1960s, a small network of clubs and correspondences already began to develop, such that by the mid-1970s, a strong and vibrant collector's market had begun. The Overstreet *Comic Book Price Guide* observes that while fans were not a dominant segment in absolute numbers, they represented a powerful one due to the intensity of their interest and their large per-person purchases. These readers were more serious about comics, were privileged with more disposable income, and some would buy several copies of one issue for investment purposes alone.[7]

Many of these committed readers ended up as artists and writers who later worked for DC and Marvel, as well as for the independent comics publishing houses in the 1980s. This tendency well attests to the impact this generation of superhero fans had on the industry. In fact, most of the well-known leading artists connected with the medium at present admit to having been fans themselves, to having grown up with their favourite superheroes and to having "been there," allowing them to develop a shrewd grasp of superhero fans' wishes and expectations. In addition, these artists regard themselves as, in some measure, still being very much a part of the field and the community: Alan Moore, Ed Hannigan, Stan Lee, Jack Kirby, David Mazzucchelli, Len Wein, John Byrne, Gene Colan, Al Williamson, John Severin, Steve Englehart, Mark Gruenwald, are some of these central figures.[8]

Two major assumptions are supported by the existence of a cultivated fan community. First, most people reading and writing commercial superhero comicbooks belong to that community; and second, they are not only broadly acquainted with, but have participated in the development of at least a sizeable proportion of what has been done and what is being done to the form and contents of superhero comicbooks throughout the fifty years of the genre's existence. In this sense, comic fans are not passive consumers of a cultural product. Indeed, they are in many ways active in its creation, more active with respect to audience interaction than with most mass-media situations such as television, the movies, music videos, or romantic fiction.[9] In addition, given the relatively close nature of the comics community, and the fact that many people now involved in the industry of producing comics came from the fandom culture, it is quite likely that the comics audience constitutes one of several direct and significant influences on the creative process and development of the genre. In his study of Batman readership, Patrick Parsons suggests an interesting point; that "contrary to the assumptions of some in both the popular and academic community, the impact of readers on the contents may be greater than the impact of the contents on the readers."[10] Concerned with the occasional neglect of the audience in the studies of cultural commodities, Patrick Parsons shows the many points of interaction between the producers and consumers of comicbooks, in particular the Batman. He sees the comics fan community as a specialised sub-culture—"a modern media-bound specialised community"—and shows how the various demographic, psychographic and ideological peculiarities of that community must be taken into consideration when critically analysing, for example, the current Batman which, for him, is "a product of a variety of cultural and industrial factors."[11]

The comicbook fans/creators themselves are the real movers behind the story of the development of comicbooks. This is as true today as it was in the earlier phases of the genre. The youngsters who grew up with comicbooks have grown up to be those most involved now in publishing houses and/or media centres. This demographic factor has greatly affected the conception of comicbook characters and narratives and, accordingly, has also changed the production and distribution of comicbooks.

THE DIRECT MARKET IS ESTABLISHED[12]

> In the early 1980s, a new wave of dealers was appearing. They'd grown up with institutionalised collecting, took new comics seriously as potential gold mines, and were starting to turn comic shops into streamlined, aggressive businesses.
>
> Gerard Jones and Will Jacobs
> *The Comic Book Heroes*, p. 245

Another influential factor in the transformation of the superhero genre is the solution the industry found to its distribution difficulties—direct sales and the specialist shop network. The first

specialized comic shops were opened in 1974 usually near univer-
sities or in the low-rent part of the city. By the late 1970s and early
1980s, these comic shops moved into the city centers and shopping
malls and, with their colorful window displays, attracted the attention of the wider public. By 1981, an interesting and most welcome
phenomenon occurred in the distribution, marketing, and selling
of comicbooks. A network of several hundred speciality comicbook stores, selling almost exclusively comics and comic-related
items, had spread out across the United States and Canada. Instead
of the usual news-stands where comics competed for space with
various other publications, the speciality shops got their supplies
directly from comicbook distributors, complete with promotional
flyers which announced upcoming issues, signalled the availability
of back issues, indicated which issues were increasingly becoming
scarce and pricier, and provided other tidbits of information for
the comic buffs. These flyers started simply as order guides for the
shops so that the publishers could estimate orders more accurate-
ly and stabilise press runs by reducing wastage from overproduc-
tion. Previously, DC and Marvel determined the number of copies
the news-stands would receive but the news-stands always had the
option of simply returning unsold issues, whether they were properly displayed or not. With the direct sales, returns could be avoid-
ed, new comicbooks could be promoted in advance, and more
importantly, reader preferences could be better monitored.

   This method of direct sales marked a switch from the traditional newsstand market to a comics culture based on collector
and fan preferences. It served to reinforce the fast emerging demographic trends in comicbook audience which involved a shift from
popular market to a smaller, more specialised audience that would
frequent and gather at the speciality shops and ask for comicbooks
using titles of issues or series, names of authors and illustrators,
dates of publication, specific cover art, etc. The efficiency afforded
by direct sales made regular acquisition of particular issues easier
compared to the previously uneven availability and operating inef-
ficiencies of news-stand distribution. This enhanced the fans'
recognition and appreciation of individual artists and cultivated an
auteur system in comicbooks. The comics community began to
know and follow the work of the principle artists and writers. The
new comicbook speciality market with its attendant collector consciousness increased the value of comicbooks and made them not

only commercially viable but attached a certain nostalgic, sub-culture-artefact prestige to them as well. In the light of the comicbooks' steadily shrinking audience, many credited the direct sales with rescuing the medium from sure collapse.[13]

In 1979, Marvel and DC sold already about ten percent of their comicbooks through specialized comic shops. It took some time though before either of these two publishers really recognized the possibilities afforded by the new situation, and to use the direct market to equalize losses from the decreasing interest of newsstands to sell comics. But soon after, the first coup of direct market selling occurred: with assiduous planning, an original issue of the historical comicbook *Action Comics #1* was sold for $10,000.00. Television caught on to the interesting trivia and the selling of comics suddenly took on the air of a financial investment. Old issues, the so-called "back issues," suddenly increased in sales or turnover due to speculation on the part of the buyers. For very practical purposes, Marvel began earnestly to pursue the new methods and possibilities of direct marketing. On March 1981, Marvel announced that, for the first time, a comicbook would be sold exclusively through the direct market. An atmosphere of a cultural event was deliberately produced. And, as if to test how unimportant the actual content of a comicbook with such a historical dimension can be, and moreover, how powerful the possibility of market manipulation can be, the choice was (of all things), *Disco Dazzler*. Marvel made the propaganda and rouse the buyer's enthusiasm, and no one seemed to be bothered by the hopelessly old-fashioned contents of *Disco Dazzler 1*.[14] With 400,000 copies sold, this comicbook outsold all other titles in March 1981. Some pubescent children, for whom investments were still a foreign concept, also started buying multiple copies of other popular comicbooks like *X-Men* with the hope that they could re-sell these for a lot more money some years down the road. The experiment went much, much better than expected and the direct market proved to be a potential goldmine.

As the number of speciality comicbook stores grew, a market developed that could support small press runs of comicbooks aimed at collectors. Smaller and creator-owned companies were motivated to produce for a more specialised market, recognising the trend that there were enough collectors and readers who could support early limited efforts by smaller independent comicbook companies. By 1983, the direct comicbook market had become so well established that a number of new independent publishers decided to try their hands at comicbooks. Many of these small publishers were former fans and collectors who financed their new companies out of their own pockets (reminiscent of the Underground Comix movement in the 1960s).

SMALL-PRESS, SELF-PUBLICATION, AND ALTERNATIVE WAYS

As Marvel and DC increasingly took the lead in the comics sales in the beginning of the 1980s, there were less known but very notable comics that were also being published. Dave Sim's *Cerebus* and Wendy and Richard Pini's *Elfquest*, both self-published, each increased their monthly sales from a modest 500 copies in 1978 to around 20,000 in the early 1980s. Even as the direct market was largely determined by superhero comics, some alternative comics also found their niches among the comics readers who, by this time, were getting increasingly well versed with the medium.

In 1980, Art Spiegelman produced the first issue of a pioneering anthology, *Raw*, which housed various and differing styles of cutting-edge comics artists in North America and Europe under one roof. *Raw* was way before its time. At this time, there were not many comics in North America that were consciously combining artistic ambitions within the medium of comics, and there were hardly comics aimed at readers over 25. The most prolific contributors to *Raw* were Drew Friedman (#1, 2 and 6), Jacques Tardis (#1, 5), Ben Katchors (#2, 3 and 6), Gary Panters (#3-6, 8) and Charles Burns (#3-8). The anthology had a roster of exceptional talents that brought an intelligence and breadth of vision to comicbooks rarely previously seen in the field, especially in North America.

In July 1982, Fantagraphics published the first issue of *Love and Rockets* by the Hernandez brothers, until then self-produced and distributed. The simple yet impressive force of Xaime Hernandez's well-balanced black-and-white illustrations first attracted the attention of readers who had heretofore only read superhero comicbooks. Each of Hernandez's sketches was a small piece of art. The characters were interesting and the stories were captivating and unfolded with an irresistible kind of humour that

Figure 29. A page from *Love and Rockets* #50. Art and script: Xaime Hernandez © 1996 The creator.

made it difficult to stop reading. *Love and Rockets* combined sentimentality and punk mentality, two dispositions not usually seen together, and "friction" between the two produced an unmistakable flavour in the series unlike any other previous comicbook. Xaime dealt with the life of Latin American immigrants in a suburb of Los Angeles; his older brother, Gilbert, demonstrated his exceptional narrative abilities reminiscent of Gabriel Garcia

Marquez as he wove tales about a Latin American town called
Palomar. The fantastic creatures and adventures displayed in the
beginning of the series decreased steadily as the stories focused
more on relationships and the daily grind of life, stressing the
eccentric "human heroes" in *Love and Rockets*. Xaime simplified
and made his illustrations a bit more abstract, devoting his time
more and more to the artful composition of the pages and stories.
Love and Rockets became a windfall for Fantagraphics and for
readers who wanted to see the new directions in North American
comics or who simply wanted to enjoy and admire the artistic abilities of "Los Bros" (the brothers Hernandez).

Besides Fantagraphics, Pacific Comics and Eclipse Comics also
experienced increase in sales although these two publishers did not
directly confront the sales impulse of the superhero mainstream.
Following in the success of Marvel and DC, First Comics took
advantage of the direct market to distribute its first comicbook in
March 1983. By October, First Comics succeeded with Howard
Chaykin's *American Flagg*, which until then was the biggest hit of
an alternative comics publisher, even though neither children nor
newsstand vendors liked this particular series. Set against the
gloomy, disconsolate atmosphere of Chicago at the brink of disaster in the the 21st century, Chaykin used a hero who once was a
pornography star. Reuben Flagg is only an actor who becomes a
hero as the borders of fiction and reality fuse together. Chaykin
picked up on an apocalyptic atmosphere and added a fetishistic
dimension to it, showing the domination and intermixing of sex
and politics and commerce in a way not seen before in North
American comicbooks.

In the following months, the number of comics publishers and
series increased steadily. Kitchen Sink Press, already well-known as
an underground comicbook publisher, entered the collector's market by offering Will Eisner's *The Spirit* and other "classics" in
comicbook form for a new generation of readers.[15] Eagle Comics
was another publisher that distributed its books exclusively to
comicbook stores and its first title was *Judge Dredd* which is a
popular British strip re-packaged for American audiences. Among
the newly published comics from the alternative publishers, two
notable ones were Matt Wagner's *Mage* (published by Comico)
and Don Simpson's *Megaton Man* (published by Kitchen Sink).

By the beginning of 1985, however, it became more and more apparent that the upstart publishers who tried to break through the comics market by emulating the Marvel action style were heading up a blind alley. In the superhero scene, it was impossible to prevail over Marvel and DC by using or copying their own weapons. Whoever wanted action and superhero comics, and like before, that was the majority of people flocking to comics shops, would eventually always choose to buy something tried and true: comics from the two predominant publishers, DC and Marvel. Due to the lack of demand, Eclipse had to withdraw most of the series it had counted on to succeed. Fantagraphics, the publisher most intent on pursuing alternative ways to the action/superhero comicbooks, had to concede that the direct market intensified the collecting impulses of comic buyers but did not (yet) awake any lasting interest in different, better quality comics.

DC and Marvel also took advantage of the new developments and started publishing for the specialised market as well, this time featuring writers and artists *by name*, previously uncommon in the comicbook industry. Since the core of comicbook fandom were proponents of the superhero genre, and so were most of the popular artists at that time, there was another resurgence in the popularity of superhero adventure stories.[16] The comics industry took advantage of an already existing, albeit dormant, interest in superheroes, while simultaneously catering to a new audience that did not have the same background knowledge of the genre: both Marvel and DC utilised the proven popularity of superheroes by revamping their major characters. This time, however, the heroes offered were markedly not mainstream in sensibility or appearance, but started showing distinctive deviations that are to characterise the more contemporary superheroes. The recent spate of graphic novels re-defined the origins and characters of heroes and villains while stirring up controversies by challenging some traditional notions of a superhero. By 1984, both Marvel and DC had started "re-inventing" or "re-vitalising" their characters to cater to a new breed of older and more knowledgeable readers. In addition, there were also totally new readers now lured to the graphically and narratively mature and more sophisticated comicbooks. Marvel issued an *Official Handbook for the Marvel Universe* (December 1985) detailing characters for collectors in the new series. Marvel also celebrated its 25th anniversary by publishing the New Universe titles, supposed to be the beginning of the second Marvel cosmotology and mythology. DC published the *Crisis on Infinite Earth* series which allowed them to re-organise and simplify the DC world with its myriad of characters and universes for new readers, tie up loose ends in their superhero mythology and history, and revitalise them according to the new, more sophisticated lines. The most successful was DC's launching of a major revision of its two main characters: Superman was updated in the mini-series *The Man of Steel* (June 1986) and Frank Miller re-made Batman into an ageing vigilante in his mini-series *The Dark Knight Returns* (March 1986). The best new series also came from DC. *Watchmen* (September 1986), by Alan Moore and Dave Gibbons, published as a series with twelve issues of 32 pages each, was a richly textured rendition of a group of superheroes who were trying to make sense of functioning as heroes in a modern world, while coping with "real world" problems like alcoholism, impotence, poverty, and so on.

By 1989, Marvel and DC still accounted for nearly seventy-five percent of all sales made in comicbook speciality stores, but there were also over seventy-five small and mid-size comicbook publishers turning out hundreds of titles.[17] As the 1980s came to an end, sales figures seemed to show that comicbooks had re-established themselves as a vital and growing medium that continued to appeal to an ever-widening and expanding audience. The new form of marketing and distribution, which gave more recognition and publicity to individual artists, inspired more creators to form their own publishing companies, make creator-owned lines of titles to be published and finally to abandon the "sweatshop atmosphere" of the two dominant comics publishers. Although limited in circulation, the independent comic books revitalised and strengthened the entire comicbook industry. Most of the innovation in style and range of narratives, as well experimentation in the potential of the medium were published by alternative or independent publishers. Many artists who were disillusioned and/or cramped by bigger publishing houses worked for these independent publishers. This resulted in the eruption of more new styles and influences than at any time in the past thirty-five years. The speciality stores and independent publishers also enabled more promotion, franchises, and regular availability of imported comics from Europe and Japan, opening a steady market for these in North America. In general, more comicbooks, in the form of graphic novels, compiled series and albums, were being sold than ever before. Since 1986, comicbooks also have begun to receive popular and critical attention and extraordinarily wide coverage in the mainstream press, in the style magazines, in the music papers, even in some business magazines. The renaissance in comicbooks and their new high media profile have altered the medium: all in all, the new releases are distinguished from their pre-"direct sales" predecessors by access to bigger budget (and consequently high-priced) status in all aspects of production, format, artwork, and above all, aggressive multi-media advertising.

HEROIC TRANSFORMATIONS

The world of North American comics consisted of almost nothing but conventional and uninspired superheroes in 1979 as Frank Miller took over the illustrations for the *Daredevil* series. An exception could be the Marvel's *X-Men*, but in general, comics were published in poor quality paper and was destined to be thrown away. Although works with potential to awaken adult interest such as Dave Sim's *Cerebus*[18], appeared on the scene in 1977, and a year later Will Eisner's *A Contract with God and Other Tenement Stories*[19], such works were marginal. These two excellent comicbooks, for example, did not start an impulse that excited anyone outside the narrow, die-hard fan scene of the Superhero comics to buy any books.

Between 1975 and 1978, DC initiated over 50 new series but at the end of 1978, more than half were again withdrawn. At this time, DC's market was smaller than 50% of Marvel's share. Not even the success of the film *Superman* at the end of 1978–until that time, Warner's biggest commercial success altogether—drove anyone to take advantage of the interest stimulated in this series. Marvel was undaunted. With its very conventional use of super-heros, Marvel aimed to dominate the comics market. Since the beginning of 1978, Jim Shooter took over the job of Marvel Chief Editor, replacing Archie Goodwin. Barely a year passed, however, and Shooter already withdrew as much as 20 series–intercepting the downward trend of Marvel. In a very authoritative manner, Shooter demanded an unconditional subordination from the writers and illustrators (following the style created by Jack Kirby in the 1960s) and the strict adherence to a monthly publication rhythm.

Despite this strictness, very many young comics artists applied to
work for Marvel, similar to the trend in the 1960s. With a certain
feel for talent, Shooter quickly lowered the average age of his
employees.

Despite the youthful batch of new cartoonists in Marvel, it was
the old and experienced Chris Claremont who recognized the signs
of the times and peppered his X-Men with features from the ubiquitous film hit, *Star Wars*. Although cosmic powers and galactic
wars already played a substantial role long before *Star Wars* in Jack
Kirby's *Fantastic Four* and *New Gods*, the young Star Wars-gener-
ation perceived the comicbooks of the team Claremont/Byrne as
current and contemporary and propelled the *X-Men* series to the
top of the bestseller's list by the end of 1970. Claremont and Byrne
knew who they were writing for—they did not only meet the expectations of young superhero-fans, but by emphasizing the personal
relationships between the varied members of the *X-Men* team,
Claremont and Byrne also managed to entice new readers outside
of the superhero-fan ghettos. By 1980, *X-Men* sales rose to over
300,000 copies per month at the same time that not one DC title
could reach the 100,000 copies per month mark.

In 1979-80, the *X-Men* was a distant bestseller although
another Marvel comicbook would have a bigger influence in the
contents of future comicbooks: *Daredevil*. On March of 1979,
with issue #158, Frank Miller took over the illustration of this
series, which until then was on the brink of being withdrawn due
to lack of success. In January 1981, Miller started to write the
scripts as well. Miller's stories and dialogue were stark and down-
right, heavily influenced by Film Noir. His illustration became
increasingly forthright and graphic, taking on an almost absract
quality that Miller would realize to its perfection years later in *Sin
City*. In Frank Miller's hands, scenes of brutality that until now
were portrayed in superhero comics as a harmless sports match,
would be explicitly depicted in ways comics readers had not previously seen. To Miller's advantage, comicbook sales had begun at
this time to be more and more independent of newsstand vendors
who would not dare alarm their customers by such portrayals of
violence. *Daredevil*, previously a problem for Marvel, became a
successful series under Miller. Miller's rendition of *Daredevil* (story
and illustration) is also crucial to the further development of North
American comicbooks. He used the fundamental battle between

Good and Evil based on the rules of superhero comics while plac-ing his characters and narratives in increasingly realistic situations. By calling attention to the seeming contradictions between super-beings and his realistic illustrations and situations, Miller showed that there were still many facets and possibilities not yet fully utilised within the superhero genre.

While Miller was opening up a road to the future of superhero comicbooks, Marvel realised that, in the context of growing manipulation in the direct market sales, Chris Claremont and Frank Miller were "winners." Artists used to be unknown and were previously perceived to be interchangeable, but the direct market made it possible for authors and illustrators to be the point of interest. Fans had stopped buying blindly, for example, simply asking for the newest *Batman* comics at the newsstands. Instead, fans started choosing by 'names' among the hundreds of Batman comics in a specialised comic shop. If a fan really liked an issue, he or she could and would ask next time for the numbers (naming the issues numbers from specific authors or illustrators). In 1982, most of the comics buyers asked for Frank Miller and/or Chris Claremont. What would make more sense then, than to let the two work together in one comics? A four-issue series of *Wolverine*[20] written by Claremont and illustrated by Frank Miller came out at the end of 1982. Wolverine is one of the most hardened or brutish members of the *X-Men*, the first one most apt to the gloomy atmosphere and dismal tone with which Frank Miller made his mark in *Daredevil*. Although, qualitatively, the work by Miller/Claremont fell short of Miller's *Daredevil*, the strategy to appeal to both *X-Men* and *Daredevil* fans succeeded tremendous-ly: *Wolverine* was a huge hit. In addition to the Claremont-Miller combination, this series also had the lure of the then new format of the Mini-Series[21] which would later be copied and proliferate in the following years.

DC reacted to Marvel's success with the start of a counter con-cept that would radically affect the entire comics market in the fol-lowing years. DC began to focus resolutely on an adult or older public that was outside the scope of Marvel's hardcore superhero locus. At the end of 1982, DC successfully produced *Camelot 3000* which transported the medieval legends surrounding King Arthur into the future by a very original rendition of fantasy by Mike Barr, illustrated with beautiful details by Brian Bolland.[22]

Camelot 3000 was published in twelve issues, and is known as the inception of what is now known as the Maxi-series, a big or long series all published more or less within a year.

DC's real triumph for the long term, however, was to have been able to snatch Frank Miller from Marvel and to let him produce his own mini-series with creative autonomy. In February 1983, Miller left *Daredevil* where he could only hint at some of his ideas due to Jim Shooter's regulations and style of producing comicbook. Five months later, DC published the first of a six-part Samurai adventure, *Ronin*[23], in high-grade quality paper on which North American comics had never been printed before. Miller wrote and illustrated a story about a solitary warrior struggling in a decaying world. The chance to experiment with graphic styles, together with the ample time for production deadlines and the quality of the paper opened up possibilities that Miller had never before imagined in creating comicbooks:

> It changed the rules. It showed me that comics have endless possibilities. I had to adapt my writing and drawing styles for the improved format. The primary difference was that, on better paper, the coloring became a vital part of the story.[24]

The different style and overall impact of *Ronin*—which clearly showed influences from Japanese *mangas* and the graphic style of Moebius—was acclaimed by critics. However, the sales figure fell short of expectations, most probably due to the book's price of $2.50 which was then unusually high for a comicbook. Nevertheless, with *Camelot 3000* and *Ronin*, DC succeeded in holding its own against its cardinal competition, Marvel, and in clearly establishing a new position within the comics scene. With *Ronin*, DC started printing "The New DC" in the covers of its comicbooks to clearly display the trademark that identified this new line. With *Ronin* and the remake of the *Swamp Thing*, DC succeeded without a doubt to produce comics with good and complex narratives, and the potential to appeal to a wider audience. The quality of the narratives not only improved, but the paper used and the overall appearance gave the impression of an ambitious artwork. All the same, within DC's increasing spectrum of titles, there was not one that could dissolve the confines of the "comics ghetto" which had developed its biases over decades and was not prepared to relinquish its predilections overnight. There was hardly anyone buying in comic shops that had not previously liked comics, or at least was already exposed to it. The media interest in comics dwindled in the mid-1980s. Marvel continued to cater to the expectations of its proven young readers (known in the industry as the "Marvel-zombies"), and the gap between Marvel and DC remained wide like before. Marvel's market share was approx. 50% while DC's share was around 30%.

But the credit for the renaissance of superheroes rightly belong to the initiative and boldness of the creators themselves rather than to the corporate decisions undertaken by the big publishing houses. It is impossible to think of the re-making of superheroes without thinking of two names: Frank Miller who did *The Dark Knight Returns* (1986), and Alan Moore who wrote *Watchmen* (1986). While both of these seminal works may be seen against the general upheaval and excitement in the field of comics around that time (*Maus* by Art Spiegelman came out in book format the same year, and *Love and Rockets* by the Hernandez Brothers in 1982), the superhero stories captured the imagination of comics audience because the new comics dealt simultaneously with something very familiar and very strange: heroes who have ceased to be superhuman, who sometimes have problems with drugs, alcohol and sex, and above all, who grapple with notions of authority, power, and evil that are not always clear and against which they do not always win. *The Dark Knight* in particular was so successful that it is recognised not only as responsible for making Batman the most popular comic book hero but as playing no small role in the incredible burgeoning of the comics industry in the 1980s.[25] After this, more and more superhero comicbooks came out which addressed political, social, and moral issues, and participated in a boom to re-define comicbook heroes and narratives. In gestures reminiscent of Frank Miller's preoccupation with transforming the heroes of comicbooks, many well-known artists participated in the rejuvenation of the genre. Citing intentions and views similar to Miller's, they acknowledged the enjoyment in both reading and creating new heroes while attesting to the increased possibilities available in transforming comicbook heroes in the context of a more mature, more serious narrative form. Interviews with those involved with the comics industry usually reveal an earnest interest and expansive awareness in what is going on with the industry and the genre, as well as in the narratives and artworks of other comics artists[26]. In these interviews, as well as in the coverage by mainstream press, there was a tone of seriousness that had been long ignored when dealing with comicbooks. Similarly, super-heroes that used to be considered ridiculous for prancing around in colourful tights were discussed sensibly, according to the new perception of heroes that now frames comicbooks. Frank Miller, for example, comments about the *Dark Knight*:

> "I was working on a revivification of a folk hero, but I was reaping all the benefits of fifty years of the hero's history. It's true also with Alan (Moore) because you couldn't really approach *Watchmen* without growing up with the Justice League of America. Now I'm trying to build walls to push against. With Batman that's easy because you know the rules of the game."

> "Even with the nuclear backdrop and the contempt for super-heroes expressed by the world at large in *Dark Knight*, I don't think *Dark Knight* is pessimistic . . . it has a hopeful ending. The book starts with Bruce Wayne contemplating suicide; at the end he's found a reason to live. He's adjusted to the times. . . . The key transition is his recognition he's no longer part of the authority. That's really the transition at the end of *Dark Knight*, this knowledge that he's no longer on the side of the powers that be anymore, because the powers that be are wrong."[27]

Although there have been many attempts to make superheroes more multi-dimensional, especially psychologically, since the 1960s, there was a marked difference in the changes in the 1980s: there seemed to be an underlying cynicism in the revamping of the genre rather than simply an imaginative elaboration of an old genre. A connection was apparent between the increased cynicism of the major superheroes and an apocalyptic impulse in mass culture and a certain impotence in dealing with it, both of which, not surprising-ly, coincides with the prevalent sentiment of the early 1990's Generation X.[28] To remain a commercially viable product, comics must react to the shifting demographics of its readers, as well as to the prevailing notions within a broader cultural setting. As seen through comicbook heroes, these notions centre around more ambiguous definitions and conceptions of authority, more com-promises in formulating ideologies, and the underlying feeling of societal decline, all of which may be witnessed in other such media as television, popular songs, and films. Both *The Dark Knight* and *Watchmen*, for example, comment directly on the post-Vietnam syndrome in the US with its ensuing loss of faith in the moral integrity of the State and its agents. For example, on page 4, Book Three of *The Dark Knight*, one sees a classic example of "passing the buck." True or not, people believe that government officials try to evade the responsibility for a problem, while hoping that some-one else can take the blame. On page 6, Book Two, people repre-senting various sectors of society give their diverse opinions about a problem plaguing America. The use of a television box to frame these voices reflects the collision of discourses in society increas-ingly made possible by mass media, as well as the ensuing confu-sion and uncertainty regarding truth claims. In addition to the loss of faith in authority and institutions, there was a pervading atmos-phere of anger, frustration and bitterness over the general signs of increasing corruption and violence in American society. This may be seen in Bruce Wayne's decision to team up with the confused members of the Mutant Gang (*Dark Knight*) and in Ozymandias' orchestrated destruction of New York city, in the belief that the world can be saved only after total annihilation (*Watchmen*).

The world of superheroes used to comfortably position its readers as white, middle-class American males—this was the ideo-logical position necessary to make sense of the superhero texts unproblematically. The best superheroes were male, white, literate (if not as superheroes then at least their alter egos); they never suf-fered from poverty, were ensconced at least in middle class values, if not of a higher social class, and (directly or indirectly) commu-nicated that violence can be justified if it is used "properly" in upholding the law. The villains were always distinguishable from the "good guys." In the end, the superhero always won and restored order, even if the most part of the comicbook was devot-ed to the eruption of crime and evil and to elaborate displays of fighting and violence. More recently, however, creators of comics have mixed up these codes and have even intentionally directed us not to submit to these old, comfortable viewpoints. In Neil Gaiman's *Black Orchid*, for example, the lead character is a female hero who is caught and exposed by crimelords within the first four pages. Although superheroes are always discovered and threatened at crucial moments, something unanticipated happens in this story.

The man who catches Black Orchid says:

> "Hey, you know something? I've read comics. . .I'm not
> going to lock you up in the basement before interrogating
> you. . .then leave you alone to escape. That stuff is so dumb.
> But you know what I am going to do? I'm going to kill you.
> Now.[29]

Then, he not only ruthlessly shoots Black Orchid in the head
but sets her on fire as well. It is a startling moment because as the
killer tells Black Orchid that he understands how the rules of the
superhero genre work, he is not merely addressing an endangered
heroine but also the readers of that genre in a way never done so
directly before. The writer clearly signals that all the familiar rules
of comic book storytelling—all those rules that insure hard-earned
triumphs for the heroes and the inevitability of justice—will not
apply in this narrative. As Mikal Gilmore observes in his
Introduction to this graphic novel:

> (In *Black Orchid*) We are not only at the beginning of a new
> story, we are at the beginning of a new way of telling such a
> story. It is not just the Black Orchid who is killed in these
> opening pages: It is also the ethos of the super-hero genre that
> is being set up for its long overdue death.[30]

Black Orchid does not follow the expected phases of a hero
adventure: it does not revolve around the heroine seeking out the
enemy; she does not succeed in exposing an organisation dedi-
cated to crime and corruption, which she was bent on doing. She
rescues the man who killed her father and destroyed all the other
heroines, but most importantly, up to the end, she refuses to kill
people who were threatening her and her "daughter" at gun-
point.

Frank Miller's *Sin City* (1991), meanwhile, inverts the usual
hierarchy of justice. The readers' sympathy is directed towards
societal outcasts like prostitutes, strip dancers and hired killers
who live in the margins of middle-class residential suburbia, and
fight against atrocities which are organised by the police, the well-
known citizens of the main city, even the archbishop who comes
from the most established family in the society depicted. Miller's
heroes are also motivated more by wrath and personal revenge
rather than by a higher sense of justice or the good of the many.
Furthermore, the stark black and white landscape of *Sin City* ren-

dered by Miller's sharp, rugged lines flaunts equally tough heroes who are far from being asexual like their predecessors in comicbooks geared for younger readers. In fact, in *Sin City* both male and female bodies are shown bare and erotic, although often in obscure and shadowy outlines due to Miller's clever use of the chiaroscura effect. In a distortion of justice, one hero, Marv, dies despite his revelation of the real mastermind behind a series of hideous murders. *Sin City* also participates in the re-creation of a new mythology for the genre where accepted customs of the superhero parables are suspended, and the moods and tones are much closer to the darker dreams and darker realities of modern-day life.[31]

By the late 1980s and early 1990s, most heroes were undergoing personality changes and character transformations. They ceased being superhuman and were shown to have problems in dealing with a darker, more corrupt modern world. Also noticeable is the hint of amorality which started to surround some superheroes as they worked more and more on the borderlines of the law. Retribution and revenge, for example, even became acceptable motives for becoming a superhero, like the Marvel Comics' *The Punisher* (July 1987) who seemed to be a walking arsenal waiting for bad news to happen. Marvel's best-selling books around this time were *Spiderman* and *X-Men* titles, both with the "new" concept of a superhero who is guaranteed neither definite triumph nor immortality. But if there is one figure most closely associated with the search for and creation of new superheroes, it would be the Batman, who has now outranked Superman as the most popular superhero.[32]

BATMAN AS A MOBILE SIGNIFIER

The Batman started as a part of the Superman tradition and a contrast to it, being much closer to the then pulp vogue for masked crime fighters such as the Shadow who, having no superpowers or guaranteed immortality, was more of a sleuth than superhuman. Other heroes would follow this path, thus establishing a sub-category within the superhero genre.[33] Unlike most comicbook heroes who were created as a result of freak accidents or who were born with supernatural powers, the Batman decided to transform himself mentally and physically. He did not find himself thrown into advantageous or extra-ordinary circumstances, but consciously and systematically laboured to achieve his position as an individual empowered to combat crime and senseless deaths. He does this in order to alleviate his anger and frustration at the brutal murder of his parents. In the more recent comicbooks, Bruce Wayne's transformation into a bat is given more mystical, more psychotic, more metaphorical overtones, making the Batman's psychology and motives increasingly complex without contradicting previous details in the Batman's mythology. It is remarkable how various writers have worked with well-known material and managed to re-define the Batman character without threatening the coherence of the fans' cherished experience and knowledge of his nature. Indeed, the multiple refractions of the Batman character seemed to have made him fuller instead of fragmenting him into obscurity.

The writer who started the Batman into his renewed direction, both textually and commercially, is Frank Miller who wrote *The Dark Knight Returns* and *Batman: Year One*. Despite the moderate commercial success of his *Ronin*-series (summer of 1983), DC still believed in Miller's potential as author and illustrator to attract a wide audience. Miller had once stated that the Batman-character has had a big influence on him, and DC made him an offer he could not refuse: Miller was allowed to extensively re-define the Batman character on his own terms and ideas[34]. Miller did not disappoint DC. With his audacious re-interpretation of Batman, he exceeded all expectations and made the Dark Knight into a dominant figure in American comics. Since *The Dark Knight Returns* is a central comicbook in re-shaping superheroes, it is discussed in more detail in the next chapter.

NOTES

1 Much of what is now known about the audience during the early period of comics developed out of scholarly and public debate about the impact of this burgeoning media on children; See, for example, Alexis Tan and Kermit Scuggs, "Does Exposure to Comic Book Violence Lead to Aggression in Children?" *Journalism Quarterly* 57.4 (1980):579–583, Judith Duke, *Children's Books and Magazines: A Market Study* (New York: Knowledge Industry Publication, 1979); Willam Marston, "Why 100,000,000 Americans Read Comics," *The American Scholar* 13 (1944): 35–44; Paul Lyess, "The Place of the

Mass Media in the Lives of Boys and Girls," *Journalism Quarterly 29.1* (1952):43–54.

2 Since the 1970s, superhero comicbooks have ranked third among the most popular comics according to sales figures; second is the category of Sci-fi/Horror, and the first is the somewhat broad category called Adult Humour which is made up of such works as "Peanuts" and "Calvin and Hobbes." See Jack Lyle and Heidi Hoffman, "Children's Use of Television and Other Media," in *Television and Social Behaviour*, Vol. 4 (Washington, DC: National Institute of Mental Health, 1979): 121–256).

3 Even the attempt to attract more female readership by creating super-heroines resulted in characters more memorable as examples of Good Girl Art in comics rather than characters whose adventures girls would enjoy following (see the section on "Masculinity and Identity" in the preceding chapter).

4 Pearson and Uricchio, "Notes from the Batcave: An Interview with Dennis O'Neil," in idem, *The Many Lives of Batman* (London and New York: Routledge, 1993): 19–20.

5 Roger Sabin provides an extensive list of current comic fanzines and journals. See Roger Sabin, *Adult Comics: An Introduction* (London: Routledge, 1993): 305–306.

6 The science fiction fandom started earlier and is more established than the superhero followers. The science fiction community also has more cross-overs to other science fiction venues like novels, short stories, television shows and movies. However, superhero comicbooks in general are more sought after and are more collectible in terms of price and nostalgia value in the comics collector's market.

7 Robert Overstreet, *The Official Overstreet Comic Book Price Guide* (Tennessee: Overstreet Publications/House of Collectibles, annually).

8 See various interviews in David Anthony Kraft, ed. *Comics Interview* (New York: Fictioneer Books, published monthly since 1984); *Comics Scene* (New York: O'Quinn Studios, published quarterly since 1985); and *Comics Journal* (Seattle, Washington: Fantagraphics Books, published monthly, n.d.).

9 An ideal example to show how influential the opinion of comicbooks fans can be is the infamous telephone poll which decided the death of Robin in 1988. For more details on the editors' decision about Robin's death, see Pearson and Uricchio, "Notes from the Batcave: An Interview with Dennis O'Neil," in idem, *The Many Lives of Batman* (London: Routledge, 1991): 20–23.

10 Patrick Parsons, "Batman and His Audience," in Pearson and Uricchio, *The Many Lives of Batman* (London: Routledge, 1991): 67.

11 P. Parsons, *ibid.*, 65–89.

12 The next ten pages are translated from a non-published essay written

148 Reading Comics

in German by Jan Philipzig.
13 Eddy Christman, "Direct Sales Rescues Comics," *Advertising Age* (June 25, 1984): 110; "Speciality Stores Increasing Share of Comic Market, Boosting Sales," *Variety* (July 8, 1987): 28; Kurt Eichenwald, "Grown-ups Gather at the Comic Book Stand," *New York Times* (Sept. 30, 1987): 1; "Biff! Pow! Comic Books Make a Comeback," *Business Week* (Sept. 2, 1985): 59.
14 The disco-fever had actually cooled out by 1981, but Marvel stayed put with this 1970s' concept. A curious, but minor, information: the illustrator of the series is Paul Chadwick who later impressed both critics and fans in *Concrete* which came out in 1987.
15 Very clearly an exception, *The Spririt* (1944) by Will Eisner reflected the current trend of superhero comics with adult elements. The Spirit looked and sometimes acted like a superhero, he even had the obligatory identity-concealing mask, but there was a sophistication in this strip that had never been seen before: "Eisner was strongly influenced by the pulps and film *noir*, and included in his stories *femmes fatales*, great deal of adult humour and settings involving beautifully-rendered shadowy cityscapes. He was also a master at conveying moods through the ingenious use of 'camera angles': 'I always saw comics as an art-form,' he later said, 'and I knew that there was a literate audience out there who would appreciate what I was doing.'" (Sabin, *op cit.*, 148). Although never a bestseller, *The Spirit* soon became the standard against which other comics would be measured, and would later be "rediscovered" by the underground, and later still by key creators in the 1980s. It is now considered as one of the classics of the medium.
16 Philip Gritis, "Turning Superheroes into Super Sales," *New York Times* (Jan. 6, 1985): 6.
17 Lisa Towle, "What's New in the Comic Book Business," *New York Times* (Jan. 31, 1988): 21; and "America is Taking Comic Books Seriously," *New York Times* (July 31, 1988): 7.
18 Cerebus began as a parody of the *Conan the Barbarian* series. Its main character is a cartoon figure living within a world full of humans (much like Jeff Smith's Bone which appears later, see Chapter Seven).
19 *A Contract with God* is Will Eisner's first graphic novel originally published in 1978 by Baronet. The succeeding volumes were re-printed by Kitchen Sink.
20 At this time, Japanese mangas were a big influence on Miller's graphic style; accordingly, Wolverine's "true love" is a Japanese woman.
21 The first mini-series from DC was *The World of Krypton* (1979).
22 Although full of twists and surprises (as expected when a medieval tale is transported to a futuristic setting), the series still revolved around the conflicting triangle of love between Arthur, Guinevere and Lancelot.
23 A young samurai avenges the death of his master by a demon. Since the

power of his sword can only be activated by spilling innocent blood and he is unwilling to kill just anyone, the samurai kills himself and then slays the demon while dying. The demon curses him to a fight again in the future. The story moves to an overly polluted New York, gripped by public unrest, and tottering on the verge of disaster.

24 *The Comic Book*, 107.

25 Pearson and Urrichio, "Introduction," in *idem, The Many Lives of Batman* (New York and London: Routledge, 1993). This transformation into a darker, more intriguing Batman is apparently also the reason for the success of the first two Batman movies.

26 The interviews of various comics artists and publishers in *The Comics Journal* provide many insights to their awareness, even excitement, in the changes occurring in the industry.

27 Chris Sharrett, "Batman and the Twilight of the Idols: An Interview with Frank Miller," in Pearson and Urricchio, *op cit.*, 34 and 37.

28 Hence the quote from one of Generation X's most popular bands, R.E.M., in the beginning of this chapter

29 Neil Gaiman, *Black Orchid* (New York: DC Comics, 1989) n.p.

30 Neil Gaiman, *Black Orchid* (New York: DC Comics, 1989) n.p.

31 There are other comicbooks that explored non-traditional ways of portraying superheroes but came out after 1990. Some of these will be mentioned in Chapter Seven.

32 That is, in terms of comicbook sales and figures from box office sales of their movies in North America which is still the biggest market for these two media. Despite the recent prevalence of Batman due to Hollywood, more people around the world might still know about the origins and myths surrounding Superman than the Batman.

33 According to Roger Sabin, *op cit.*, 146, the quality of this sub-category should not be exaggerated, however, since a crucial difference between the superhero and detective is that the former replaced a certain cerebralness of detective fiction with a greater degree of action, thereby appealing to a much younger readership.

34 Frank Miller says: "I was lucky enough to have almost complete autonomy and produce something that for me was ultimately very personal." (*The Many Lives of Batman*, p. 34).

itself, although in different forms than its 1930 prototype. This chapter will discuss how the changes and development in comic-books, especially the construction and properties of superhero comicbooks, can be correlated much more closely with the fanta-sy wishes and consumer caprice of readers than most other com-mon forms of popular narrative like television, cinema or romance fiction. Some reasons for the close relation between comics and its readers are: the cheapness of comicbooks as a commodity; the gen-eral low opinion of the product which bonded those who favoured it and also fostered a strong underground movement; its well-developed community of fans; the way comicbooks were produced and distributed; and, most importantly, the nature of the superhero figure and his adventures and exploits which made it easy and pos-sible to incorporate almost any "neat" idea proffered by those in the industry as well as its readers.

At the height of its popularity in the early 1940s, the super-hero comicbook was a unique visual phenomenon. In most cases, it was in a standard 64-page magazine format and celebrated the exploits of superheroic characters in action-packed, vividly coloured covers that children found hard to resist. The superhero dominated the pages of the early comicbook. These were mostly muscular men in brightly coloured tights shown performing remarkable feats of strength and defeating strange villains one after another. The heroes also had all the traits a child could dream of: speed, strength, power, and knowledge. The recurrence of this sight and theme in the minds of thousands of children and adoles-cents over a fifty-year period must have helped the American (male) youths to a better understanding or recognition of their fan-tasy goals as they related to their personal ideals. Interestingly, what primarily appealed to the visualised fantasies of childhood provided the twentieth century with a pantheon and mythology comparable to those of previous cultures. The superhero figure has developed into a lasting and vigorous presence in American and European popular culture such that the recognition of the Batman or Superman, for example, by millions who have never read a Batman comicbook or seen a Superman film is ensured.[2]

The lasting popularity of superheroes is rather unexpected if we consider the characteristics most familiar to superhero comics: a) the plot, characterisation, and theme are relatively simple; b) they rely frequently on formulaic plots and traditional symbols; c) there

CHAPTER SIX
Frank Miller's *The Dark Knight Returns* (1986)

"Everything is exactly the same, except for the fact that it's all totally different."

Alan Moore Introduction to the bound issue of *The Dark Knight*

"Then the world at large discovered it—people who've never been in a comic shop were coming in and asking for this new Batman thing—and it went to third, fourth, and fifth printings."

Gerard Jones and Will Jacobs
The Comic Book Heroes, 297

The title of the first issue that came out in March 1986 would give Batman fans pause: *The Dark Knight Returns*—returns? In his distinct costume, the most foreboding of all superheroes had been appearing monthly to control Gotham criminals and bring them to justice. But Miller's Batman was coming out of retirement. Was Miller implying that the Batman comics that had appeared in the last years, some of which were dutifully collected by fans, insignificant and meaningless? That was exactly Miller's intention. *The*

Dark Knight Returns brings the Batman to the modern present that had changed drastically, and takes him away from the stagnation of the issues sold since the 1970s. Miller's daring re-interpretation of the Batman begins in a Gotham City almost unrecognizable in its desolate atmosphere with the duskiness and melancholy distinct to Miller's illustration.[1] More importantly, Miller's Batman is an aging anti-hero who does not blindly conform to the current power status, but actually questions it.[2] As Alan Moore clearly states in his introduction to the book:

> As the naivety of the characters and the absurdity of their situations become increasingly embarassing and anachronistic to modern eyes, so does the problem become more compounded and intractable.[3]

In Miller's departure from traditional superheroes, Alan Moore did not see a decline but instead the elevation of superheroes into legends.[4] Miller changed the superhero engaged in nothing but endless and repetitive fighting by lending it the dimension of time.

> Miller managed to shape the Batman into a true legend by introducing that element without which all true legends are incomplete and yet which for some reason hardly seems to exist in the world depicted in the average comicbook, and that element is time.
>
> All of our best and oldest legends recognise that time passes and that people grow old and die... With *Dark Knight*, time has come to the Batman and the capstone that makes legends what they are has finally been fitted.[5]

This chapter provides an analysis of how the elements of time affects, and concretely manifests itself in, the narrative structure of *Dark Knight Returns*.

BATMAN RETIRED

In the beginning of the graphic novel, a much older Bruce Wayne alias Batman lives in a world safeguarded by his money "in a million-dollar mansion miles away" (Issue 1, p. 5). While the city suffers under a heatwave and a spate of horrible crimes, Bruce Wayne is in a car race, whereby a newscaster comments "I'm surprised anyone can even think of sports in this weather" (I, 2). In withdrawing his Batman identity a decade ago, Bruce Wayne also seems to have departed from present reality. By recasting his Batman mask into a racing helmet, Miller seems to comment on traditional Batman comics where the hunt for criminals gives an impression of being only a sports competition, without once making any headway on actually squashing the roots of criminality.

Even within the arena of a dangerous sport, Bruce Wayne remains dissatisfied and is thrown into a mental and emotional tumult. The first page hints at his desire for suicide (perhaps a desire to withdraw from the current world) as he intentionally turns off the computerized gadget in the car and pushes the race car into suicidal speed, thinking: "This would be a good death... but not good enough" (I, 2). A life beyond reality proves to be impossible for Bruce Wayne, a reality he had nevertheless only learned to confront with his Batman mask on. His hesitation in the thought: "This would be a good death... but not good enough" reflects the duality of the Bruce Wayne-Batman character: a good enough death for a more or less normal man like the retired Wayne, but not good enough for Batman.

Just in the first page of the comics, we can see the motifs that will run through the narrative:

- Allusion to the dual identity of the Bruce Wayne-Batman figure
- The possibility of death gives the dimension of a past and the appearance of "real" time in the life of Batman who never aged in the last 50 years
- Bruce Wayne-Batman has to comprehend and deal with the present times
- Television reports only sensationalism and does not dig into the core of truth; therefore, the second identity of Bruce Wayne is preserved

Two pages later, it is clear not only to fans but also to novice Batman readers that there is only one way out for Bruce Wayne: he must concede to his Batman identity which had been suppressed until then. At one point, Bruce clicks glasses with Commissioner Gordon, who says: "You've certainly learned to drink" (I, 4). The retraction of his Batman identity unsettles Bruce, drives him to drink, gives him suicidal tendencies and feelings of torment not unlike those of a schizophrenic: "... in my guts the creature writhes and snarls and tells me what I need. . ." (I, 4) that push him to return into the Batman's costume. Gordon totally misinterprets Bruce's anxiety, as he suggests: "You just need a woman." (I, 4). In one interview, Frank Miller expounds on his view on Batman:

> His sexual urges are so drastically sublimated into crime-fight-ing that there's no room for any other emotional activity.[6]

This obsession never left Wayne-Batman in his retirement and makes it impossible for him to have a meaningful relationship with other people. "I am a zombie" Wayne says, "A dead man, ten years dead. . ." (I, 4).

BATMAN RETURNS

From the start, it is very clear that Wayne's inability to have a ful-filling life without a Batman identity necessitates the latter's return. The return itself probably represents the artistic culmination sum-mit of the story, and Miller shows it in three phases: The Murder of His Parents, The Fall into a Cave, and The Bat Breaks Through.

I. The Murder of His Parents

The Batman is a creature of the night. Wayne suffers nightly anxi-eties from the writhing, snarling creature in his gut and it is no dif-ferent this evening after he and Gordon part ways. While walking in the city streets that night, Bruce Wayne experiences a modern version of what led to Batman's birth 40 years ago. His turmoil propels him to the now dilapidated place where his parents were murdered after the three of them watched the film *The Mark of Zorro*. Of the former place, only a street lamp remains, and Bruce seems hypnotized by its light. He is swallowed up in the past, where the impelling force of his Batman existence lies, as he gets mugged once again, precisely in the same place. The young mem-bers of the Mutant gang who assault him are not identical with the previous murderer, but to Bruce Wayne, "These—these are his chil-dren. A purer breed ... and this world is theirs" (I, 6). As the force of the present lawlessness impels Bruce Wayne to his knees, the awakening of his alter ego becomes imminent. The same place and similar circumstances compel, for the second time, the birth of Batman. Only in his mask and costume can Wayne thrive to meet the challenges of present reality.

Another night, Wayne is again thrown into the traumatic experience of his parent's murder as the television shows a re-run of an old film, *The Mark of Zorro*, the film he saw with his parents the night they were killed. (I, 14) In two pages without any text, Wayne re-lives the murder which served as the origin and catalyst for Batman's genesis. Although Wayne tries to thrust the notion aside by changing channels, there is no escape from the force of Batman. Impressions of the past mix with the crimes of the present (I, 16) and the suppressed motif wins: "The time has come. You know it in your soul. For I am your soul. . .You cannot escape me... You cannot stop me—not with wine or vows or the weight of age. . ." (I, 17) Batman will not be denied, this is becoming clear to Bruce Wayne, who is reduced to a physical shell without his alter-ego. The schizophrenic character of the situation is obvious: Wayne can no longer stop his second self. The creature of the night wins.

II. The Fall into a Cave

Chronologically, the focus of this section happens between the two experiences mentioned above. Wayne is dreaming of a scene from his childhood. His parents, Martha and Thomas Wayne were still alive and a six-year-old Bruce was running after a rabbit in their garden. Bruce was suddenly confronted with the purpose of the innocent game with a question from his mother: "Bruce, what are you going to do with it when you catch it—don't go into that hole! Bruce!" Nevertheless, Bruce falls in while simultaneously losing the rabbit which was the purpose of his chase. He falls into an abyss where the rabbit, which he would not have caught anyway, no longer plays any role. The cave is not the world of his parents, nor their questions, nor the rabbit, but the world of bats which first frightens the young Bruce, "No! Go away!" (I, 10) However, in a few moments, a fascination with the torpid cave takes over, and Bruce stares in wonder at one bat that symbolizes the cave's lack of development:

> "Gliding with ancient grace... eyes gleaming, untouched by
> love or joy or sorrow... breath hot with the taste of fallen
> foes... the stench of dead things, damned things... surely the

fiercest survivor—the purest warrior... glaring, hating...
claiming me as his own" (I, 11)

In the world of the bats, Bruce feels secure from the questions
of adults that must be answered outside the cave, safe from having
to confront the purpose of his games. He perceives the bat as a
warrior, hardened in vast emptiness, and unafraid of anything new
or unknown. In a series of eight frames, the bats approaches the
frightened yet fascinated child, until the bat's shadow initially covers Bruce, but eventually fills up the whole panel (I, 11). For Miller,
assuming a Batman identity is also an expression of a defensive
and parrying stance against the unknown—this will have a sexual
connotation for Bruce years later. Bruce Wayne transforms this
same cave into a secret Batcave where he takes on the traits of bats
and becomes Batman. The cave also acts as a mother's womb
where he comes back after his nightly patrol for justice. The cave
is the base of Batman's operations: "... huge, empty, silent as a
church. . ." (I, 11) empty and still, diametrically opposed to actual relationships or attachments.

In the lower half of the same page, a graying and half-clothed
Bruce Wayne stands in the Batcave, compelled by the Batman
inside him: "Brings me down here when the night is long and my
will is weak. He struggles relentlessly, hatefully, to be free. . ." (I,
11) The costume of the bat allows Bruce a retreat from a world full
of human relationships in constant motion which he cannot control. Bruce never learned to live in this world. His costume functions as a fetish, a substitute for real, live relationships. The role of
the costume and mask in the divided Bruce Wayne/Batman personality becomes even clearer when Bruce gets out from his car
after his visit to Gordon. He bristles against conceding to his
Batman identity: "I can't stand to be inside anything right now,"
(I, 4)—not inside a car, nor in a costume, much less "inside a
woman." Alan Moore elucidates on this psychological disposition
of masked superheroes and their stilted relationships with women
in his maxi-series, *Watchmen* (see also Chapter Four of this book).

Miller's Bruce Wayne tries to resist the need to find personal
fulfillment in the identity of the Dark Knight, but only the Batman
outfit and identity offer a relief from the creature's nightly challenges. The death of his former sidekick Robin made Bruce
Wayne form a resolution to cease the nightly activities that
would give him peace: "I gave my word. For Jason. Never. Never

again. (I, 11). But as the action progresses, Batman's vow to Jason would find a different expression in the selection and development of his follower, and no longer in the Dark Knight's renunciation of its nightly combats. The creature of the night stirs and the retirement that never really applied to Batman, ends.

III. The Bat Breaks Through

One night at home, Wayne listens to the messages left by Harvey Dent (Two-Face), Clark (Superman), and Selina (Catwoman) in his answering machine—Batman is essential for both friends and foes. As Bruce stands before a window, an approaching bat casts a shadow on him through the window's frame which crosses out his face. The bat breaks through the window and flies into the Wayne Manor premises, its open mouth and bared teeth filling the last page of this issue. Bruce Wayne's current existence which denies his second identity finds an end with the intrusion of the bat.

The actuality of this scene is vague, but it is not important if the bat was real or existed only in Bruce's mind. The scene is reminiscent of the Batman's origin as first revealed in *Detective Comics # 33*: as Bruce Wayne was thinking about his parents' murder and what he could do to avenge this and stop similar atrocities, a bat flies through a window and appears before him. Wayne gets the idea to become a fearless creature of the night, and fight crime dressed like a bat. This time is no different: in the lower panels of this page, Bruce Wayne's face changes from an expression of doubt and surprise to resolution and conviction. The bat did not just break through the closed window in Wayne's mansion but breaks through the "lies" in Bruce's mind that he can keep his other personality suppressed.

After the scene with the bat, Miller moves us to a dark, stormy night in Gotham. A power outage has thrown the city and its suburbs into total darkness—a perfect setting for the re-appearance of Batman who thrives on stealth, concealment, and darkness. Two assaults are stopped by an invisible figure, but we get glimpses of gloves and shoes in the grey-blue colour of the Batman (I, 19-20). As the third assault loomed, intended for two young girls, a dark blue glove so familiar to American readers is raised right before Batarangs pierce through an assailant's arm and one other attacker is lifted in the air.

In the third assault, Batman saves a young girl, Carrie, who will later fight by his side as the new Robin and lead the aging vigilante into the modern times.

BATMAN'S FOES

I. The Joker

On page 6, a row of four frames shows the first phase of the return of the Dark Knight. This is mirrored on the other side of the spread by another series of four pictures: in a psychiatric clinic, known to Batman fans as the Arkham Asylum, the blinds roll up to reveal the face of the oldest and most well-known of Batman's adversaries, the Joker. Batman's renaissance is attended with the simultaneous revival of his main protagonist who, during Batman's absence, was tucked away in Arkham Asylum. In one interview, Miller describes the Joker as Batman's "antithesis,[7] a force of chaos", which is directly opposite to Batman's being a "control freak."[8]

The close link between Batman and Joker is shown again when the television reports on the return of the Dark Knight. Eight frames (I, 33) demonstrate the gradual transformation of the previously soporific and lifeless facial expressions of the Joker. His reawakening can be seen in his mouth, as it spreads into a broad grin, a distinctive trait of this popular Batman-enemy, that Jack Nicholson made even more popular to millions of people later in a Batman movie. The grin gets wider and wider that it breaks through one frame and becomes two frames wide. A similarity of comics with film is shown in this instance: the series of pictures just mentioned simulates the zooming in for a close-up shot. At the same time, Miller shows a feature distinct to comics—the film or movie cannot go beyond the frames of the screen.

Within the series of these pictures, the parasitic dependency between Batman and Joker becomes evident. The Joker awakes while watching a report that the Batman is back, and the first words that break out of the Joker are "BB. . .BBBat. . .Batman. Darling." (I, 38) as he "naturally" falls back into being the Batman's antagonist. From this time on, one can see a vitality and life in the Joker, making the Batman also responsible for the existence of his most intimate enemies, at the same time that he is trying to conquer them. This interpretation of the Joker is not new. Already in 1973, the Joker himself states in Dennis O'Neil's *The Joker's Five-Way Revenge* (*Batman #251*): "Without the game that the Batman and I have played for so many years, winning is nothing!"

This game, interrupted by Batman's withdrawal, has already started for the Joker as his psychiatrist, Dr. Wolper, encourages him to "Just be yourself" (III, 18) during their appearance together in the *Late Night Show*. The Joker follows exactly the doctor's prescription and gasses the psychiatrist, David Letterman, and all those present in a gruesome act so typical of the Joker. This scheme is meaningful in various levels:

- The Joker confirms his unchangeable destructive character; proving he is incurable and his atrocity is an immutable trait
- The television is shown once again to prefer sensationalism over responsible awareness

Figure 30. *The Dark Knight Returns* shows a grim Batman who breaks a promise he made 30 years ago never to kill anyone. *The Dark Knight Returns*. Art and script: Frank Miller © 1986 DC Comics

- The Joker, who thickly applies his own red lipstick before coming out on stage is shown as an embodiment of the homophobe's fear

The third aspect is also demonstrated in the way the Joker continuously calls Batman "Darling" and "My sweet" in the final pages of the third book. Batman answers in the beginning of the final book by unequivocally killing the Joker.[9]

Frank Miller was criticised by, among others, *The Village Voice* for mixing homosexuality and wickedness and immorality in the figure of the Joker. The censure was not totally unfair as there is no other, more positive homosexual figure in the book to counter the blatantly destructive figure of the Joker. All the same, the critique must be placed in proper context: for Miller, the Joker does not represent an absolute evil autonomous of his surroundings—much of his conduct is closely linked to that of Batman's.

Like Bruce Wayne, the Joker becomes "different" by an accident. Falling into a vat full of chemicals distorted his appearance and gave him his singular smile. Joker's reaction to this mishap is in direct contrast to Wayne's reaction to his parents' murder. The Joker vowed revenge by overthrowing all structures of the civilized world and to let chaos reign. Batman, on the other hand, overcame his trauma, by trying to rid the world of disorder and confusion which made his parents' murder possible. While the Joker pushes for discord, Batman fights for order—one's reaction to a private trauma is the other's aversion and outrage. When the Joker creates chaos, the guardian of peace becomes his natural enemy. And when the Joker wants to undermine this self-appointed custodian of the law, who has never come to terms with his own sexuality (and for years was swinging together nightly with another guy in colorful tights), the most proven way is to play up to his homophobic fears and force the Batman to reflect on his insecurities.[10]

II. Two-Face

Another Batman foe, Two-Face, is deemed ready to rejoin to society after a 12-year stay in Arkham Asylum. He underwent psychiatric treatments and plastic surgery to restore his disfigured face, after which the same psychiatrist who treated Joker, Dr. Wolper, says: "You're fit to return to society... "(I, 7). Frank Miller's graphics, however, belie this view: Two-Face's close-up spans two frames, the middle gutter splitting him. Moreover, his experience of oneness or entirety in the last picture is based solely on a mirror-reflection, and the *mirror phase* proves to be a misguided process of self-realization for Two-Face.

A short detour to Jacques Lacan helps elaborate this scene. Jacques Lacan is a French psychiatrist and post-structuralist who analyzes the interpendence of consciousness (also, sense of self) and language. He defines the mirror phase of a child as the first perception of its incompleteness. When a child looks into a mirror, it perceives its reflection as an "Other" separate from its own self, and the child perceives a difference between an imaginary self and a perceived real self. After the plastic surgery but before seeing himself in a mirror, Two-Face doubts his recovery, "Maybe Gordon ...is right about me ..."(I, 7: Commissioner Gordon, who is skeptical about the whole process done on Two-Face, vocally states on television that Two-Face will never recover.) Upon seeing himself in the mirror, Two-Face comments: "Oh, my God. . ."(I, 7).

This complete, undivided "God" (the "other" as reflected in the mirror) is separate from one's body and is not identified with the self, according to Lacan: together, they do not make a whole. On the contrary, the mirror phase induces or brings about a quest for an Other. Two-Face, unable to resolve his outward appearance with his inner self, then directs his attention to, of all things, the likewise divided Batman-Bruce Wayne personality. The orientation Batman provides as Two-Face's "Other" is obviously questionable—it becomes impossible to overcome the divided self since the patient has fixed its orientation for recovery and its search for completeness on a personality that is also divided. The next step, according to Lacan, is the entry to language—but since in Two Face's case, the "Other" is a split personality itself, this next step is problematic for him: "What can I say?" (I, 8). Which part of the split personality is the language supposed to express? Two-Face is rendered speechless by the inability to make a choice. As the reader turns over the page, the reader encounters only a new phase of the book but not a new page in the life of Harvey Dent (aka Two-Face). The plastic surgery changes his outward appearance, but his psychological recovery fails.

In an interview, Frank Miller states that he considers Two-Face as Batman's *Doppelganger*. "Two-Face is identical to Batman in that he's controlled by savage urges, which he keeps in check, in his case, with a flip of a coin. He's very much like Batman."[11] Two-Face first appears in August 1942 (*Detective Comics* #66) as the popular Defense Attorney Harvey Dent. Because of his good looks, the press called him "Apollo" until a criminal whom Batman turned over to justice threw some corrosive chemicals which permanently disfigured one half of Harvey Dent's face. At the brink of going mad, Harvey Dent scratches one side of a coin which he uses to decide his behaviour and ultimately, the fate of his victims: after a coin toss, leniency if the unmarked side emerges, and atrocity or death for the disfigured side.

Bruce Wayne also developed a split personality after his parents' murder: on one side a carefree playboy, on the other, a Zorro-inspired vigilante in a bat outfit. If the Joker serves as Batman's antithesis, Two-Face parallels the superhero's having a split personality. Like Harvey Dent, Bruce Wayne developed an alter ego although the objectives of their alter egos vary extremely. The biggest difference between Batman and Two-Face is the way each reacted to a traumatic experience, as Miller says: "Anyone can be a victim ... It's how one uses the evil inside. Batman makes his devils work for the common good."[12] Bruce Wayne had sponsored Harvey Dent's treatments. Contrary to Gordon's skepticism, Wayne publicly states his reason for sponsoring the treatments: "We must believe that our private demons can be defeated ..."(I, 9). This remark seems more like a wish he expresses for himself. In the next panels, we see Bruce Wayne dreaming of his parents, falling into the batcave, and struggling with his own demons. Just like him, Dent is unable to leave his personal "demons" behind.

Harvey Dent's "recovery" becomes a media spectacle and a newscaster reports: "A new life begins today for Harvey Dent... and he looks great." (I, 8) Then we see a beaming and good-looking Dent holding up a new, shiny coin, unmarked at both sides. (I, 9) Dent speaks about remorse, absolution, and a new life of serving the public. Significantly, the four pictures showing the superficial and media-ready face of Harvey Dent are divided into two different pages of the book, split in two halves. This is an example how Miller ingenuously uses a technique offered to a comic writer/illustrator not available to a conventional author or a film director.

On page 13, we see Dent already back in the underworld, signaled by a coin scratched on one side falling onto a table full of playing cards, money, and guns. From this page on, Two-Face is only shown with a fully-bandaged head covering the plastic surgery and the face he cannot live with.[13] When Batman later finds a coin scratched on both sides in the scene of a crime (I, 32), his hopes for Dent's recovery evaporates. It is clear from the fully marked coin that the external success of the plastic surgery was totally subjugated by an inner malice. Whereas before, Two-Face's split face mirrored the divided urges within him, now, his perfectly pretty face only hides completely damaging intentions. The age of television demands superficial perfection, but the results are horrible.

The first chapter ends with Two-Face falling from a tower in the city, until his doppelganger Batman comes and catches him and observes. "We tumble like lovers." (I, 46). Two-Face confirms their reciprocality with his words: "I've been a sport... You have to admit that—I played along." (I, 47). In the middle of page 47, two rows of four panels each divided by the middle of the spread, give the impression of a mirror reflection: the first row shows Two-Face's head, the second shows Batman's face. The third frame in the first row shows Batman's vision of Two-Face " ... As he is." Right below the third picture of the second row, we see a sinister-looking close-up of a bat. Their demons are reflections of each other, as ordered by the pictures. Batman himself is aware of the parallel: "... I see ... a reflection, Harvey. A reflection." (I, 47).

COMMISSIONER GORDON AND THE PREVIOUS BATMAN

Police Commissioner Gordon, who has been in service since 1940 and has since then become a regular in the Batman comics never grew any older like all other regular supporting characters in the Batman series. Miller shows Gordon just 1 month before his retirement. Another significant deviation from traditional Batman comics is that Batman's real identity is no longer a secret to Gordon, as a result of a deep friendship that had developed between Gordon and Bruce Wayne.

In this book, not only is Gordon almost retired, but his views are also outmoded and old-fashioned. As an example, at the beginning of the second chapter, Gordon bemoans the time when a car was still "a symbol of wealth and power." (II, 2). These cars,

together with the other material possessions of the rich and powerful, were exactly what Batman protected between the years 1939
and 1986. In *The Dark Knight*, Bruce Wayne realizes (as the story
progresses) that with such a perspective, he only upholds status
quo and does not really get to the roots of crime. Gordon, however, is not able to learn nor accept the changes wrought by modern
times.

   Another example is when Gordon finds out that the next
Police Commissioner, his successor, is a woman. His reaction: "A
woman. Christ almighty. . ." (II, 16) Gordon proves to be extremely conservative, intolerant of progressive ideas, almost a fossil of
the war years as he and Batman were originally conceived. In *The
Dark Knight*, Gordon represents the ideology of the traditional
Batman figure of the last four decades. At the beginning of this
mini-series, we still see this traditional Batman figure right after he
came out of retirement, before he is directed into modern reality by
the new Robin. In the first two books, Miller shows some parallels
between Gordon and Batman to clearly illustrate the relationship
or similarities between the two. Both men are incapable of a ful-
filled life outside the pursuit of criminals (II, 12); because of their
ultra-conservative views, both are held responsible (in television)
for the present crimes (II, 5), their old styles of fighting crimes go
against the changed consciousness of the people. Critical voices
descry the superhero of Gotham City as a fascist: "The only thing
he signifies... is an aberrant psychotic force—morally bankrupt,
politically hazardous, reactionary, paranoid—a danger to every
citizen of Gotham." (I, 33).

   The next pages bear out these charges as we see a brutal and
churlish Batman throwing one of Two-Face's cohorts through a
window pane: "You've got rights. Lots of rights. Sometimes I
count them just to make myself feel crazy. But right now you've
got a piece of glass shoved into a major artery in your arm." (I, 37)
Even as Batman's principles still prevail during this time and he
refuses to kill, his methods of interrogation and detention are not
in accord with basic human rights. One cannot just dismiss the
arguments of his adversaries: "Makes me sick. We must treat the
socially misoriented with rehabilitative methods." (I, 37) The
observation of the parents of the new Robin, Carrie, runs:
"Obviously a fascist. Never heard of civil rights." (I, 37) Batman's
attitude and procedures that have been familiar and accepted by

readers for many years now begin to grate against modern realities. Even the new generation of policemen does not accept Batman's previously tolerated vigilante-style of justice and wants to arrest him (I, 28). The traditional superhero totally lost his positive image in Miller's rendition of Batman as he initially sides with the dominant power and refers to the petty gang criminals or thieves as "punks." Only much later does Batman realize that the present is much too complex for a clear delineation between good and evil.

The first chapter ends with a interim climax—the confrontation between Batman and Two-Face. The Dark Knight fights with a US Military-issued weapon, but he starts distancing himself from what has been his ideology until then: "It was developed by the military during one of our more contemptible wars." (I, 41) But at this point, Bruce Wayne alias Batman is still searching for his own point of view. His momentary bewilderment gives rise again to a wish for death, cut short by Batman's feelings of responsibilities to the citizens of Gotham City: "... a fine death. But there are thousands to think of." (I, 43)

The second chapter shows Batman reaching a turning point in comprehending the new situation, as he maneuvers a confrontation with the "Mutants" in the slums of Gotham City. Batman first appears in the dump within the protection of an impenetrable tank (a modified Batmobile) and gets the chance to shoot the leader, but, at this point, Batman still refuses to kill. Eventually, and against his better judgement, he gets out to fight a hand-to-hand combat with the mutant gang leader (II, 19), his old body betrays him, and he loses to the Mutant gang leader. In leaving the tank, Batman starts to move away from the ideologies that kept him siding with the dominant powers in the past. Doubting the certainty of the morals that had previously guided him, Batman becomes vulnerable and loses to the gang leader. Significantly, Batman is saved from death by Carrie, alias Robin. In Miller's narrative, this is the turning point for Batman where we see that his traditional ways of thinking and fighting do not guarantee his victory over the new breed of scoundrels, and he has to depend on Carrie. From this point on, we see Batman starting to leave his antiquated beliefs and being ushered into the modern realities from a child of the media generation. Batman begins to understand the decisive role that Carrie can play for his own development: "She's more than a child." (II, 37) He stops sharing Gordon's conservative outlook and is re-born a second time—this time born into the 1980s. As usual, Batman retreats into the cave and takes strength from seeing a bat, but this re-birth does not mean a withdrawal from reality. "Then... something shuffles, out of sight ... something sucks the stale air ... and hisses"(II, 31). On the contrary, this time, it is a breakthrough into the realities of the present. The next time we see Batman, he is explaining to Alfred his choice for the new Robin and optimistically planning how to finally stop the Mutants: "Carrie. She's perfect. She's young. She's smart. She's brave. With her, I might be able to end this mutant nonsense once and for all." (II, 37).

ROBIN AND THE NEW BATMAN

Carrie is a young girl who is in touch with the trends and developments of her time. For example, she is particularly interested in computer studies (I, 22), and wears green-tinted eyeglasses, which, at first glance, are not unlike the glasses that identify members of the mutant gang. Although Carrie, in direct contrast to Commissioner Gordon, is up-to-date with the times, she has not mutated into or been reduced an uncritical consumer of her period but has retained her individuality. While the many-colored glasses of the mutant gang are mere slits, which hide their eyes and simultaneously narrow their capacity to see, Carrie's eyewear have big lenses through which clearly show her alert eyes. While she belongs to a generation bombarded with images from computer and television, her opinions are not limited to the ideology relayed by the media. When TV reporters are interviewing people about Batman's reappearance, Carrie is the only one who did not stare wide-eyed at the camera and give sensational reports about him, like: "... Wild animal. Growls. Snarls. Werewolf surely." or "Monster! Like with fangs and wings and it can fly ..." Carrie says: "Reality check ... he's a man." (I, 26) Carrie is capable of being critical of the TV as a mass medium, without shutting off the developments of her time. Even Batman's authority is something she does not blindly obey. Instead, through her ability to decide for herself, she manages to effectively help him in his battles, and to even save his life (III, 24 and 25).

The Mutants, on the other hand, the mutants are absolute products of modern society devoid of any individual characteristic. They "mutate" by watching TV (IV, 11 and 17), their perspectives are completely influenced and decided by the artificial and colorful world of the media age. Outside this illusory world, there is no stability and truth are absent, and the mutants' confusion is manipulated by their gang leader. The senseless killing of a cat (I, 6) shows a deprivation of a natural respect for life, defiling a church shows scorn for any religious worth. There are no logical, understandable motives for the mutants. The attack of Carrie and Michelle seems to be nothing but an imitation of a bad horror film, as one sees in the use of a power saw and the video arcade setting (I, 23).

This passive and uncritical consumption of media products is not exclusive to the mutants as a marginal group, but extends to the average citizen of Gotham City. Batman was described as a "huge man dressed like Dracula," (I, 24), others believed in having seen a werewolf or a monster (I, 26). Legends conveyed, even created, by television influence the perception of reality. Batman must come to terms with this condition—how perceptions can be influenced and changed—if he is to prevail upon the children of media. If he insists on remaining with the rules of the past and keep denying the present, he will never gain the respect of these children: "Young people these days . . no respect for history." (II, 18) For the Mutants, and younger citizens of Gotham, Batman can only truly function as a legend and become a myth if he is current and up-to-date. Batman had the potential for myth right from the start: "A recent survey shows that most high schoolers consider him a myth." (I, 3). In the second chapter, Batman finally makes use of this potential as he defeats the Mutant gang leader in a dramatic duel covered live by television (II, 42-46). Miller's introduction of the element of time is central to *The Dark Knight* in two levels. Not only are Batman and Gordon older, and the city of Gotham changed with time, but as the narrative unfolds, Batman learns increasingly to deal with modern realities. He realizes that one can only influence the media generation if one is presented as a figure or legend marketable to and consumable by TV audiences.

During the match, the Mutants wear T-shirts which state "My name is Rob" (II, 44). After his impressive, albeit staged, triumph, Batman rises as a legend for the media generation. The "Rob" becomes "Rob-in" as the Mutants now become fascinated with the

Dark Knight and form "The Sons of Batman" gang. A mutant, having replaced his slit-like glasses with the Batman insignia, declares on TV: "The mutants are dead. The mutants are history. This is the mark of the future. Gotham City belongs to the Batman" (II, 46). The change does not go smoothly. As "Sons of Batman," some Mutants start dispensing "order" brutally, in a way even more extreme than the old Batman which was publicly perceived as oppressive and despotic. To stop the "Sons of Batman" from using excessive violence, Batman once again makes an appearance in the dump, this time sitting atop a horse while he smashes a rifle into pieces, saying: "*This* is the weapon of the *enemy*. We do not *need* it. We will not *use* it." (IV, 21). The declaration does not lose its desired effect, since Batman has learned to work within the medium appropriate to his TV-saturated audience. He is perceived as an authentic legend: "You know—like in a Western." (IV, 23)

Although, and partly because, he succeeds in winning the Mutants over to his side, Batman finally realises: "I've become a political liability ... (IV, 24) as the television and police force more than ever detest him and perceives him an anomaly in the present times. Batman decides to end his unwanted Batman-existence, and turn over his fight to Carrie: "Right there—in that saddle—is all the reason I need. She has decades—decades, left to her. . ." (IV, 34). Batman then stages a fight with Superman, the prime supporter of the dominant power, stages his own pseudo-death (IV, 43), and sanctions the media to announce his demise (IV, 45). After the official wake and funeral, Batman is dug up from his grave by Carrie—and Batman's new existence is closely linked to the young generation.

Bruce Wayne's new reality is portrayed in the last page of the fourth and final chapter: he lays aside his Batman garb because he cannot deny the present: "here, in the endless cave, far past the remains of a crimefighter whose time has passed ... It begins here— an army—to bring sense to a world plagued by worse than thieves and murderers ... This will be a good life good enough." (IV, 47). Wayne does not consider it his task anymore to protect the "Haves" (moneyed or propertied class) from petty thieves which he, in the meantime, considers as victims of the reigning power structure and relations. He aims for a bigger plan. Wayne had always gone back alone to his "Batcave" to plan his next moves away from any company and influence, now he shares this

"Batcave" with Carrie and the former Mutants who were his enemies at the start of the book. The retreat to the Batcave no longer means a withdrawal from or denial of the ever-changing world and points of view—close alliance with the young generation assists him in finding a position to counter past hierarchies and traditions that make up the ruling political conditions. With this shift, Bruce Wayne heeds Carrie's ideas and principles. From the beginning, Carrie was the only figure who was simultaneously engaged in the present and in a position to critically reflect on this present.

DARK KNIGHT SUMMARY

The strength of Frank Miller's works, before and after *The Dark Knight*, does not lie in the incisiveness and entirety of the ideological concepts he presents. Although *The Dark Knight* questions supremacy and explores the need to come to terms with the young generation, for example, Miller still ends with Bruce Wayne as an authority figure that is male, imperious, and patriarchal (II, 38; III, 11; III, 32; IV, 47). Miller also shows a female influence necessary to lead Batman into his new position in the modern world, but Batman remains a figure devoid of any intimate relations with women. In fact, references to sexuality are mostly negative (I, 4, 21; II, 39; III, 23, 27, 32, 37). One weakness in *The Dark Knight* is the treatment of the relations between authority and power that comes across as unresolved and not thoroughly thought out. Despite these weaknesses, Miller manages to enthrall readers with themes that address the current times. By exploring the power of media and the fear of political renovation in *The Dark Knight*, Miller shows how actual sociological and political phenomena may be intertwined into a critique of the superhero genre.

OTHER BATMAN NARRATIVES

In America, *The Dark Knight* would be the impulse behind the commercial success of the Batman film three years later. In turn, the movie's success had a big impact on the comics market during the late 1980s and early 1990s. Because of the uncommon demand for these issues, *The Dark Knight* series was collected and published in book format after the four issues were completed. This practice has now become the norm rather than the exception.[14]

Known as a "graphic novel", *The Dark Knight* enjoyed 38 weeks
in the New York Bestseller list, the first superhero comicbook to
have ever been included in the list. Miller succeeded where comics
publishers and other comics artists have not—he broke through
the limits of the comics ghetto and managed to get people to buy
a comicbook—people who were unaware of this medium or who
have not touched a comicbook since their childhood. *The Dark
Knight* became a media event and comics were suddenly the talk
of the town.

With the sensational success of his Batman narratives, Frank
Miller proved something that had long been lacking in this medium, in particular, the superhero genre—that there are readers who
are interested in seeing complex aspects of modern life dissected in
comicbooks. In the following years, current political, ecological
and sociological problems found their way into American comicbooks, albeit quite late compared to other media.

The Dark Knight was not the first comicbook intended for
adult readers. Its novelty and consequent success lie more in the
radical way it eroded the traditional superhero genre from within
the genre. Miller did not create an alternative comics whose potential sales would be suspect in a market dominated by superhero
comics. Instead, he used Batman—second oldest of all superheroes[15] and very popular in America—to vitalize his pioneering
ideas and produced comics that would be accessible to a wider
public. Consequently, there would be other attempts in using the
Batman to show innovations in comicbooks, as well as to tackle
issues more serious than have ever been included in earlier comics.

Grant Morrison's *Arkham Asylum*, for example, plays with
very ambiguous standards for sanity and insanity. Two narratives—the personal and scientific journal of a brilliant psychiatrist
Amadeus Arkham and the Batman's tribulations in the Asylum
more than half a century later—effectively intertwine and confuse
the boundaries and relations between intelligence, sanity, insanity,
and memory. Unlike most previous superhero stories, narrative
privileging is not conferred on the hero, Batman. Instead, the tale
constantly shifts between Dr. Arkham's memories, the accounts of
the current inmates in Arkham (most of whom are confined there
because of the Batman), and the Batman's encounters with these
bizarre creatures, as he struggles to go through the tunnels of the
asylum for a better understanding of himself and his enemies. With

the variety of languages and points of view that are textually and visually built into *Arkham Asylum*, it is difficult to determine whose story is being told, to whom, and why. In the expectations and myths which superhero comics tend to create and reinforce, a privileged mode of expression usually emerges as the narrative unfolded. There can be languages that take prominent places in turns, but eventually, there is only one that is chosen to speak the truth and advance the narrative to its accepted conclusion. A very common, though largely unnoticed, privileging in superhero comicbooks presents the narrative through the perspective of the ubiquitous crimefighter. In this way, specific narrative devices grant the superheroes narrative centrality and, in addition, often cede to them narrative authority through point-of-view frames, first person narration and other textual and graphic cues which foster reader identification with him and his exploits. This process emphasises the hero's hegemonic role and function and fosters the reader's acceptance of the hero's hegemonic traits and ideas.

But in *Arkham Asylum*, a systematic privileging of the Batman, either textually or visually, is not conspicuous in the tale. The Joker, for example, who leads the rebellion of the inmates against the asylum's authorities, comes across just as imposing as the Batman, and is even described by a psychotherapist as:

> (The Joker is) a special case. Some of us feel he may be beyond treatment. In fact, we're not even sure if he can be properly defined as insane.
>
> It is quite possible we may actually be looking at some kind of super-sanity here. A brilliant modification of human perception. More suited to urban life at the end of the twentieth century.[16]

Dave McKean's richly-textured illustrations and use of photo montage, in addition to the sombre colours and tight, overlapping panel formatting and multi-tiered page lay-outs, leave a very cryptic and erratic impression of the total narrative. The ending, as well, is very vague—Batman's "freedom" and the permission to leave Arkham alive is not gained through victory but granted through a whim by one of his demented enemies, Two-Face.

Arkham Asylum is an excellent example of a "post-modern" texture manifested in an increasing number of contemporary

graphic novels which employ textual and visual pastiche of material from books, newspapers, paintings, songs, scientific reports,
advertisements.[17] In only eight words, the Batman's origin is re-
told through a series of dreamlike and seemingly unrelated images
juxtaposed with the Batman's controlled suffering and the Joker's
delight during a psychiatrist's interrogation (this particular re-
telling of the murder of Bruce Wayne's parents, however, assumes
a great deal of prior knowledge of the Batman's origins from its
readers). Two narratives about the journey to madness—that of
Dr. Arkham's and the Batman's—alternate and intertwine in this
book sub-titled "The Passion Play, As it is Played Today."
Citations and images from other books abound and overlap in
this text, particularly from Lewis Carroll's *Alice's Adventures in
Wonderland*. As well, references to real people like Carl Gustav
Jung lend realism to Arkham's personal and professional journals.
All throughout, however, no certainty is ever given the reader as
to the rationality of any of the characters in the book. An under-
current of volatile violence, delicately held in check, runs through
the whole narrative. Arkham allows a dangerous and demented
patient, Mad Dog Hawkins, to roam free. In a session with
Arkham, Hawkins claims that the Virgin Mary instructs him to
mutilate only the faces and sexual organs of his victims. Hawkins
also states that he cuts himself with a razor "Just to feel. Just to
feel something!" Later, Arkham comes home to find his wife and
young daughter butchered by the Mad Dog. Nevertheless,
Amadeus Arkham again accepts Hawkins as a patient and, one
year to the day of his family's massacre, straps him to the elec-
troshock and burns him—an incident treated as an accident by the
psychiatric community. Arkham also kills his mother with a razor.
But he was not locked up in the asylum, however, until he
attempted to kill his stockbroker. Arkham's memories haunts the
asylum, driving the present Dr. Cavendish to free the inmates and
to kill the Batman. Lost in the jumble of recollections of others as
well as his own, the Batman impales his palm with a piece of broken glass to remind himself of the present and dull his anguish
over his parents' murder with physical pain. All these are punctuated by the laughter and the jesting of the Joker, who reveals his
profound knowledge of the Batman and the other inmates of the
asylum in his wisecracks and badinage. A multitude of voices,
memories and dreams battle to relate the story of Arkham, but the

reader is left to his/her own resources as the Joker proclaims: "Let the Feast of Fools begin!"

Batman is shown to have a special relation with, but also a strange fear of Arkham Asylum, which is featured in many of the new graphic novels published by DC, even those which do not belong to the Batman series. The asylum is now treated as a repository of dark secrets, undisclosed life stories, revelations from raving lunatics, but nevertheless a place which superheroes—the Black Orchid, Sandman, and the Batman, for example—have to confront if they want to possess precious information unavailable anywhere else. Access to information is increasingly becoming an important object for control, power, and victory in the present batch of superheroes who depend more on craft and cunning than on brute strength. Whereas in previous comics, the seat of information was usually some governmental or institutionalised centre, proper information in the newer tales is accessed from unexpected places like Arkham. *The Killing Joke* by Alan Moore, for example, exemplifies the lack of information about the Joker, either in the Batman's elaborate computers or in Gordon's precinct files. The Batman usually has to make the rounds of the tougher spots in town—bars, jails, the red light district, even talk to some crime lords—in order to trace the Joker's whereabouts.[18] The Sandman not only went to Arkham Asylum, but conferred with three witches and wandered the slums of London in order to learn how he could regain the power-amulets that were stolen from him.[19] Arkham Asylum seems to incarnate the inversion of standards and the blurring of boundaries in the new graphic novels which attempt to reflect the confusion in today's existence. This is addressed by Dr. Arkham as he remarks:

> I see now the virtue in madness, for this country knows no law nor any boundary. I pity the poor shades confined to the Euclidean prison that is sanity. All things are possible here and I am what madness has made me. Whole. And Complete. And free at last.[20]

Another Batman comicbook, *Night Cries* by Archie Goodwin, reveals qualms about the existence of a social reality that can still be understood in relatively stable categories, and the underlying structures that invisibly organise these categories. *Night Cries* deals with drug use and child abuse and explicitly shows that these problems are experienced across social classes. In the overpowering sense of futility in both Commissioner Gordon and the Batman as they deal with the crises in this tale, there are echoes of an unstated conviction that the prime determinant of social order is economic and political. However, social class, which previously was a key in both analysing and solving social problems, is revealed to be a weak link in the cases spanning from the poor, black families from "the Heights" to the rich, white families with famous names. The identity and motivation of the criminal is logical, but unexpected in that he is not as marginalized as villains in superhero comics usually are. Another noticeable inversion in this story is the hint that Bruce Wayne's money seems more effective than the Batman in being able to deter child abuse. As well, the usually upright Jim Gordon is portrayed ambiguously as trying to solve a crime concerning child abuse that he himself is shown to have suffered and now seems to be prone to repeat. The building up of the situations and circumstances which prevent direct action from either Gordon and the Batman in the tale's conclusion produce some discomfort, uncertainty, and an active desire in the reader to think through contradictions in *Night Cries*, not only in textual terms but also in the reader's social experiences.

Comicbooks like *Night Cries* show that, although certain conventions within superhero narratives pull towards tradition and repetition, and towards a particular brand of individualism and faith in authority, there is nevertheless nothing necessarily conservative in the medium per se. Different writers do, and have always done, very different things with the medium's generic constraints; this space of free choices has resulted in the development of more sophisticated graphic novels available now. There is presently a growing number of artists who continue to display exceptional talent with the medium—in telling sophisticated stories with innovative narrative techniques, both visually and textually. With the loss of constraints that used to bog the medium down—regarding length of narratives, styles of illustrations, and what may or may not be written or illustrated—comics now demonstrate that they can be used to effectively and artistically explore social issues and abstract concepts while remaining entertaining and accessible to a wide audience. In today's world with rapidly and constantly shifting landscapes, readers demand new themes, new insights, and new characters. The more recent comicbooks show that the medium can more than meet this challenge.

NOTES

This Chapter was mostly translated from a non-published essay written in German by Jan Philipzig.

1 In the following years, this gloom and doom would be copied and become an almost typical mark of "modern comics".
2 *The Many Lives of Batman*, p. 39.
3 Introduction by Alan Moore to *Batman: The Dark Knight Returns* (New York DC Comics, 1986).
4 Moore's appraisal of the superhero genre changed as time passed (see the section on :Crisis and Nostalgia" in Chapter Seven).
5 *Ibid.*
6 *The Many Lives of Batman*, 38.
7 Even clearer than Miller, Grant Morrison, in *Arkham Asylum*, would interpret that Batman's opponents are simply the suppressed parts of his own personality. Thus, it is not a coincidence that Batman's revival this instant is poised against the recovery of the Joker—the one cannot exist without the other.
8 *The Many Lives of Batman*, 36.
9 DC had always maintained that Batman, despite all his fights and use of violence, never killed and will never kill—but Miller went against this canon. Among Batman fans, *The Dark Knight* is a "closed" book or a book on its own, and not part of the Batman universe so that the Joker does not disappear from other Batman issues despite his unequivocal death in *The Dark Knight*.
10 Miller in *The Many Lives of Batman*, 37.
11 *The Many Lives of Batman*, 36.
12 *Ibid*, 44.
13 Two-Face only removes the bandages during his last confrontation with the Batman, as he admits that he never really felt he was cured.
14 Some comics shop owners and sellers say they prefer having the bound collection of complete stories because they take up less shelf space and can be sold for a longer period of time than individual issues.
15 Batman is second only to the original superhero—Superman who came out in the Spring of 1939.
16 Neil Gaiman and Dave McKean, *Arkham Asylum* (New York: DC Comics, 1989): n.p.
17 In *Watchmen*, for example, quotes from the Bible, Nietzsche, Elvis Costello, William Blake, Bob Dylan, Carl Gustav Jung, to name a few, litter the text. Newspaper clippings, scientific reports, pages from a diary, pages from *Treasure Island*, posters, postcards and letters are incorporated into the book. From Chapter Three onwards, the tale in the comicbook of a boy in the sidewalk who reads about the moral decline of a shipwreck survivor runs parallel to the commentary a news

vendor gives about the decline of American society. In *Black Orchid*, one of the main characters constantly sings and the texts of the songs act to move the narrative forward. He also judges the personality of another character through the latter's choice in the jukebox.

18 *The Killing Joke*. DC Comics 1988. Alan Moore (Story); Brian Bolland and John Higgins (Illustration).

19 *The Sandman: Preludes and Nocturnes*. DC Comics Vertigo, 1991. Neil Gaiman (Story); Sam Kieth, Mike Dringenberg and Malcolm Jones (Illustration).

20 *Arkham Asylum, op cit.*, n.p.

CHAPTER SEVEN

A Glimpse at the Comics Scene after 1986

"Who cares that 20 years ago they used to actually have dialogue in their pictures? The kids don't like that anymore, obviously. They want books that have 22 blank pages. Who are we to argue with them?

I don't have a long concentration span, you know what I mean? I don't read *Sports Illustrated* because the articles are too long."

Todd MacFarlane,
founder of Image
Comics Comics Journal #152,
p. 52 and 63

DC RIDES THE WAVE OF SUCCESS

After *The Dark Knight*, DC Comics enjoyed a wave of success and for a short time, even rose to be the number one comics publisher in North America. In imitation of *The Dark Knight*, Batman editor Dennis O'Neil started lending an increasingly dark and grim atmosphere to other, more conventional series like *Batman* and *Detective Comics*. Unfortunately, he only managed to imitate the surface, and the grit and realism of the mini-series turned into increased violence and brutality.[2] Miller's transformation of the Batman narrative ends 50 years of the traditional series, or at least is a deep cut in the constancy of this character. However, DC did not feel compelled to follow this step, since the *Dark Knight's* success also increased the sales of other, more conventional Batman stories.

Another attempt to give previous products an aura of being new and trendy was the re-production of the classic Superman, with an alleged new start in a series entitled *Superman #1* (January 1987). In addition to playing with material from their long-established or traditional material, DC also produced new and innovative works like Alan Moore's maxi-series *Watchmen* (Sept. 1986 to Oct. 1987). While Miller's *The Dark Knight* showed some contradictions in authority and power in superheroes but still hinted at hope for Batman's ideals in the ending, Moore goes further and shows that humans have no need for superheroes whatsoever, and that superheroes are even detrimental to society. This type of reflection on the superhero genre, however, could not win readers over who were not previously familiar with superheroes. Nevertheless, the radical theoretical concept of the *Watchmen* should be considered as a milestone in the history of comics.

By the end of 1986, there was renewed media interest in comics. Articles about comics appeared in mainstream magazines like *Times* and *Newsweek*, and *Watchmen* was mentioned on television. A TV report, (hypocritically) shocked over Catwoman's portrayal as a prostitute in *Batman: Year One* drew the obligatory cry for censorship from some Christian conservative groups. DC reacted by printing "Recommended for Mature Readers" on the covers of those comicbooks intended for older readers. This decision adversely affected DC in the long run—its two most successful money earners, Frank Miller and Alan Moore, did not conceal their anger over DC's concession to the advocates of censorship. Moore declared he would never work for DC again, and has abided by this statement until now. After *Batman: Year One*, Miller bade farewell to DC and chose Dark Horse as his new publisher.

THE BLACK-AND-WHITE BOOM

During 1986-87, other publishers benefited from the fact that comics were suddenly "in," especially those producing black-and-white comicbooks. Eclipse came out with *Destroy*, a giant-sized comicbook from Scott McCloud, which was an overt parody of the superhero genre. In *Destroy*, two superheroes leave a trail of destruction in an amusing and facetious portrayal of explicit violence. The cover of *Destroy* even advertised the "truth" saucily: "32 pages of meaningless, overblown violence, mayhem and destuction!" (Plus one Naughty Word)." First Publishers landed a hit with the adaptation of a classic *manga* (Japanese comicbook) *Lone Wolf and Cub*. Kazuo Koike and Goseki Kojima's classic comics were first published in Japan in 1970. Frank Miller liked the originals very much—he wrote introductions and did the covers for the first 12 issues for the North American market which helped increase sales. Other well-known comics artists who did covers are Bill Sinkiewicz (#13-24) and Matt Wagner (#25-36). Mirage Studios, who had published a black-and-white series *Teenage Mutant Ninja Turtles* since 1984, shot up in sales with its four, pizza-eating turtle heroes, and led the expansion of comics into a multi-media experience such as the world had never known before. Three commercially successful films, about 2 million toys and action figures, and an animated TV series came out from this simply drawn comicbook. Kitchen Sink registered surprising success with a cartoon-style illustrated erotic soap opera, *Omaha the Cat Dancer*, that positively portrayed sexuality, and gay, bi- and disabled issues in a discerning manner. Dark Horse came out with Paul Chadwick's intelligent stories about a boulder-like superhero, *Concrete*, who continuously seeks to understand his body and capabilities, his environment and the people who populate it. The eco-sensitive stories trigger reflection on our environment, show big city isolation, and feature an alternative romance in Concrete's impossible love for the scientist assigned to him (see *Figure 31*). Not all of the new black-and-white comicbooks at this time were laudable, but Miller's success and the overall increase in quality and quantity of comicbooks gave a considerable push to the budding collection of fans and assisted in the commercial sales of even some inferior quality books.

MARVEL AND THE KIDS

As the superhero genre was cleverly deconstructed by Miller, Moore, and McCloud, DC and Marvel reacted to the trend differ

Figure 31. *Concrete #4*. Art and script: Paul Chadwick © 1987 Dark Horse Comics, Inc.

ently. A disparity in their outlook regarding the future of comics became noticeable between the two mainstream publishers. Marvel held on to superheroes as the measure of all things, and focused all the more on young readers with each issue. Marvel had neither an intellectual interest for deconstructing the superhero genre nor a concern for current political or sociological events. Instead, Marvel's focus was to cater to the graphic preferences of children surrounded by computer games and television. While DC sought to lure older consumers to read comics, Marvel concentrated on the changing expectations of its proven young buyers (known to the industry as the "Marvel zombies"). In April 1987, a Canadian, Todd McFarlane, illustrated *The Incredible Hulk* and, with his impressive poster-like illustrations, became a big hit for kids who grew up bombarded by colorful and dynamic MTV images. McFarlane's upbeat and lavish illustrations for *The Amazing Spiderman* not much later were an even bigger hit, propelling McFarlane's popularity. In addition to fast-paced graphics, action and violence were also being offered to the same audience of video games and television, without any pretense of putting the violence in a realistic—psychological or sociological—context. Chris Claremont loaded his action-full adventures with more violent scenes, and Marvel readers reciprocated with even more increased sales. Marvel recognized this trend and dispatched a merciless avenger with Steven Grant's *Punisher*, relentlessly cold-blooded in a way comicbook readers had never seen before. The portrayal of violence in comics reached a new level. In 1988, Marvel came out with a series, *Punisher War Journal*, full of guns, explosions, fighting, and deaths. Illustrated by Jim Lee, the pages also boasted of women with perfect "silicone" figures, mimicking the ideal of beauty being peddled in television, films, and video games. By concentrating on the appetites of adolescents immersed in mass media, Marvel advanced pass DC to claim the first place once again in the bestseller list..

DC AND THE ENGLISH CONNECTION

DC did not allow Marvel to completely monopolize the lucrative teen-age entertainment scene without a fight and successfully came out with a new series for *Justice League* in May 1987. However, DC was simultaneously attempting to win over more mature readers. Already in 1980, DC made a contract with Brian Bolland, Dave Gibbons, and John Bolton—all illustrators from England. The average age of comics readers has traditionally been higher in Europe than North America, and this tendency fits the market DC was trying to target. If there was any skepticism that British illustrators and writers would catch the interest of North American readers, Alan Moore put these to rest with *Watchmen* and *Saga of the Swamp Thing*. Moore proved that British authors and illustrators, with their different perspective and sensibility, could lend an impetus to American comics. By late 1980s, Karen Berger was officially given the responsibility to search for more British talent and bring them over to North America. There followed something akin to a "British invasion." This did not immediately resulted in a series of hits, but in the 1990s, this move would pay off for DC.

Alan Moore had gained fame in England for his contributions to *Warrior* and *2000 A.D.*, as well as his maxi-series *Marvelman* and *V for Vendetta*. After taking over from issue 20, Moore began to steer the *Saga of the Swamp Thing* with a concept different from its previous issues. He re-wrote the origin story of the *Swamp Thing* and gave the creature vital psychological dilemmas that the series never had (#21). The biggest change was the way Moore portrayed horror —instead of alarming the readers with superficial sensationalism, the dread now came from sensing that horror lies in the core of man's inner self or psyche. Moore's subtle stories did not bring the *Swamp Thing* near the sales figure of the *X-Men* but this marshy creature made an astonishing comeback with the older comicbook readers. In addition, a relatively unknown Moore began to rise as a superstar in North America and proved that British authors can contribute to the vitality of the North American comics scene.

Berger employed a friend of Alan Moore, Jamie Delano, and gave him Detective Constantine to work with, a character that Alan Moore introduced in the *Saga of the Swamp Thing #37*. In January 1988, DC launched a new horror series, *Hellblazer*. Under the influence of various British authors and illustrators, this series gained a collection of devoted fans. Delano dominated the first 40 issues,[3] where he likened horror to social ills and decay. After issue 40, an Irish, Garth Ennis took over and focussed on Constantine's shattered psyche and inner life, at the same time that "he really piled on the gore and nastiness, which made the comic more successful."[4]

Neil Gaiman, a British journalist, became aware of the possibilities of comics when he interviewed Alan Moore for a newspaper. Gaiman's first comicbook, *Violent Cases*, together with Dave McKean, earned them both some fame in England.[5] Alan Moore

chose Neil Gaiman to take over *Marvelman,* a series Moore started. This series appeared under the title *Miracleman* in North
America and introduced Neil Gaiman to American readers. Next,
Gaiman wrote a three-part comicbook *Black Orchid* (again illustrated by Dave McKean), which showed traces of film noir and
played with the superhero genre in the tradition of *Watchmen.*
With hindsight, Gaiman says: "I thought *Black Orchid* was something important, so I treated it as such, as a result of which it is
lumpy and overly portentous, and it thinks too much."[6]
Nevertheless, Gaiman managed to pull some narrative tricks to
perplex the readers–for example, the superheroine already dies on
page 6–and made his mark as a talented storywriter. January 1989
saw the first issue of another series from Gaiman, *Sandman.* It
started with lean sales, and was almost withdrawn, but the title
slowly gained popularity and even became the third most successful production for DC, next only to Batman and Superman. The
centre of the stories is *Sandman* as the Lord of Dreams. Set in the
dreamworld, any semblance to reality is ignored in this series.
With its unusual perspective, *Sandman* gained the interest of many
readers who have never read or were never interested in comicbooks before, including female readers who traditionally shy away
from comicbooks.

Much like Neil Gaiman, Grant Morrison's introduction to
comics in his native land was through Alan Moore—by reading
Moore's contributions to the British series *Warrior*[7] After
Morrison began to illustrate for comics (*Captain Clyde*), he tried
being a storywriter in both the series *Warrior* and *2000 A.D.* In
1986, Morrison offered DC his ideas for *Animal Man*–a vegetari-
an superhero who fights for the animal world–and *Batman:
Arkham Asylum.* Animal Man started in September 1988. In a
completely post-modernistic situation in issue 26, the hero
becomes conscious of the root of all evil as he meets his own creator, Morrison himself. A drug-induced vision in issues 18-19, has
Animal Man seeing the readers of the comics looking at him. In
Animal Man, there is built-in satire and even reflection on the form
of comics. With characters conscious reflecting on the comicbook
nature of their reality, the naïve suspension of disbelief disappears
the conventions in the medium are deconstructed. Later, Morrison
would go one step further in his contributions to the *Doom Patrol*
(Feb. 1989 to Jan. 1993). In a surrealistic manner, he liberated

superheroes from any vestige of reality—contrary to the way Miller and Moore had intentionally maneuvered realism within the genre into a dead end.

BATMANIA AND SPIDER-MAN #1

While only some older readers were interested at the start of the British influences in American comics, two major events stirred up the comics industry. On May 1989, after an extravagant publicity campaign, Tim Burton's *Batman* film played in moviehouses and became one of the most commercially successful hits at that time. DC's conventional and mainstream series hardly profited from the widespread Batmania that resulted—many fans of the film were not comic buffs and only asked for products matching Burton's production of Batman, with its contemporary irony and detached attitude. DC had expected this reaction, however, and had already engaged Grant Morrison for his concepts in *Arkham Asylum*. If Morrison had taken away realism in the world of superheroes in *Animal Man* (and later in *Doom Patrol*), he offered the opposite in *Arkham*: "... my vision was of it being ultra-real to the point of being painful."[8] What he rendered realistic was not the characters but each psychological realm that each character represented. Dave McKean's abstract illustrations contrasted with the realistic elements of the story, and the resulting product visually impressed many who were already fans of the Batman film. Upon reading the book, however, it turned out the story was not easily accessible to people who were not real Batman fans because the narrative depended a great deal on prior knowledge of the Batman mythos and his cohorts. In addition, the symbolisms of Morrison did not completely harmonize with the visual symbolisms of McKean. Nevertheless, the book sold excellently and inspired many series of Batman "graphic-novels." On the other hand, this trend also started the critique against the overuse of symbolisms in comicbooks, an impression that critics predicted would eventually hurt the targeted readership.

In November 1989, DC began a new Batman-series that took advantage of the title of Miller's revolutionary comicbook, as well as the popularity of the film: *Legends of the Dark Knight*. This was a succession of mini-series where various comic artists had a great deal of freedom to present their individual interpretations, compared to the more conventional Batman-series that kept on coming out monthly. The quality of the short stories varied greatly in the following years depending on the author and artist.[9] It is also interesting to note a sales strategy that DC used for the first time: Issue #1 was published in four different covers with different colours. Because of this trick, many collectors bought all four copies the resulting sales easily cleared the million mark.

Besides the Batman film, a second major event shook up the comics industry. Todd McFarlane's big and impressive illustrations in *Amazing Spider-Man* pushed the stories more and more in the background, and Marvel decided to market *Spiderman* two ways: the *Amazing Spider-Man* series was to retain the narrative or storytelling tradition, while Todd McFarlane was allowed to start his own series, keeping the poster-like illustrations that were so popular with the kids. What other title could give his first issue the atmosphere of a big media event: *Spider-Man #1*. This issue hints at the other, darker side of the American dream in the form of Spiderman's opponent, Lizard. Instead of an alien or an anomaly to the human race, Lizard is portrayed as rising from America's ghettos set to a rhythm that is uncontrollable yet hypnotizing. In black-and-white morality, Lizard is deemed unequivocally evil in the tradition of a series like *The Punisher*. McFarlane explained the superfluous role of an author in the introduction to this issue: "I don't profess to be a writer, but I do think I can tell a story. What this means is that most of the issues will rely heavily on the artistic side." For his honesty, McFarlane won the sympathy of the kids.[10] *Spider-Man #1* was illustrated with McFarlane's typical flashy illustrations, teeming with prolonged and full-page fight scenes. The issue was done in various covers with different colors, some copies were sealed in plastic bags while some were not. All of these lent an air of speculation and investment to *Spider-Man #1*. When the issue appeared, McFarlane fans brushed shoulders with curious speculators in comics shops, andd the sales of this issue catapulted to a dimension unthinkable before: 3 million copies were sold.

In the 1990s, there was a type of speculation in comicbooks in a way the industry never had before. The young, amateur speculators were interested less and less in the contents of a comicbook; their main interest was only in being able to profit from selling an issue some years after buying it. *Spider-Man #1*, for example, in sealed and mint condition, jumped in value shortly after it came out and fueled the speculation scene.[11] Shops began to keep a big part of the new issues in their back rooms to artificially keep an impression of short supplies. Marvel and DC took full advantage of this buying frenzy and started to publish one product with minor variances that urged a collector to buy multiple versions of one issue. But since the narrative contents of the comicbooks were slowly but surely relegated to the background, the new speculators did not seek "good" products, but mostly only those cited in television or magazines, or those with extravagant or new-fashioned covers.

IN THE SHADOW OF THE SPECULATION BOOM

Television reported the start of a new Batman or new Spider-Man series, but there was no news about lesser-known titles from small-press and alternative publishers. While, in general, the sales figures of the comics industry rose, the smaller publishers who could not publicize their wares and characters in film or television suffered from the attention focused only on mainstream comics. Eclipse and First Comics declared bankruptcy, and Tundra went out of business a few years later. However, Kitchen Sink and Fantagraphics proved that focusing on alternative titles for a more mature audience was a viable choice for a comics publisher in the late 1980s/early 1990s.

In addition to the Hernandez brothers, Fantagraphics succeeded in getting contracts from two more excellent comic artists: Peter Bagge and Dan Clowes. Dan Clowes came out with his first series, *Lloyd Llewellyn*[12] in 1986, and then with the exciting series *Eightball* in October 1989, where he showed his talents both in the visual and narrative domain (*see Figure 32*). Between 1986 to 1987, *Lloyd Llwellyn* came out in six issues, and in 1988, Fantagraphics followed with a "one-shot" issue. *Lloyd Llwellyn* showed influences of the 1950s visual style and Clowes' love for kitsch from this era, as well as some elements that will be typical for Clowes later on: strange characters, absurd handling of situations, and predicaments that are not totally resolved or explained. For this series, the parody of the 1950s middle class lifestyle seemed to have been done more with a sense of fun rather than for any relevance to the present times. In *Eightball*, the stories took on more complexity, and the parodies covered more topics (example, in *Pussy*). In *Like a Velvet Glove Cast in Iron*, Clowes developed a dreamlike, distanced, and more abstract way of dealing with everyday subject; but exactly in its surrealistic and abstract

Figure 32. *Eightball* #2. Art and script: Dan Clowes © 1990 Fantagraphics.

moments, Clowes offered a discerning view and social commentary on American life. *Ghostworld*, about two girls on the verge of changing or breaking up their friendship as they grow up, is Clowes' least surrealistic work. Here, Clowes goes in different direction than in earlier works, but we still see a comment on social life. As a whole, Clowes ventures into the abyss of modern America's soul, showing direct and piercing pieces of everyday life with a detachment reminiscent of David Lynch's films. Like in Lynch's movies, not all secrets are solved, and not all questions answered. This uncertainty is highlighted by Clowes' artwork which sometimes takes on a haunting quality.

From 1985 to 1989, Peter Bagge's *Neat Stuff* stirred reflection on family values during the Reagan and Bush era by showing the everyday life of the Bradley family through an uncanny selection of seemingly unimportant topics and details. By showing a more or less regular family, a bit messed up but not totally dysfunctional, Bagge provided glimpses into the aspects of American life not usually shown in comics or television then. In the Fall of 1990, Bagge came out with *Hate*. This series focused on a Bradley family member, Buddy, who moved to Seattle and survived the assumed apathy of the Grunge generation through his abundant supply of cynicism (see *Figure 33*). Bagge's biting commentary on modern life, combined with humourous and highly entertaining scenes, make *Hate* one of the bestsellers for Fantagraphics. While at the beginning of the *Hate* series, the humour was based on situations that came from the clash of very different characters, in the later issues, the focus shifted to the development of one or two established characters, in particular Buddy and his girlfriend, Lisa. Although there is character and situational development from issue to issue, Bagge made sure each *Hate* issue may still be read alone without any loss of its entertaining value. In Summer 1998, Bagge finished the *Hate* series with issue 30. Together with Robert Crumb, the Hernandez brothers, Dan Clowes, and Chester Brown, Peter Bagge is without a doubt one of the greatest cartoonist of the past two decades.

By the 1990s, the roles were clearly divided among comics publishers: the alternative publishers targeted the readers who are in their twenties or older and, with its superhero focus, Marvel concentrated on teenagers and younger readers. DC found itself in-between and started losing its younger readers to Marvel, while having sporadic success with their titles "Recommended for

Figure 33. *Hate #12*. Art and script: Peter Bagge © 1993 The creator.

Mature Readers." Neil Gaiman's *Sandman*, at least, became a big commercial success. But in 1992, DC's overall market share of comics sales dipped under 20%.

After leaving DC and Marvel, Frank Miller moved between the alternative and mainstream scenes like Neil Gaiman. After having provoked a lot of ideologically motivated critique in *Dark Knight*, it is clear that his Dark Horse series, *Give Me Liberty* (1990-91, illustrated by Dave Gibbons), made an effort to deliver a politically correct adventure. However, the ideological positions were too obvious in their two-dimensionality: Maria Washington (poor, female, black) overcomes many obstacles that came with her black origin, to fight for justice and democracy. In the process of the story, Martha loses her mannish traits and after each obstacle, becomes a personification of the American dream. Miller succeeded only in a handful instances to lighten up the ideologies with humour.

After the extremely brutal, and at the same time not so original, beginning of the three-part series, *Hard Boiled* in 1990[13], Miller started a new series called *Sin City*.[14] Frank Miller had previously attempted to use hard-boiled storytelling influences within the superhero-genre, but only in *Sin City* did he really manage to transpose brutish elements in film and literature into the medium of comics. *Sin City* is Miller's first black-and-white comicbook. It is also the series where he honed his now distinct and impressive black-and-white graphic style that meld seamlessly with his narratives. *Sin City* boasts of very tough heroes, unusually cruel and cunning villains, as well as *femme fatales* of every kind, while institutions like the government, police force, even the church, are shown to be rife with corruption. Of all black-and-white series in the late 1990s, *Sin City* became the most successful series (of the black-and-white series published regularly, the most successful is *Bone*.)

Miller plays with the aspects of gangster literature much like he played previously with the superhero genre. His heroes, not unlike his superheroes, are rather odd but always able to overcome physical and mental tests through their individual abilities and audacity. Miller's characters, however, remain stylized.[15] Despite these parallels to his early works, Miller developed in two areas:

- He managed to smoothly blend his graphic style and narratives like never before, and
- He found access to the clandestine world of the big city underground that his Batman and Daredevil approached

but could not live in within the superhero genre. *Sin City* begins where *Dark Knight* ends, in direct confrontation of authority.

THE HIGH POINT OF SPECULATION

In almost all series, Marvel extended the use of the "West Coast Style" popularized by Todd McFarlane and Jim Lee. This new style was based on the techniques used for fight scenes and action sequences in earlier, well-known Marvel series, without the old irony and playfulness. Instead, it showed a new standard in the glorification of violence. Subtle reflections of the genre, like Ann Noccnti formulated in *Daredevil #254-291*, were not in demand. In demand were muscles which would shame the most serious bodybuilder, and breasts that even the *Baywatch*-babes would envy. Taking full advantage of the speculators who were led to think that comics with Issue #1 marked on the covers would be good investments, Marvel followed the manipulated success of McFarlane's *Spider-Man #1* with Jim Lee and Chris Claremont's *X-Men #1*. As if following a proven formula, this issue came out in different covers and was toted as a new series to run parallel to the established *X-Men* series. By this time, the list of Marvel Hits was pre-programmed.

The buying frenzy was hyped up even more by magazines like *Wizard* which contained nothing but price lists, increase in value of specific issues, blatant investment suggestions. *Wizard* told their very young readers exactly what they wanted to hear: the new Marvel Comics must be bought as fast as possible, for within a short time these would be sold out but could be re-sold with an impossibly high profit. However, if one really paid attention to how many numbers of copies were printed for *X-Men #1*, one knew at once that this issue will never be rare or in demand. The comics shops played along with the speculation game, keeping boxes of copies in their backrooms. All those involved in the ruse profited for a time. Perceived as investments, the time when comics were part of a subculture seemed to be over.

By the early 1990s, Marvel celebrated its biggest and most successful artists—the creators of the West Coast style, all from South California: Todd MacFarlane, Jim Lee, Rob Liefeld, Marc Silvestri, and Erik Larsen. Full of confidence from their success, these creators arranged a meeting with then Marvel president, Terry Stewart, to fight for creator rights, for more appreciation and recognition, and for more better remuneration. While enjoying its success, however, Stewart believed that it was the Marvel characters and tradition that were drawing the readers, and therefore, artists and writers were replaceable. He did not respond to the demands sufficiently and was penalized for his presumption: the five Californians walked out of Marvel and founded the Image Studios (together with Jim Valentino who also worked for Marvel).

True to McFarlane's belief expressed in *Spider-Man #1* that writers are superfluous, Image did not hire writers. They trusted in the imposing illustration style for which they became known. Even the medley of characters in superhero teams reflected the characters in the titles each artist had worked on in Marvel, only the names and some minor details were changed. MacFarlane alone managed to come out with a comic that was not merely a copy of Spider-Man. *Spawn* was distinct, although overall not a totally new concept: a tormented superhero, a grim atmosphere, a contract with the devil, an unfulfilled love, an impressive rival opponent. Nevertheless, Todd McFarlane's *Spawn* was a big hit, especially among the young comic fans: *Spawn #1* sold 1.7 million copies in May 1992. McFarlane may not be the best storywriter, as he himself admits in an interview with Gary Groth in *The Comics Journal #152*. But his sense of rhythm for moments of suspense and revelations are astounding, surpassed only by his impressive illustrations made up of vivid colours, numerous full-page scenes, and excellent use of layered frames and overlapping graphics. The lack of substance in the stories did not matter as long as MacFarlane did not tackle topics that were too complex for his style. Issue #5, for example, only handles the topic of child abuse in an unacceptable superficial level, reminiscent of an early afternoon television talk show. But whatever aspect of intelligent criticism was thrown at *Spawn* did not affect its fans. In fact, since the heroes and villains in *Spawn* were extremely appropriate to market as action figures and other toys, the comics crossed over to other products. McFarlane proved to have a good business sense and founded his own very successful toy line, *McFarlane Toys*. In addition, the comics was turned into two movies, one had live actors and the other was animated.

While the first issues of *Spawn* were ovedrall credible, the other first issues of Image founders were nothing but overblown fighting orgies without rhyme or reason. The least proficient were the totally uninspired and amateurish works by Liefeld. Nevertheless, issues still sold simply because these were part of the Image line and marketing strategy. The big "i" Image Trademark on the covers stood for "in", for California, for dynamism, for a new generation of younger people who will not bow down to the system (i.e., Marvel). At the beginning, the sales of all Image titles were in the million-dollar area,[16] and since there were no producers to cut into their profits, the Image founders became the richest comics artists at that time. Image was suddenly close behind Marvel and DC as a third powerful player in the industry. Still, no real writers were hired for Image. *Spawn* was again the exception where well-known writers like Alan Moore (issue 8), Neil Gaiman (issue 9), and Dave Sim (issue 10) made guest appearances.

As Image celebrated sensational success, Marvel initially did not seem to suffer from losing its West Coast cartoonists. On the contrary, Marvel even expanded. Taking full advantage of the speculation boom, it published more and more series that, by the end of 1993, Marvel was publishing 150 issues per month. The multiple covers were done in holograms, glow-in-the-dark, multiple colours, and so on until all marketing tricks were used up. DC, meanwhile, lost its second place to Image in 1992, and its market share dropped to under 20%. Nonetheless, DC remained convinced that knowledgeable, older readers were the way to the future. Against the mainstream market flow, they held on to this conviction and made it visible with the Vertigo line which more or less took over the comics marked with "Recommended for Mature Readers."[17] Some exceptions were *Animal Man* and *Doom Patrol* which were superhero material but published under the Vertigo line.

To stay alive in the mainstream market, DC also felt compelled to come up with a "media event" in order to profit from the speculation market. The decision was the ultimate strategem: in issue 75 of the new Superman series, the oldest and best-known superhero died after a magnificent Image-style grand fight. As expected, the issue with Superman's death took on an aura of a cultural event which attracted a lot of media attention. Even people who have never bought a comicbook before, reached for the collector's edition, platinum edition, news-stand copy, or the direct sales copy, and naturally, some simultaneously bought one of each. Six million copies were sold as people speculated on the increase of value and investment returns for an issue that was made to be and became a cultural event. It did not matter that Superman came back to life a few issues later. What did matter to the speculators was that the six million copies that were sold did not increase in price at all the next year, or any year after that. This was not the first time that comicbooks hailed as profitable investments did not become more valuable, but this time, too many people were duped and comics publishers simply went over the top in exploiting their market.

CRISIS AND NOSTALGIA

In 1993, Image comics sales figures, though still very good, had just started to slide past its peak. Marvel began to withdraw some of its 150 monthly titles. The speculation fever had been abused heedlessly and the fans were catching on.[18] Neither *Legends of the Dark Knight #1* nor *Spider-Man #1* nor *X-Men #1* nor *Superman #75* or any other issue #1 from Image increased in value. What were encouraged in price guides hardly interested anyone anymore, especially those issues that were lobbed to be good investments. Increasingly, first issues found themselves marked down or in rummage sales because the shops had to get rid of them somehow. Just as the speculation boom drove away older comic fans who did not like the cynical commercial approach to comics, the younger fans now started turning away. The manipulated speculation market had not yet totally burst by 1993, but the symptoms for its collapse increased.

Amidst the comic covers full of bulging muscles, older fans started longing for the time when comics still had stories. The stories of 30 years ago may not have been too complex, but there was nevertheless the effort to have a story. Looking around in a comic shop in the early 1990s, it was clear that the comics industry had molded itself to the consumer culture of the young. The cool Westcoast style magazines were only a succession of fight scenes. The contents of the issues aimed no further than to look like investments and to participate in the competition for consumer dollars. By the end of the speculation boom, older comic fans longed for more innocent superheroes without the brutality that was becoming increasingly popular among the younger readers. In addition, older fans wanted more stories. They wanted a return to a time when illustrations of fight scenes were used as parts of a narrative. However, this desire for comics from a more "innocent time" could only lead to a dead-end: the naïve superhero narrative could never be a new direction for comicbooks. Superhero comics had always propagated the view that fighting and winning over the enemy is a symbol or a realization of the American dream. The situation in 1993 was only an ensuing continuation, albeit a bit extreme, of the idea that perpetual victory is good. The origins of this belief may be found in the same capitalistic society that gave birth to the idea of the powerful superheroes. The comics industry had become the victim of an ideology which gave birth to it, which it represented, and from which it had never detached itself. With this as a background, one can construe the trend of nostalgia induced by older readers in 1993 as something like "selective remembering," enshrining a past that was actually never totally "innocent." Despite this ideological objection, this sense of nostalgia produced some of the more interesting comics of the early 1990s.

Once again, it was Alan Moore who recognized the trend. In 1993, he came out with the first comicbook of the nostalgic movement titled *1963*[19] published by none other than Image Comics who previously flooded the market with the dullest orgies of violence and brutality. In *Watchmen*, Moore had actually intended to retire superheroes, but he observed in the following years that the effect of *Watchmen* and *Dark Knight* turned into another direction: the prevalence of superheroes could be confined within limits but they cannot be totally removed or destroyed. Instead, their fight scenes had only became more brutal and the atmosphere (if the artist even tried to create an atmosphere) became more and more sinister.[20] In *1963*, Moore reacted by recreating the seemingly harmless naivete of the early days. Having despaired of the grim and downbeat superhero comics that *Watchmen* and *Dark Knight* spawned, Moore took to the opposite by pretending it was 1963, down to the fake ads and editorial pages, and produced a pastiche of early Marvel comics in all their enjoyable simplicity. Excellent artists such as Dave Gibbons and Steve Bissette, John Totleben and Rick Veitch imitated the style of Jack Kirby and Steve Ditko. The "affectionate parody" functioned quite well in all six issues of the series, with each issue focusing on different charac-

ters, some with intended superficial similarity to Marvel characters.

In the same year, James Robinson and Paul Smith threw a
glance at the post-war era in DC's four-issue mini-series *Golden
Age*. The superheroes, stripped of all missions by the end of the
war, grappled with internal conflict within America. A year later,
Marvel followed suit with the four-part series *Marvels*, where the
genesis of the Marvel universe is re-lived through the eyes of a
photo-journalist, Phil Sheldon:

> Like his ordinary fellow-men, Phil has come to terms with the
> appearance of superbeings and the effects they have on day-
> to-day life. Through him, his family, colleagues and strangers,
> we see mankind's fear, insecurity, helplessness and prejudice
> laid bare by these awesome Marvels whose conflicts wreak
> millions of dollars of property damage with apparent disdain
> for the misery heaped upon affected innocents.
>
> (Marvels) is an adult comic in the true meaning of the word,
> with neither an ounce of exposed flesh nor exposed innards
> in sight.[21]

In *Marvels*, Kurt Busiek presents a low-key and understated
narration of a well-researched story,[22] wonderfully complemented
by Alex Ross's excellently painted artwork. The most conservative
story of the nostalgic wave came from Mark Waid with his four-
part series *Kingdom Come* published by DC, and illustrated
(painted) by Alex Ross. Waid's view of the future was a dismal DC
Universe where traditional heroes like Superman and Batman have
retired (and were not accessible to the public anymore). The world
was overrun by a new generation of superheroes resembling the
West-Coast style heroes of Image and Marvel. When the young
breed of heroes caused a nuclear catastrophe, Superman comes
back to lead the older superheroes to discipline the new brood and
to control chaos through the old order. The clamor for father figures was intensified by Ross' graphics which depicted the old
heroes in a style reminiscent of national socialistic propaganda
material—the hero-figures were often lit from below and shown
from a worm's eye view. *Kingdom Come* sold 200,000 copies at a
time of crisis for other comic sales.

The year 1993 marked a turning point in the development of
the direct market sales, as well as in the history of modern

American comics. In the following three years, the concept especially represented by Marvel and Image—to target a specific group of readers and to exploit them using all kinds of trick—collapsed. Marvel started withdrawing one series after another, and had to let go of half of its employees by 1996. From 1994 to 1995, the sales and turnover in the comics industry were reduced by a third, and in 1996, it lost half of its customers from the previous year. Many kids noticed that they had been had and turned away in big numbers from the comics scene. From the 10,000 comic shops of 1993, only 4,000 remained three years later.

ALTERNATIVES TO SUPERHERO COMICS

> When I was about seven, literally, I was given these huge boxes of Marvel and DC comics and I read them. I came to the conclusion that basically, fight scenes in comics work if either you hit the bad guy a lot and then you win, or you hit the bad guy a lot and he wins, but next issue you come back and you hit him a lot and you win. And that seemed to lack suspense.
>
> Neil Gaiman
> *Comics Journal #169*, p. 58

> Books which are self-published (at least initially), such as Bone...are among the books which are setting the trends which are bringing in new readers...(A)nd in a couple of years, we just might even be dating girls.
>
> Paul Tobin
> *Comics Journal #188*, p. 118

Fortunately for the American comics, there were activities in the industry of the 1990s other than the muscle-bound heroes and the increasingly insipid fight scenes that dominated the market. In the late 1980s and early 1990s, there were some notable Canadian cartoonists who came into the North American comics scene. Joe Matt produced noteworthy contributions to the underground anthology *Snarf* (Kitchen Sink, 1987-1990) before he successfully started his own series, *Peep Show* (Drawn and Quarterly) in 1992. In *Peep Show #4*, Matt portrays himself in his everyday life beset

Figure 34. *Peepshow* #1. Art and script: Joe Matt © 1993 The creator.

with sexual obsessions and a lack of motivation/inspiration to work. The author's courage shows in his portrayal of himself in a not-so-positive light, without playing on the readers' sympathy (see *Figure 34*).

Another Canadian, Seth, took over the illustration of the series

Figure 35. *Palookaville #4*. Art and script: Seth © 1993 The creator.

Mister X (Vortex, 1984-88, Seth since 1985) from the Hernandez brothers. In 1991, he started his own series, *Palookaville*, for Drawn and Quarterly. Seth's comics show a quiet, introspective narrative-style with elegant illustrations similar to the cartoons in the *New Yorker* of the 1930s and 1940s. Seth reflects on this influence in *It's a Good Life if You Don't Weaken* (*Palookaville #4-9*).

In *Figure 35*, where Seth is talking to Chester Brown, the author indulges in meta-text as he discusses the techniques and styles of illustrations he admires, at the same time that his own illustrations show influences of *The New Yorker* style he was praising.

The most expressive cartoonist from Canada, Chester Brown tackles difficult stories with simple yet very perceptive choice of details and in exceptional ordering of frames. His *Yummy Fur* (Vortex 1986-1991, Drawn and Quarterly 1991-1994) is littered with autobiographical elements. Especially in the later issues of this series, Brown manages to lend a magical dimension, simultaneously humourous and melancholy, to his childhood, the central themes being his perception of adults and repression of sexual feelings. Brown is a master in visually rendering feelings of uncertainty, fear, lust, and shame. He uses a wide assortment of narrative tricks available in the medium, without letting these tricks interfere with his stories: the way he lays out the pictures on a page, his choice of pictures, the viewing angles and perspectives of each picture, textless pictures, repetitive pictures, slight variations in gestures and expressions (see *Figure 36*)—all narrative tricks fully serve the atmosphere and clarity of the stories. The visual impact of Brown's comics is a phenomenon of modern comics. His new series, *Underwater* (Drawn and Quarterly since 1990) leads the reader through a world experienced through the eyes and ears of new-born twins, with the dialogue starting out as gibberish and slowly becoming familiar as the twins begin to understand a word here and there. The interesting concept fails to be sustained, however, since the first issues prove to be rather inaccessible to readers who are thrown into the orientation of newborns, an experience not many readers crave. Time will tell if this series will, in the long run, reach the high degree of its predecessor, *Yummy Fur*.

Juliet Doucet's *Dirty Plotte* (since 1990) is another distinctive comicbook from Drawn and Quarterly, and Juliet Doucet another artist that extends the limits of the medium, especially regarding themes and characters. Doucet has a lovely and unique graphic style, unbridled imagination, and complete lack of inhibition—menstruation, castration, and cutting one's self with a razor are just some of the topics she has set to comics with unfeigned emotions. Debbie Drechsler's *Daddy's Girl* and *Nowhere* are also produced by Drawn and Quarterly (*see Figure 37*). *Daddy's Girl* is a harrowing series of vignettes about growing up with sexual abuse

Figure 36. *Yummy Fur* #29. Art and script: Chester Brown © 1992 The creator.

told with unflinching honesty; while *Nowhere* is a chronicle of childhood executed in a striking two-colour style. Drechsler's illustrations are deceptive in their simple lines, but the overall effect is

Figure 37. *Nowhere* postcard. Art: Debbie Drechsler © 1997 The creator.

startling in the way they direct responses to her works. Securing Adrian Tomine from the self-publishing scene was one of the latest coup for Drawn and Quarterly. With *Optic Nerve* and *Sleepwalk*, Tomine sets about spinning dry but affecting tales of ordinary life, sleekly rendered in a Clowesian style (*see Figure 38*). Tomine was born in 1974, was reading *Love and Rockets* by the time he was

Figure 38. Cover of *Optic Nerve #4*. Art and script: Adrian Tomine © 1997 Drawn and Quarterly.

Figure 39. A page from *Optic Nerve #3*. Art and script: Adrian Tomine © 1996 Drawn and Quarterly

13, and started *Optic Nerve* the summer between his sophomore and junior year.[23] Quite remarkable for a very young man, he provides perceptive vignettes of relationships and tantalising glimpses into lives, told with a unique detachment (*see Figure 39*). With an exceptional roster of talents, Drawn and Quarterly proved that money can be made with high-quality comics. Co-publisher Chris Oliveros proudly states in the summer of 1998: "We've never had a finer time financially in our existence these last eight years."[24]

In addition to Peter Bagge, Dan Clowes, and the Hernandez brothers, Fantagraphics succeeded in adding more first-class comic artists to its list. Some examples are: Bob Fingerman (*Minimum Wage*, since 1995), Chris Ware (*Acme Novelty Liberty*, since 1993), and Roberta Gregory (*Naughty Bits* and *Artistic Licentiousness*). Chris Ware's Acme Novelty Library (*see Figure 40*) is "an astounding publication, presenting comics that engage the intellect, and managing from the first issue to do so in a accessible manner, thus succeeding where *Raw* failed."[25] Ware's artistry is impressive: his illustrations are clear and simple but convey a wide range of emotions, his colors are striking, and he has a total concept for each book, complete with fake ads and cut-out paper toys reminiscent of another era (see *Figure 41*).

Pioneering cartoonist Roberta Gregory takes on pornography, shopping, yuppies, dating, and office life with a central character that is "permanently PMS'd and PO'd embodiment of the female id".[26] Gregory sex comic about human-looking, normal people with imperfect bodies and are as fucked-up as the rest of us; *Naughty Bits* is a scathing and hilarious dissection of the relations and frustrations of the thirty-something woman in the 1990s (*see Figure 42*). Gregory gives us a cast of human-looking, normal people with imperfect bodies, irritating manners and yearnings and failures that are familiar to us. The aggressive character of Bitchy Bitch often engenders accusations of being man-hating but this assertion is absurd. Gregory's sarcasm spares no one, and female characters are portrayed no less flattering than their male counterparts.

Beyond the list of Fantagraphics and Drawn and Quarterly, there were other cartoonists contributing considerably to the changing face of the comics industry. Another dynamic female cartoonist is Donna Barr with her *Desert Peach* (published by MU Press/Aeon). The series centres on Pfirsich Rommel, the gay,

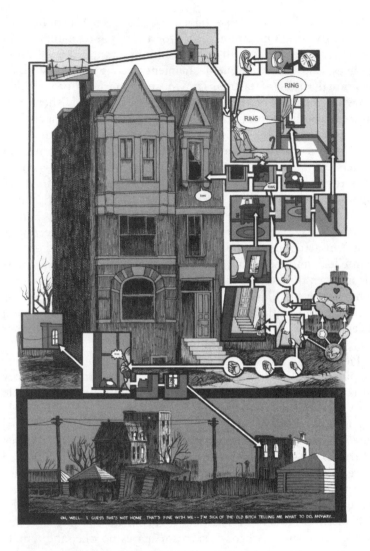

Figure 40. A page from *Acme Novelty Library #1, vol. 5*. Art and
script: Chris Ware © 1993 Fantagraphics Books.

younger brother of WWII Field Marshal Rommel (*see Figure 43*).
Pfirsich Rommel commands a battalion of diverse and trouble-
some characters who make up the cast of a politically astute and
gleefully politically incorrect series. Barr's work is characterised by

Figure 41. An advertising page reminiscent of another era; from *Acme Novelty Library* #1, vol. 5. Art and script: Chris Ware © 1993 Fantagraphics Books.

delight in shaking the reader's complacency and splendid indifference to "what the neighbours will think."[27] Meanwhile, Alison Bechdel's *Dykes to Watch Out For* (Firebrand books) provides graphic commentary on the quirks, crises, and joys of contempo

Figure 42. *Naughty Bits* #26. Art and script: Roberta Gregory ©
1998 The creator. Her web page is www.robertagregory.com

rary lesbian life. Through the anger and anxieties of her characters,
Bechdel dispatches quick-witted and incisive social commentary in
a light-hearted approach, but the difficulties and politics of gay life
are never far from the surface. Since 1994, Slave Labor has published an anthology, *Action Girl*, with a very diversified roster of

Figure 43. *The Desert Peach* #16. Art and script: Donna Barr ©
1991 The creator.

cartoonists, boasting of notable contributions from Sarah Dyer,
Jessica Abel, Ariel Bordeaux, Patty Leidy, Chris Tobey, and
Carolyn Ridsdale (*see Figure 44*). This is a women's only series
which, due to the differences in style, and length and depth of narratives from various contributors, sometimes suffer from overall

Figure 44. Cover of *Action Girl Comics #1*. Created and edited by Sarah Dyer © 1994 Sarah Dyer

inconsistency where insipid contributions sometimes jump out. In general, though, the issues are energetic and sufficiently diverse to be enjoyable.

Kitchen Sink, meanwhile, remained active above all in the 1990s through the publication of Alan Moore's *From Hell* (illustrated by Eddie Campbell). They took over the series starting with issue #4 after Tundra went out of business in 1994; the last issue was #10 in 1996. *From Hell* is a very well-researched story about Jack the Ripper's murders in the late 1880s where Moore delves into the descent of human soul without moralizing. His detached and analytical narrative style suits the recounting of the gruesome murders in this series. However, the same style did not quite work when employed in *Lost Girls* (Kitchen Sink, since 1995, artwork by Melinda Gebbie). Instead, this attempt to produce intelligent comics about sex gave the impression of being too insensible and excessively stylized. Since 1995, Kitchen Sink has also been publishing Charles Burn's fascinating and disquieting series, *Black Hole* about a disturbing sexually transmitted virus that only affects teenagers. Burn's well-balanced graphics and storytelling that he had only used in short stories until then were very apt to a longer narrative about the horror of high-school social interaction.

Even beyond the alternative publishers that were increasingly becoming established, there were more master works being published. David Mazucchelli, who had worked together with Frank Miller in *Daredevil* and *Batman*, turned away from the mainstream and, with a complete change in style, managed to self-publish an ambitious project, an annual titled *Rubber Blanket*. A small publisher, Adhesive, published an existentialist hero in Shannon Wheeler's *Too Much Coffee Man*[28]. The hero is "a paunchy guy with a massive coffee-cup helmet on his head and that permanently caffeinated bug-eyed look."[29] His relatively dull life is punctuated with some superhero-style fighting which are travesties of the "real" ones, and commenting on the meaninglessness of such fights. Paradox Press, a New York-based publisher and a subsidiary of Time-Warner Company, came out in 1995 with Howard Cruse's *Stuck Rubber Baby*, a graphic novel with 210 pages about a teenager's gradual awareness of his homosexuality set against the emergence of the gay movement and fight for racial equality. *Stuck Rubber Baby* achieves a fine balance between tackling weighty themes, the use of convincing art, and providing good entertainment. Another self-published success is David Lapham's *Stray Bullets*. Each issue in the series focuses on a different set of characters with their own stories. Nevertheless, the series still manages to weave a complex story between the issues. Lapham provides subtle variances in forms of violence while developing his characters involved in strange situations like the dysfunctional childhood of Ginny, the violent urges in Joey who was mentally handicapped, and the "troubled *ménage a trois* on the run from the Mob."[30]

THE MARKET LEADER IN THE 1990S

What about the market leaders? Image had come to realize that it is unwise to simply depend on spectacular but shallow action and the illusory speculative value of comics. The sales figure for Image titles, which had soared from nothing to the second most commercially successful comic publisher, had fallen from 700,000 in 1992 to 200,000 in 1994. Image knew it must raise the standard of its publications so as not to disappear just as quickly as it appeared on the comics scene. Alan Moore's *1963* was followed in the same year with Sam Kieth's *The Maxx* (since 1993, dialogue by

Figure 45. *The Maxx #1*. Art and script: Sam Kieth © 1993 The creator.

Bill Messner-Loeb), a complex comics which places the schizo-phrenic implications of the superhero-genre quite effectively in relation to modern big cities realities (*see Figure 45*). The stories are intriguing, constantly shifting from a big urban American city to "The Outback" while delving into the thoughts, motivations, and feelings of the Maxx. *The Maxx* is a very good comicbook, not only in the complexity of its narratives but also in its illustra-tions, layout, and dark, vivid colors that resonate with emotion and beautifully set convincing atmospheres.

In 1995, Image managed a major coup when it took over the publication of Jeff Smith's fantasy series, *Bone* (originally from Cartoon Books since 1992).[31] Smith's ability to render his charac-ters and scenery in simple, clean lines is reminiscent of big names in cartoon illustration like Walt Kelly (*Pogo*) and Bill Watterson (*Calvin and Hobbes*). *Bone* is a charming story about three cousins who were run out of their town and find themselves living near a forested village with strange, mostly likeable characters. The sto-ries are bustling with elements familiar to experienced fantasy fans which are nevertheless revitalized by a delightful humour brought about by the interaction of cartoon figures and human creatures. Underlying moments like the great cow race and the attempts of Kingdok and the Lord of the Locusts to get Phoney Bone, is the love story between the cartoon figure, Bone and the mortal princess, Thorn—an amusing love story with timid emotions that keeps readers glued to their comicbooks (*see Figure 46*).[32]

In 1995, Image also came out with Kurt Busiek's *Astro City* (illustrated by Brent E. Anderson) which delighted many old school superhero fans with its deliberate, well-planned concept. Busiek expounds on his idea of a superhero in an interview in the *Comics Journal # 188*:

> "The superhero becomes a symbol, a simple character con-cept into which, as Scott McCloud would say, we project our own identity."[33]

> "The superhero genre has historically been limited to the adven-ture thrillers, actions stories that can be sold easily to boys in their teen years or younger. But that's a self-imposed, market-driven limitation, not any sort of creative limitation of the genre, and I wanted to explore the rest of the genre, celebrating the power it has to make ideas come to life and seeing what it can do."[34]

Figure 46. *Bone Vol. One: Out from Boneville*. Art and script: Jeff
Smith © 1996 The creator.

In *Astro City*, readers can identify not only with the superheroes, but more so with the ordinary citizens whose perspectives
provide the insight into the superheroes. Busiek takes the whole
superhero genre as a tapestry of the familiar and the unknown. He

Figure 47. *Astro City: Life in the Big City*. Art and script: Kurt Busiek. Astro City™ © 1999 Juke Box Productions. All rights reserved.

presents well-known markers: secret identity, sidekicks, a corporate hero, and an ever-growing clash of values in modern era, but we get to know these though the varying viewpoints of ordinary citizens like us. One example which won an industry award: the portrayal of human conflict arising from a city full of superheroes is very well depicted in issue #4 where Busiek explores the identity crisis of a woman belonging to an immigrant family. When her office suddenly turns into a battlefield for the superbeings, this initiates an evaluation in the woman about the big city, the values in her "old" world, and where her she wants to take her future (*see Figure 47*). Starting 1996, a new publisher founded by Jim Lee, Homage, released a second series of *Astro City* with the same high level of art and entertainment as the previous one.

Another feather to Image's cap was the start of the series *Soulwind* by C. Scott Morse in 1997. Issues 1-4 were stories about a young boy transported to a far-away planet he was supposed to save. There are traces of aspects from McCloud's *Zot,* Jeff Smith's *Bone* and the *Star Wars* films all mixed towards a fantastic, varied and expressive adventure. Morse's blend of art styles is refreshing: Japanese drybrush art opens the book, then he shifts to a more western style for the main story. He narrates the stories well with shifts in subject matters, some vagueness in characters, and unexpected turns of events that keep readers wanting more.

In 1994, as the superhero-dominated comics market was coming apart, another publisher had been leaning towards the alternative scene—Dark Horse became the fourth most successful comics publisher in terms of sales behind Marvel, DC and Image. One of their smartest moves was taking over Mike Allred's *Madman* which until then was published by Tundra.[35] Although Allred had previously produced *Madman* for another publisher, it was not until *Madman Comics* (published by Dark Horse Comics) that he wielded the graphic style that would include him within the group of acclaimed comic illustrators. Unlike Frank Miller and Alan Moore who deconstructed the superhero-genre through realism in the hero's situations and problems, Allred revealed the shortcomings of the genre by using an imperfect hero who was continuously confronted with the absurdities of pop culture and who dealt with reality only on an abstract level (*see Figure 48 and 49*). *Madman* was infused with the spirit of 1950s science-fiction films, with bespectacled scientists and robots and eccentric inventors that heightened the popularity and visual appeal of the comics. Allred reflected on the state of superhero comics by making his everything else but heroic Madman well-aware of his insufficiencies. Despite his short-comings, Madman is able to triumph over his surreal and strange environs because he never tries to drive the absurdities away from his world but accepts it as part of his identity and existence. Any nostalgia in Madman is dissimilar in ideology from the nostalgic sentiments in *Kingdom Come* which situate the latter within mainstream superheroics. In *Madman Comics*, Allred spiced the pleasure in familiar superhero elements with a contemporary and fitting irony that illustrates, the handling of superheroes rests neither in insipid, hackneyed, banal brutality nor in disheartening nostalgia.

In the same year, Dark Horse produced Mike Mignola's first *Hellboy* mini series (*Seed of Destruction*, 1994) where a demon originally summoned by the Nazis comes back years later to deal with fantastic phenomena as a gruff private detective. Like in the following *Hellboy* series, Mignola's strong visual expressions are especially convincing, certainly more appealing than the lack of logic in some stories or the bizarre resolutions presented to some problems—"(Mignola's) artwork is stunning: bold and dramatic, with colors by Mark Chiarello that make each panel flow like a stained-glass window."[36]

In contrast to *Hellboy's* spectral realm, *The Tale of One Bad Rat* by Bryan Talbot (Dark Horse, 1994-95) subtly and delicately deals with the difficult topic of sexual child abuse without moralising or sprinkling the story with superficial solutions or shallow judgments. The story is told from the perspective of the victim, Helen, as she runs away from home and comes to terms with the paternal sexual abuse she has suffered. Through her journey, her constant companions are a pet rat and a fascination with Beatrix Potter. Helen ends up in the scenic and uplifting surroundings of the English Lake District where she finally is able to confront her father (*see Figure 50*). This mini-series is a very good comicbook and an excellent example of comics that is not limited by any genre and can appeal to a wider audience outside the comics community.

In 1998, Frank Miller came out with a new series *300*, which is his first historically-oriented work, narrating stories of the past without using the moral standards of today. In contrast to the West-coast style of using large illustrations, Miller uses splash pages and big graphics to effectively serve the narrative, lending a rhythm, an almost a musical quality to the narration. *300* was one

Figure 48. *Madman Comics, Yearbook '95.* Art and script: Mike Allred © 1995 The creator.

of the biggest hits of 1998. By this time, Dark Horse offered a wide spectrum of topics and styles in quality comicbooks. In addition, this publisher also took advantage of the popularity of media cross-overs and the profit to be made from it—Dark Horse augmented its income through the self-production of films like *The Mask* (starring Jim Carrey).

In DC Comics, meanwhile, the *Sandman* series was nearing its last issues in 1996. However, DC's Vertigo line managed to extend its success with the *Preacher* series that started in 1995. Its Irish author, Garth Ennis, injects the road-movie style stories with moments of extreme physical violence. In its postmodernist handling of violent elements, the *Preacher* is suggestive of Quentin Tarantino's films. Like the films, Ennis' simultaneously shocking and entertaining use of violence comes from an astute reflection of modern pop culture. The violent elements, like all other parts of

Figure 49. *Madman Comics, Yearbook '95*. Art and script: Mike Allred © 1995 The creator.

Figure 50. Helen confronts her abuser in a sensitive and well-written scene from *The Tale of One Bad Rat*. Art and script: Bryan Talbot © 1995 The creator.

the narrative and graphics, are used as building blocks to enthrall and startle. Unlike TV talkshows or traditional crime novels or conventional superhero comics, however, the use of violence in *Preacher* or Tarantino films is not framed by sanctimonious moralising. Rather, it is used to expose that the regularity and degradation of violence have become morally neutral building blocks of pop culture. Like Tarantino's film *Pulp Fiction*, *Preacher* is simultaneously a product of pop culture as well as an attempt to provoke reflection on the reality of this pop culture.

An offshoot from Batman, *Hitman # 1* (DC, since 1996) is about a contract killer hired to bump off superheroes. Here again, Ennis reveals a postmodernist handling of violence. Right from the start, Ennis shows his typical postmodern approach to violence with the hero's comments: "Cheap supervillains. I dunno. But I gotta admit; if it wasn't for them, I'd be out've a job" (page 4). Ennis' narratives critically reflect on violence and other aspects of the superhero-genre, without undermining the genre's commercial success and popularity as a product of pop culture. Without the Batman series, for example, Ennis knows that he could not have worked on *Hitman*. Without the superhero-genre, the rise and popularity of American comics would have been unthinkable, and Ennis would certainly not be in a position to make his living from writing comicbooks. Garth Ennis is one of the most successful comics authors of the late 1990s. Among his many publications, his sense for dark humour, knack for gripping and realistic dialogue, and his awareness of the comics medium as vital for pop culture come most alive in *Preacher* and *Hitman*.

In addition to Garth Ennis, DC Comics focused on Grant Morrison in the latter half of the 1990s. Although Morrison's earlier abstract interpretation of Batman in *Arkham Asylum* met with some criticism, his conventional and not-so-original series for the *Justice League of America* in 1997 was welcomed by both fans and critics. Morrison learned from his experience with *Arkham* that superhero fans are not keen on abstract and deep psychological analysis of established superheroes. Rather, fans wanted appropriate conformity to established elements with some updates or twists that provide easy access to entertainment. Morrison met the fans' wishes with *JLA*, while at the same time working on a personal and innovative project not aimed at the superhero crowd, *The Invisibles* (DC, since 1994). The *Invisibles* turns the good vs. evil schema of the superhero genre on its head, as the "good guy" in this series is an anarchist group active world-wide, and the "bad" are those wearing the hats for law and order.

In contrast to the three publishers mentioned above, Marvel did not expand much out of the superhero ghetto. In 1996, only six Marvel series showed increasing sales figures: *Uncanny X-Men, X-Men, X-Force, Thor, Fantastic Four* and *The Silver Surfer*. However, between 1994-95, all of these series already suffered some loses that even the profit in 1996 could not make up for. Marvel had to cancel many other series. In 1995, Marvel's decision to stay with superheroes had already started causing them serious problems:

> Marvel's sales on *Spider-Man* and other Marvel superheroes were at their lowest in 30 years. In addition, Marvel released figures on May 7 (1996) which showed that their revenues after expenses fell 4.4 million.

> In a recent Compuserve posting, Marvel stockholder Mark Steven Long gave his account of the company's May 21 stockholder's meeting. He related that Marvel CEO Bill Evans claimed that Marvel will reverse their *long-running downturn* by posting a profit for the second quarter of this year. If that does happen, it may be due in part to the company's restructuring in January, when they cut 275 jobs and eliminated titles that were selling poorly.[37] (*emphasis mine*)

The ruthless manipulation of direct market sales in 1993 annoyed fans, caused a downward trend in sales, and eventually forced many small shops and retailers to close down. The loss of Marvel readers and the closing down of so many retail shops affected the comics industry in general. The comics industry concedes that, since 1993, its consumer base has been shrinking.

THE CURRENT STATUS AND THE FUTURE

More and more, there is consensus in the industry that mainstream-comics have analysed and deconstructed superheroes from every angle imaginable, and that the next sensible steps for advancement in comics lie beyond superhero comics. As always, the well-known and most established superheroes like Batman, X-Men, Spiderman, Superman and others like them make it still easy to earn a buck when the author plays with tradition (as long as the changes are not so revolutionary!). An author like Alan Moore, for example, takes advantage of this situation and from time to time, creates superhero-based comicbooks without much intensive work. With the profit, he finances more ambitious or more personal projects like *From Hell*.[38] Since 1990, Fantagraphics has had another line—"Eros," that had been coming out with pornographic comics. Apart from very few exceptions, the issues have low standard which nevertheless enabled Fantagraphics to finance other, more excellent magazines which otherwise would have been withdrawn due to insufficient commercial or mass popularity.[39]

The one who suffered most from the recent apathy to mainstream comics is the publisher who depended only on superheroes: Marvel. In 1997, *Wizard* published a status that considered the total money made for comics publishers, Marvel was behind DC for the first time since it was founded: Marvel had 24.81% and DC had 25.78%. Number three was Image with 14.58% and next was Dark Horse with 6.50%. Marvel's "fall" seems to show that, in the long-term, comics' chances lie in being freed from its "ghetto" of readers. The collapse of the speculation market supports this: modern comics cannot live off its superhero fans alone, hence, there is a need to attract wider readership.

In many areas, especially in the future-oriented domain of electronic media, entertainment products are increasingly tailored towards younger audience at the same time that this crowd's buying power is increasing. Electronic distractions like video games, for example, have superior ways of delivering that form of entertainment that appease pubescent appetites. In view of this competition, comics will find it increasingly hard to attract new readers and gain acceptance among very young customers. Since 1995, the average age of comics readers had gone up to 18-20 years old instead of the previous 11-12. The speculation disaster turned off many young comics readers, and 1995 saw a big decrease in sales and turnover for superhero products. Overall, there have been some radical changes to the comicbook readers: in the 1940s, the readers of comics was estimated at a couple of million, and in 1992-92, there was about 200,000 real readers (not counting speculators buying multiple copies). In 1996, there was only about 100,000. 1995 saw a big decrease in sales for superhero products, while alternative publishers like Fantagraphics showed some small growth. DC's Vertigo line also profited from its shift in readership focus. But, while older readership and general dissatisfaction with the mainstream may be a boon to alternative publishers, the loss of young readers who later might pick up alternative comics, will affect the total number of readers.

As the readership changed, the end of the speculation boom also changed and improved the contents and the format of comic-books: trade paperbacks became increasingly popular as well as bound comic books (collected series published after the original format). During the speculation boom, trade paperbacks never became an object of financial speculation (these were not "frag-ile," had no nostalgic element, and were usually reprinted). Trade paperbacks were actually bought for the narratives as the format allowed for longer storyliness. The end of the speculation boom gave rise to a surprising number of high quality, excellent comics. The current offering of the medium is more multi-faceted, with a bigger range in styles and topics compared to the start of the direct market 20 years ago.[40] The number of comics publishers has also increased, breaking the single dominance of Marvel. In addition, comicbooks are now being sold in bookstores like Virgin Megastores and Tower Books.[41] But notwithstanding the improved quality, decades-long of cultural prejudices about comics cannot be removed overnight. There is still a lack of female read-ers, whether children or adult, although there has been an increas-ing number of comics of potential interest to them. As a medium, there are still many preconceptions that rule the perception of comics and unfortunately, the industry does not have a history of sufficiently addressing these misconceptions.

Scott McCloud, a comicbook "theoretician," believes that comics can survive the collapsing reader market by a crossover to new media like the internet. He believes in the potential of digital comics in 10 to15 years. However, computer-native comics would allow comics to grow in a new shape, as long as it is not just a mat-ter of slapping an old form onto new media. In addition, this new form can allow the expansion of comics appreciation into the ever-expanding computer market. There is still a big need to explore this venue because so far, "digital" comics are merely comics in their old forms archived into a CD-ROM.[42]

In the coming years, however, the future of comics is still in being a printed material. However, there will be a pronounced rise in the quality of North American comics. The improvement of quality will lie more in the internationalization of the market and comics scene, rather than depend on big changes in American self-publishing or alternative scene. Even today, it is much easier to find exceptional American, European, or Asian comics using the internet than browsing in the comic specialty shops. Even now, the format of American comics draws nearer to the Japanese *mangas* and the European album-format as the number of graphic novels and trade paperbacks grow yearly. More and more elements of the Japanese *mangas* are found in North American comics, even as American publishers have only started to scratch the surface of a powerful reservoir of foreign talents. Only a handful of non-English European artists have so far managed to make a name in the States (for example, Herge, and Moebius). The magazine *Heavy Metal* contributed a lot to introducing European artists, but it was a slow start for a relatively small publisher who reprinted works of artists like Enki Bilal, Jacques de Loustal or Miguelanxo Prado as graphic novels. There is a need to open up comics from Europe and other parts of the world to North American readers. Some believe that the English-speaking audience may not be privy to the best comics the world has to offer, mostly due to the limitations of language, but also because there are no sufficient efforts in the industry to translate, publish, or sell foreign comics. There is still a relative isolation in which the North American market operates. While comicbooks from North America and other parts of Europe are regularly available in European stores, there are hardly any foreign comicbooks regularly made available in North America.

NOTES

This chapter translated from a non-published essay written by Jan Philipzig.

2 In the last issue of *Animal Man*, Grant Morrison comments on the "grim and gritty" comics following the success of Miller's *Dark Knight*: "... we thought that by making your world more violent, we could make it more "realistic," more "adult." God help us if that's what it means." (*Animal Man* #26)

3 Delano's streak would be interrupted by guest contributors like Grant Morrison (#25 and #26, together with David Lloyd) and Neil Gaiman

(#27, together with Dave McKean). All three issues were highly successful artistically.

4 Frank Plowright, ed. *The Slings and Arrows Comic Guide* (London:
   Aurum Press, 1997): 266. After Ennis, Scot Eddie Campbell did a short
   4-issue stint with Hellblazer, and was replaced by Paul Jenkins, writer
   and Sean Philips, illustrator. The series is currently not as popular as it
   was before.

5 In *Violent Cases*, (also later in *Mr. Punch*), Neil Gaiman tackles the
   topic of childhood memories and traumas, he intertwines these in
   myths, parables, and the gangster stories (for Mr. Punch he uses a pup-
   pet play). In *Sandman*, and *Books of Magic*, Gaiman places mythology
   in the centre of his comicbooks more than in his previous narratives.

6 Comics *Journal* #169, p. 100.

7 Morrison interview in *Comics Journal* #176, p. 56.

8 *Comics Journal* #176, p. 64-5.

9 The first story that was sufficiently convincing was Matt Wagner's
   Faces (#28-30). It is also noteworthy to mention the contributions in
   this series from: James Robinson and Tim Sale (#32-34), Bryan Talbot
   (#39, 40), Mike Mignola (#54), Ted McKeever (#74, 75) and Garth
   Ennis (#91-93).

10 In reading most of the Marvel comicbooks in the 1980s, it was clear
   that there were no pretenses to tell any stories but nobody had admit-
   ted to it yet.

11 That comics have to be sealed and in mint condition to fetch a hand-
   some price meant that the buyers could never open or read the issue at
   all. In some ways, this contributed to the decline of the need for good
   narratives in comics at that time.

12 Dan Clowes explained his title: "I'd had the name Lloyd Llewellyn
   ever since I was a little kid, because in the old Superman comics, . . .
   they had this weird obsession with the double Ls. They were always
   making a big issue out of the idea, 'Isn't it strange that Superman's girlfriend is Lois Lane, and his arch enemy is Lex Luthor and then there's
   Lucy Lane,' . . . and they would underline the two Ls. Things like that.
   I found that really strange and fetishistic as a kid, and I thought, 'What
   if someone was named Lloyd Llwellyn? He would be the greatest
   Superman character of all!" (*Comics Journal* #154, p. 64).

13 In *Hard Boiled* (1990-1992), Miller did not succeed in putting the
   extremely detailed and violent graphics into any kind of perspective to
   aid the readers' understanding. The attempt to position the spectacular but superficial issue as black comedy did not work either.

14 The first *Sin City* stories started in *Dark Horse Presents Fifth
   Anniversary Special* and continued in *Dark Horse Presents* #50-62.

15 The solitude of the figures who inhabit *Sin City* find direct expression
   in the depiction of their surroundings: no building or backdrop appear

twice, the reader is never provided an orientation point or map to the city and can get lost anytime. Meanwhile, the characters are portrayed as remote and isolated. Frank Miller says "I've deliberately made *Sin City* a very bleak place, giving you few landmarks, so that it's a place of very lonely people." *Comics Journal #209*, p. 66

16 In contrast to McFarlane's *Spawn*, the other Image titles profited from taking full advantage of sales gimmicks like multi-covers and different versions with very slight variations, a trend which the direct market created. Only *Spawn* would last as a series, the other titles were stopped after a few issues, and new "first" issues would be produced to lure readers into buy these "investments."

17 DC got rid of this labeling by mid-1990s.

18 As John Davis comments on the "Decline of the American Comics Industry": "...it's a combination of things: the cover price going up, the fact that Marvel was putting out so many titles...In addition to the fact that the content wasn't strong for a lot of the titles, the price seemed to go up steadily at a high rate and there was just more to buy. Instead of having three Spider-Man, it was six; instead of having three X-Men titles, it was eight. So whatever you were into, Marvel was asking you to buy more and more of it just to keep current with the storylines." (*Comics Journal #188*, p. 39).

19 There was no consensus in Image if a complex project like *1963* or *The Maxx* was the right response to the problematic situation they found themselves when sales dropped. Moore's *1963* did not become a commercial success as expected.

20 Since 1986, DC re-created almost all of its superhero series to give each one an external appearance according to the "grim 'n gritty" trend.

21 Adrian Snowdon in a write-up about *Marvels* in *The Slings and Arrows Comic Guide*, ed. Frank Plowright (London: Aurum Press, 1997): 365-6.

22 Busiek further explores the style he used in *Marvels* with *Astro City*. In *Astro City*, he creates his own universe of new superheroes, but the characters are strongly influenced by the classic heroes, "And for the main heroes of *Astro City*...we tried to look for the archetypes underneath things that work, and build a new character out of that. So certainly, Samaritan is very Superman-like. . ." (*Comics Journal #188*, p. 89).

23 Adrian Tomine in *The Comics Journal #205: The Young Cartoonist Issue*, pp. 45-76.

24 *Ibid*, p. 10. Oliveros does temper this optimism by adding these remarks in the same interview: "My bigger concern would be: 'Will there be a market in two or three years?' It always seems that things could fall apart any day."

25 Frank Plowright write-up about *Acme Novelty Library in The Slings and Arrows Comic Guide*, ed. Frank Plowright (London: Aurum Press,

1997): 3.
26 *12th Annual Fantagraphics Ultimate Catalogue*, p. 11.
27 Howard Stangroom in a write-up about Desert Peach in *The Slings and Arrows Comic Guide*, ed. Frank Plowright (London: Aurum Press, 1997): 157-8.
28 The character, Too Much Coffee Man also appeared in #92-95 of the *Dark Horse Presents* series.
29 Frank Plowright in a write-up about *Too Much Coffee Man* in *The Slings and Arrows Comic Guide*, ed. Frank Plowright (London: Aurum Press, 1997): 596.
30 David Roach in a write-up about *Stray Bullets* in *The Slings and Arrows Comic Guide*, ed. Frank Plowright (London: Aurum Press, 1997): 548-9.
31 Jeff Smith self-published the first issues. Issue #1 came out exactly the same time that *Spider-Man #1* came out, and was lost in the hype generated by the latter. It took six months before *Bone's* merits were finally recognized by comics readers.
32 As of the writing of this book, a movie has been planned for *Bone* which will take its commercial success to another dimension. Nickelodeon Movies have already obtained the rights to the film, and Jeff Smith himself will illustrate and direct.
33 Page 89. Kurt Busiek interview.
34 Introduction to *Astro City: Life in the Big City*, p. 8.
35 Tundra published *Madman* in three parts in 1992, and a three-part *Madman Adventures* in 1992 to 1993. Before this, Mike Allred had already used the main character, Frank Einstein, in *Creatures of the ID* (Caliber, 1990), *Graphique Musique #1-3* (Slave Labour, 1990) and *Grafik Muzik* (Caliber, 1990-91).
36 Fiona Clements in a write-up about Hellboy in *The Slings and Arrows Comic Guide*, ed. Frank Plowright (London: Aurum Press, 1997): 267-8.
37 Greg Stump, "The State of the Industry 1996" in *The Comics Journal #188*, p. 33.
38 Moore earns fast-money when he uses the popularity of series like *Spawn* and *Wild C.A.T.S.* Sometimes, he publishes his own mini-series of an established character, like he did for the evil Violator from *Spawn*.
39 Eros still shows profit although the pornographic comics market had had to take losses since 1995. *Penthouse* and *Hustler* shelved their comics series in 1998. In the same year, Fantagraphics had to withdraw some of the less profitable regular series as Eros' profit shrunk.
40 Comicbooks have also started winning non-industry recognition awards. In addition to Spiegelman's *Maus* winning the Pullitzer Prize, Joe Sacco won the American Book Award 1996 for *Palestine*, a piece of journalism in comicbook form where he records his experiences in

travelling through the West Bank and Gaza Strip while the conflict raged over there.

41 Being sold in bookstores allow more exposure for comicbooks than being sold in specialty comics shops. More people regularly wander into bookstores while only those already exposed to comics would go inside the comic shops.

42 The *Spirit* by Will Eisner is published in a CD-ROM format and distributed by mass market companies like Time Warner. Copies of old issues of *The Spirit* are archived into this electronic format which allow readers on-line viewing. While the attempt is laudable for archiving old, hard-to-get issues, putting comics into this form will not advance the medium as a whole—this CD-ROM is a classic case of a new medium simply imitating the old, taking the form of the old one as its contents.

Index

232

Index